ALASKA'S GREATEST OUTDOOR LEGENDS

T0321236

DOUG KELLY

WITH A FOREWORD BY CHRISTOPHER M. BATIN

University of Alaska Press, Fairbanks

ALASKA'S

GREATEST OUTDOOR LEGENDS

Colorful Characters Who Built the Fishing and Hunting Industries

Text © 2016
University of Alaska Press

Published by
University of Alaska Press
P.O. Box 756240
Fairbanks, AK 99775-6240

Cover and interior design by Kristina Kachele Design, llc

Cover image: Considered the original Kodiak Island hunting guide, Madsen shows his strength by holding up a brown bear near Karluk Lake in the early 1930s. Photo from the Harshman Collection, Kodiak Historical Society, P-612-2-3.

Opening image: The Ketchums's cabin in 1985 on Bulchitna Lake up the Yentna River west of Anchorage. Photo courtesy of Ketch Ketchum.

Back cover images:
Nellie Neal Lawing, who first arrived in Alaska at the age of forty-two, staying warm in a fur-lined parka. Photo courtesy of Doug Capra.

A fly rod, a floatplane, and waders were all Ray Petersen needed to explore and catch fish. Photo courtesy of Sonny Petersen.

Rene "Frenchy" Lamoureux guided in the Arctic for polar bear hunts. Photo courtesy of the Lamoureux family.

Library of Congress Cataloging-in-Publication Data
Names: Kelly, Doug, 1949–
Title: Alaska's greatest outdoor legends : colorful characters who built the fishing and hunting industries..
Description: Fairbanks : University of Alaska Press, 2016. | Includes bibliographical references and index.
Identifiers: LCCN 2015049263 | ISBN 9781602232990 (pbk. : alk. paper)
Subjects: LCSH: Hunters—Alaska—Biography. | Fishers—Alaska—Biography.
Classification: LCC SK15 .K45 2016 | DDC 639/.109798—dc23
LC record available at http://lccn.loc.gov/2015049263

To those whose hearts are in sync with the soul of Alaska

CONTENTS

Foreword · *xi*

Introduction · *3*

1 Nellie Neal Lawing, 1873–1956 · *7*

2 Frank Glaser, 1887–1974 · *25*

3 Bill Pinnell, 1898–1990, and Morris Talifson, 1909–2000 · *33*

4 Sam White, 1891–1976 · *45*

5 Hal Waugh, 1909–1973 · *55*

6 Ray Petersen, 1912–2008 · *65*

7 Sidney Huntington, b. 1915 · *73*

8 Dick McIntyre, 1917–2009 · *87*

9 Rene "Frenchy" Lamoureux, 1921–1990 · *93*

10 Jay Hammond, 1922–2005 · *101*

11 Jim Brooks, 1922–2006 · *111*

12 Lindley "Ketch" Ketchum, b. 1923 · *129*

13 Jim Rearden, b. 1925 · *141*

14 Sam McDowell, 1927–2013 · *149*

15 Keith Johnson, b. 1932 · *155*

16 Cecilia "Pudge" Kleinkauf, b. 1936 · *167*

17 Dick and Mary Bishop, b. 1937 · *175*

18 Dennis Hay, 1940–2015 · *185*

19 Jim Bailey, b. 1940 · *197*

20 Wayne Heimer, b. 1943 · *207*

21 James Williams "J.W." Smith Jr., b. 1943 · *219*

22 William C. Gasaway, 1943–2011 · *229*

23 Bob Stephenson, b. 1945 · *239*

24 Jim Lavrakas, b. 1952 · *249*

25 Chris Batin. b. 1955 · *259*

26 John Beath, b. 1960 · *269*

27 Andy Mezirow, b. 1964 · *275*

28 More Legends of Alaska's Great Outdoors · *283*

Bibliography · *291*

Acknowledgments · *293*

Index · *295*

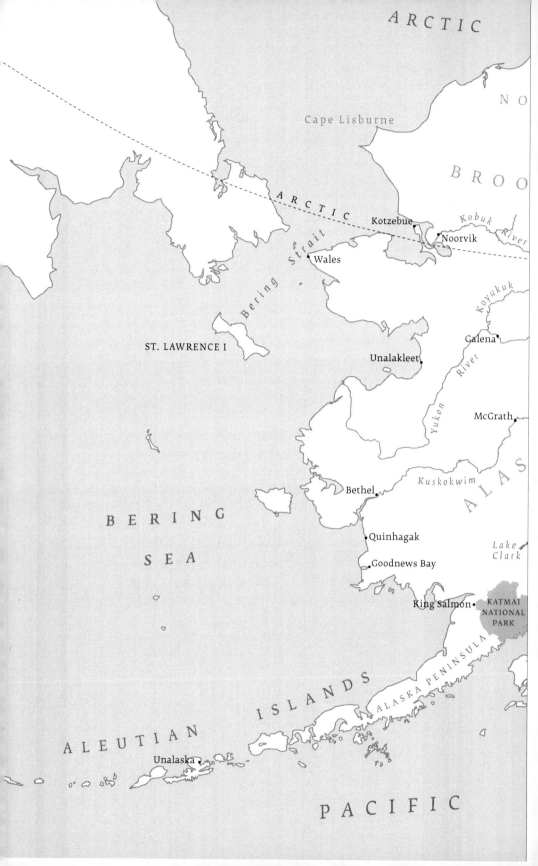

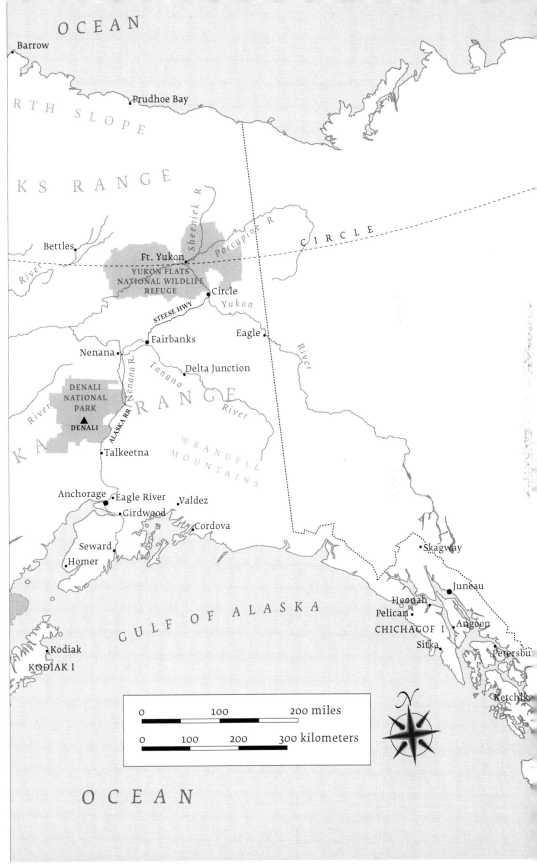

FOREWORD

Single incidents or stories alone don't make an Alaska fishing or hunting legend. It's a lifetime of experiences in Alaska that count, such as running the race in its entirety rather than just a leg. The men and women of *Alaska's Greatest Outdoor Legends* fit in a category by themselves, a group so small as to be almost unnoticeable. That's the way most, if not all of them, would want it.

Legends encompass a narrative based on popular stories about people who exhibit or possess qualities beyond the norm. A legend can also be a popular history, a people, a place that inspires, or a story that educates about a person, personality, spirit, culture, or morals. These defining criteria qualify the men and women in *Alaska's Greatest Outdoor Legends*.

This book is as much historical narrative as it is riveting entertainment. Doug Kelly draws from his personal experiences, authentic anecdotes, and generations of photos, which breathe life and credibility into these stories. He's collected supporting documentation and anecdotal references from individuals who personally know these legends. These sources provide credible insight and detail far removed from today's armchair writers, Internet trolls, and top-of-the-head commentaries.

This doesn't mean Alaska legends are perfect. They oftentimes fail more than others do because they invariably live more dangerously, take more risks, and push the envelope harder than most people, or quietly plug away behind the scenes, bit by bit, for decades. The secret to legends, however, is that they get up each time they fall and push on—stronger, wiser, better.

Like the hero archetypes in cinema and literature, Alaska legends also embody the fundamental characteristics of the quest: perseverance and transcendence. Alaska legends endure. They adapt and, like high-octane gasoline, have a bit of a kick to them. They easily ignite on the adventure and don't ping out when the going gets rough. They embrace the challenges of not only existing, but also living the life they choose to live in the forty-ninth state, whether on a remote mountaintop, as a guide, or a representative of the people.

In this book, no two legends are the same, just as no two Alaska streams are the same. But let us be careful not to glorify legends in a superhuman way. They merely coach us with their deeds and examples in the marathon of life, remaining as quiet as falling snow or commanding a presence that would make a grizzly back away.

Though different in many ways, legends do have a common foundation: They did not start out as legends. Many began as I did, possessing only a dream. They gravitated toward some aspect of Alaska's outdoors and excelled in a variety of social and professional skill sets. In the final analysis, these Alaskans tapped into a supreme passion for fishing and hunting, challenging the toughest conditions the outdoors could dish out, and loving the experience enough to return, day after day, year after year, giving it everything they had and then some.

I'm betting that a century from now, those with the curiosity and desire for Alaska wildness will search out this book and marvel at the lifestyles and adventures of these legends, much like we marvel today at the lifestyle and freedom of frontier pioneers and mountain men.

Doug brings to this book the skill of the veteran editor and journalist with the insight of an investigative outdoor reporter in researching the people, facts, and places of Alaska's historical and living legends. I've eaten moose and salmon with him. We've walked Alaska forests, crossed remote streams, and fished together. He is the professional scribe we need to tell the story of this generation of *Alaska's Greatest Outdoor Legends*.

I therefore encourage you to kick back, relax, and enjoy the stories in this book. You may cry, shake your head, laugh, swear, or marvel. You may also become inspired to find your own "life way," and when someone asks if it was worth the trouble, your answer will be heartfelt and without second thought: "What trouble?"

CHRISTOPHER M. BATIN
The Alaska Angler/Alaska Hunter
Talkeetna, Alaska
ChrisBatin@AlaskaAngler.com or www.AlaskaAngler.com

ALASKA'S GREATEST OUTDOOR LEGENDS

INTRODUCTION

Not everyone bothers with an introduction for a book. A lot of people skip it even if one is present, so I appreciate the fact that you're reading this. In turn I would like to provide some inside details into how this process evolved.

When the initial email blasts hit the in-boxes of over a thousand Alaskans requesting candidates for *Alaska's Greatest Outdoor Legends*, I didn't know what to expect. Would only a handful of nominations be offered? The answer soon came back loud and clear: Alaskans weren't a bit shy in sharing opinions about those who they felt qualified as genuine legends. Suggestions poured in about past and present anglers, hunters, guides, journalists, lodge owners, bush pilots, and biologists who have contributed in remarkable ways to the enormous popularity of fishing and hunting in Alaska.

The "possibles" list ballooned well beyond a thousand, requiring a whittling-down process that consumed most of two years.

Notice that not all chapters are the same length. Some run a good many pages, others just a few. My reasoning for that is quality, not quantity. Just one lifetime can constitute a book or even several volumes, so it became a matter of deciding on the most interesting and colorful outtakes that relate to the central theme of how he or she raised the profile of fishing and hunting in Alaska. To assign the same number of pages to everyone would be cutting some people short and stretching other chapters to the point of boredom. The last thing I want this book to do is bore you.

An example of eschewing any cookie-cutter chapter lengths is the story of Nellie Lawing. Since she passed away in 1956 and because most of those who knew her well have also long departed, I first summoned all available biographies on the Internet, on websites, and from articles to complete a rough draft. But after doing so, I ordered her autobiography, "Alaska Nellie." I figured her book would be simply a matter of pulling some fresh quotes that haven't already appeared in print. Instead, I discovered that much of the existing representations I'd found about her life were incorrect: wrong dates, wrong place names, wrong people. And so, I completely rewrote the draft to make it accurate, finishing the process by having the chapter vetted by a historian intimately familiar with Alaska Nellie's life.

I point out the foregoing not for self-aggrandizement but to express how any responsible journalist should dig beyond the representations that merely digest what others have written. That takes more time, and time is money, but reputation is even more valuable.

In addition, I chose the chapter characters in the same manner I'd think about a game of chess. I envisioned the endgame first and went from there, meaning that if the available background information was too skimpy, biased, or unreliable, I crossed that person off the chapter list. Doing it this way ignored the balance of geography, to be sure, but in my opinion weighing each chapter subject with a "material meter" made more sense than going by a map to cover every area of Alaska.

Another challenge involved deciding who qualifies as a legend or a pioneer. Chris Batin eloquently addresses that topic in the foreword. Indeed, Alaska has spawned innumerable bush pilots, biologists, fishing and hunting guides, lodge owners, and the like. Therefore, the challenge was to include in each chapter enough biographical information, work history, and contributions to Alaska's outdoors to offer perspective while providing insights that raise him or her above the norm.

But I'll also state what this book is not. It's not an encyclopedia of Alaska records boasting who shot the biggest this or caught the largest that. It's also not a "how to" or "where to" book—the bookshelves are already crammed with manuals on techniques and guides to hotspots. Instead, *Alaska's Greatest Outdoor Legends* is a compendium of legendary men and women, each chapter offering a treasure trove of interesting insights, colorful anecdotes, and tales of adventure and misadventure—mini biographies of each legendary person's life. The final chapter includes snippets on many others worthy of mention but, for one reason or another, lacked enough available material for a full chapter.

That said, tales about field and stream experiences as well as images depicting the same are unapologetically included in the chapters—after all, catching fish and shooting game is what anglers and hunters do. And yet *Alaska's Greatest Outdoor Legends* mainly tells stories about people, not fish or bears or the instruments to take them. It relates what these characters forged singularly and collectively in various eras to clear a trail through the alders of Alaska's history and lore.

Be assured that a great deal of due diligence went into this effort. Besides my own considerable experiences in Alaska over the past thirty years and countless hours combing through online resources, I've also visited libraries, historical archives, tourism offices, and chambers of commerce in pursuit of background materials. I've sat down with some of the characters themselves in their homes throughout Alaska, interviewed spouses or surviving relatives, obtained irreplaceable family photographs, and acquired untold newspaper and magazine clippings. The result has been a monumental effort but one deserving of those who became legends. And if any element is amiss, it's a product of the necessity at times of depending upon imperfect memories for stories and information.

Of course a historical book always has significant challenges. The limits of existing records, disinterested ancestors, or cameras that didn't function in bad weather reduced the scope of deserving characters. For those reasons and because of the obvious boundaries of book length, I would never claim that *Alaska's Greatest Outdoor Legends* is all-inclusive. However, I believe that most of those who read the book will agree that, in their own ways, the men and women depicted in the following chapters certainly did much to elevate the status of Alaska's fishing and hunting in the United States and the world.

In that vein, I'd like to think that someone from Boise or Baton Rouge or Barrow fifty years from now will pull this book off a dusty shelf in some antique shop filled with old "real" books and go home with it. I want every character in the book to suddenly become suddenly contemporary in that person's mind, not because it may glorify this man or that woman but because Alaska's history—every part of it—must live on to be enjoyed and envied and loved, even if vicariously.

I'm particularly pleased that many of the descendants of my subjects expressed gratitude for the chance to carry forward their relative's legacy. A good example is an email I received from Beatrice Brooks, the daughter of Jim Brooks depicted in chapter 11, after I'd asked her to look over the chapter draft and provide some images: "As I went through my dad's stuff—pictures, letters, work-related speeches—I found photos from as far back as the 1930s. My dad's generation is gone and their exploits and feats will not be replicated or remembered by new generations without books like yours. Times have changed, civilization is much larger and the wilderness is so much smaller now. Your correspondence served as a catalyst for me to go through the souvenirs of my dad's life, and it brought back to life that fabulous era to me."

I hope you feel the same way as Beatrice after reading *Alaska's Greatest Outdoor Legends*.

DOUG KELLY
March 1, 2016

1

NELLIE NEAL LAWING, 1873–1956

Lawing, Alaska

Born a Missourian who endured hardships in the gold mining towns of Colorado as a young adult, she staked out a new life in Alaska as a roadhouse contractor for the new Seward-to-Fairbanks railroad. She arrived in Alaska alone, middle-aged, but full of fire. Her operation of way stations enabled greater access to fish and game for Alaskans and visiting sportspersons.

The allure of Alaska tugs at the heartstrings of all those with a spirit of adventure. Some don't tarry for even a day in moving to The Last Frontier to fish, hunt, trap, prospect, escape the law, or just create a new reality. Most never make the move at all; others do it much later in life. The latter category fits the curious case of Nellie Trosper Neal Lawing.

Because of multiple marriages that changed her last name, I'll refer to her simply as Nellie.

Nellie would not set foot in Alaska until 1915 at the age of forty-two, well past what most consider their prime. But when she did arrive, she commenced tackling the Alaska wilderness with a rare grit and perseverance for someone reaching middle age, much less a wispy five-foot divorcee. But before delving into the portion of Nellie's life that would make her an iconic figure in Alaska's history, let's review her life before she stepped off the boat in Seward.

Nellie Neal Lawing, who first arrived in Alaska at the age of forty-two, staying warm in a fur-lined parka. Photo courtesy of Doug Capra.

She came into this world in 1873 as Nellie Trosper in Saint Joseph, Missouri. Her father, Robert N. Trosper, was a Civil War veteran who married Jennie Jane Gibson. Named Nellie after Ulysses S. Grant's daughter, she was the eldest of twelve children, two of whom died when quite young.

The hardships and disarray of the Civil War still hung in the air as Robert and Jennie soon left Saint Joseph and moved to Platte County near the town of Weston, Missouri. There they bought a timber-bordered farm with a five-room log cabin. Even on a farm, it was undoubtedly a formidable task for such a large family to keep food on the table and everyone clothed. As Nellie toiled with household and farm chores and helped raise her siblings, she heard tidbits about Alaska—quite likely from an occasional traveler who happened through town or perhaps from newspaper accounts.

However the news about such a magical land came into her psyche, it resonated. She longed for a less-mundane life, and Alaska became the dream that promised exactly that. For the next half of her life, that idyllic dream grew stronger. In her autobiography, *Alaska Nellie*, published in 1940, she described this vision of Alaska at an early age:

"My father and mother asked me what vocation I would choose when the time came for me to make my own way through life. When I told them of my desire to go to Alaska, to live in a log cabin, hunt big game, run a trap line and catch beautiful furs, they thought that I, like most all young people with freakish dreams, would outgrow them."

She and her brother Harry ran a trapline along Bee Creek for raccoons, skunks, weasels, possums, and other small game. Nellie also enjoyed hunting, fishing, and riding horses with her coonhound, Hot Foot, frequently tagging along.

When her mother died in 1898 and her father remarried two years later, Nellie took on the role of being both a sister and a mother to her younger siblings. Despite her father's misgivings in general about Nellie's leaving the family homestead and specifically her goal of living in Alaska, she nonetheless closed the door behind her for good on May 30, 1901. She boarded a train for Green River, Wyoming, where she'd already lined up a job running a lunchroom for the Union Pacific Railroad. That job didn't last long as soon afterward she accepted a better-paying position at Glenwood Springs, Colorado, for the Denver & Rio Grande Railroad. From there she bounced to Denver, where, on October 20, 1903, an employment agency directed her to an opening at a boarding house near Pike's Peak in Cripple Creek, Colorado.

She arrived the next day at one of the world's largest gold-mining camps. But as she would later write in her book, "Could I have seen through the coming years I would not have taken this trip, as it led up to one of the greatest struggles of my life."

Cripple Creek was in constant turmoil due to conflicts between angry unionized miners and intransigent mine owners. Nellie remained neutral, but the strife propelled her to quickly ditch the boarding house in favor of opening her own place six miles away in Victor. However, the violence shifted practically to her front door, and Nellie—not one fond of flying bullets and bomb explosions—sold her place in Victor and bought a thirty-room hotel called the Courthouse Club back in Cripple Creek.

By then she'd met Wesley Neal, a former Missourian doing a thriving business as a gold assayer. They went from friends to lovers, and they married on February 26, 1906. Doug Capra, a historian of Alaska and an author from Seward who's writing a biography about Nellie, discovered an interesting bit of information that suggests she had been previously married. "Her marriage certificate in Cripple Creek lists her name as Nellie Bates and not as her maiden name of Nellie Trosper," Capra wrote in an email to me. "That suggests she was married when living in Saint Joseph, Missouri, but I can find no record of that at all."

Nellie's hotel operation flourished, but the incessant lawlessness of Cripple Creek made for a stressful and sometimes traumatic existence. On one occasion she nearly lost her life when a thief tried to kill her in the hotel, and on another she had to shoot it out with a would-be robber in Wesley's assay office.

If the constant threat of violence wasn't enough, her marriage also deteriorated. Wesley had too strong an affinity for rum, which led to his mental and physical abuse of Nellie. And so on November 12, 1912, she packed up her belongings and went back to Denver to the same employment agency that had previously helped her. This time it set her up for a job with the Oregon Short Line in Huntington, Oregon.

After nearly two years in Oregon, Nellie grew restless. On a visit to Seattle in 1914, she heard about the U.S. government's plans to build a railroad from Seward to Fairbanks, a project that would be unveiled in the coming spring at the Panama-Pacific International Exposition in San Francisco. Excited at the prospect of finally getting to Alaska, Nellie took a temporary position with the Southern Pacific Railroad in Carlin, Nevada. In early spring of 1915 she set out for San Francisco; in late

June she bought a ticket on the *Admiral Evans*, a steamship bound for Seattle, where she transferred to the steamship *Alameda* for the seven-day trip to Seward.

It had been fourteen long years since she'd left home, and now she'd be going to Alaska. The journey north was like a blood transfusion as Nellie stood on deck while the *Alameda* passed Vancouver and cruised the Inside Passage on the way to Seward. The sweep of the snow-tipped mountains and the sight of gliding eagles and breeching whales framed by glaciers could only have entranced her. Nellie must have relished the cool, fresh air washing over her face, thrilled that a lifelong dream was about to be realized.

Nellie stepped onto the pier at Seward, Alaska, on the evening of July 3, 1915, filled with exhilaration and hope. Immediately, she secured employment as a housekeeper with a local family and sometime later hired on as cook for Jim Hayden, the operator of a gold mine and mill. Hayden owned a beautiful log home, named Oasis, located twenty-six miles from Seward and five miles west of the railroad in the mountains.

En route to Oasis on the Alaska Central Railroad, Nellie disembarked to stretch her legs at the tiny village of Roosevelt at Mile 23. Along the route, she had noted that the marker numbers represented the miles north of Seward. Nellie felt an immediate, almost-spiritual heart tug while admiring Roosevelt's beautiful vistas and the inviting log house standing on the edge of shimmering Lake Kenai.

Nellie worked hard at the Oasis, starting at fifty dollars a month and soon advanced to a hundred—a healthy income for that era in a remote portion of Alaska. When summer passed and ice shut off the flow of river water to the mill, everyone left Oasis for Seward. Not Nellie. She'd previously stumbled upon an abandoned cabin while hunting ptarmigan, and in December 1915 she moved into it. Living alone thirty miles deep in the mountainous wilderness, she savored the white silence of winter and the calming solitude for the next three months.

That spring, the U.S. government bought the bankrupt Alaska Central Railroad. It became the Alaska Northern Railway, the precursor of a Seward-to-Fairbanks railway project. Nellie sought a contract to operate a roadhouse—a combination hotel and diner—and suggested Mile 45 as a central location for the 114-mile Seward-to-Anchorage division. She hoped to be the region's Fred Harvey, the famous entrepreneur who, in 1875, started America's first restaurant chain by opening cafes along the western railways that cooked good meals served by young, attractive waitresses.

Nellie secured the contract, taking over a four-story roadhouse where she prepared meals and offered lodging. Rather than accepting the designation Mile 45, she decided to name the spot Grandview, an appropriate placename due to the great natural beauty of the surroundings. Nellie was tasked with obtaining all needed supplies in Seward and oversaw the cooking and innkeeping. Besides a dining room, thirteen bunks provided sleeping arrangements for men, and Nellie lived in a small room over the kitchen. Two trains each week stopped in Grandview, where travelers could join miners in relishing Nellie's excellent cooking.

Time went by, and after sixteen months in Alaska, Nellie had found her niche and discovered her soul. In her book she puts it this way: "I could never express how deeply attached I had become to this great frontier country. It had truly exceeded all my expectations. The brilliant

"Alaska Nellie" seated at far right with a rifle on her lap and a small portion of the mounts that filled her museum. Photo courtesy of Doug Capra.

Nellie Neal Lawing and Trophies. Lawing Alaska.

night of my imagination was now made doubly bright by personal contact."

Nellie quickly acquired the skills to be a successful innkeeper and cook, and those qualities put her in good stead. But another reason for her rising reputation became founded on a willingness to help others even at her own peril. One night when snow had stalled a train two miles to the north, fifty railroad men worked eighteen hours straight to clear it. Nellie prepared ham-and-egg sandwiches, donuts, and coffee, packed the food on a dog sled, and headed out into the night—even though it was twelve below zero. Much to their collective delight, Nellie reached the men, and the nourishment provided a jolt of energy that helped them to finish digging out the rails.

Although weather conditions were often daunting, that didn't deter Nellie. She'd barge into the wilderness to deliver meals to spike camps or even spend all day trudging with snowshoes to Seward to fetch someone's medical supplies. When such stories reached the locals as well as visitors, they earned Nellie respect. And guests knew they'd be taken care of at Grandview. It was a clean and dependable place to sleep and the delicious preparations of fish and game made her place a regional favorite. She also entertained guests with tales of her heroics, even if some were embellished for the sake of a good story.

The more that Nellie experienced the challenges of the Alaska wilderness, the farther her skills advanced. After only a few years in the territory, she could already fish, hunt, trap, and mush with the best of them. And from her decade in Cripple Creek, she had the ability to relate well with the many gold prospectors coming through the area.

Of the many stories Nellie wrote in *Alaska Nellie*, two of the more-often quoted ones involve the rescue of a mail carrier and her entrustment with a fortune in gold. The first occurred in January of 1920 when Henry Collman's dog sled was late in delivering to the train several sacks of correspondence that included documents vital to Seward. Nellie took off with her dog team into the teeth of a massive blizzard and somehow found Collman nearly frozen to death along the railway. She could waste no time collecting his mail sacks and pouches, or he would die before getting him to Grandview.

She did just that. Her book describes just how critical was Collman's condition: "He was thawing out too rapidly. After filling a washtub with snow, I packed his feet with snow, then applied snow packs to his face and hands, keeping him warm at the same time so the snow would melt fast. He took hot drinks and I applied kerosene, which has a healing effect on frozen parts."

But that's half the story. Knowing the importance of mail to everyone in the territory, at 3 A.M. she left Grandview and traversed huge snowdrifts to go back and get the sacks and pouches. Nellie stopped at the roadhouse and, after finding Collman still asleep, she went on to the next train flag stop, where she arrived just in time at 7 A.M. The mail delivery was made, much to the relief of Collman, the railroad, the postal service, and everyone in Seward. Later that year, just before her third Christmas in Alaska, Nellie received a package. The town of Seward recognized her extraordinary heroism with a gift of a pendant of solid-gold nuggets centered with a diamond—a personalized treasure she wore for the rest of her life.

The events in the second story occurred on a cold December day when U.S. marshals named Cavanaugh and Irwin and two other men came to Grandview after a long trip. Badly in need of a night's rest before continuing on their journey, the exhausted travelers found just enough energy to remove heavy wooden boxes from their sleds and bring them inside the roadhouse. Nellie learned that the boxes contained $750,000 in gold bullion fresh from the Iditarod mining district.

The men asked Nellie where it could be hidden for the night, and she said to slide it under the dining room table. As all four men quickly dozed off, Nellie sat up all night in a rocking chair beside the fireplace because all the beds were taken. She knew all too well from her days in Cripple Creek what evil effect gold had on the integrity of men, and she wasn't about to let anyone touch this bullion. It's doubtful the marshals would have entrusted such a mega-fortune to anyone else than Nellie. All that gold remained safely secured until the next morning, when the men loaded it back onto their sleds and mushed on to Seward.

Everyone who visits the wilds of Alaska ends up with bear stories, and Nellie had her share. Once when hunting, she stumbled on two black bear cubs up in a tree, and she knew the mother would be ready to kill any creature in the vicinity. Sure enough, a large female emerged, rose onto its hind legs, and would have surely charged her had Nellie not killed it with one shot to the chest. She retrieved the motherless cubs—left on their own, they would have died— and turned them into pets, which for many years offered great amusement and fascination to many visitors. Nellie would likewise later discover another pair of black bear cubs – this time without a momma bear around. They became her pets too.

In her most horrific and dangerous bear incident, a brown bear came onto her property and killed Mike, her only remaining black bear cub at the time. Nellie had discovered Mike's collar and bloodstains where the cub had been chained, and followed bear tracks down a trail until running into a massive brown bear. Wishing she'd brought her rifle along, Nellie ducked behind a half-fallen tree as the beast charged, barely missing her. She took off for the horse barn at the camp and made it inside just before the beast closed the distance to kill her. She broke three fingers in the jam and bruised her knee as the bear slammed into the door. The intensity of the bear's attack and ferocious growling and snarling terrified Nellie, as it would anybody.

When the bear gave up and Nellie heard it leave, she bolted to her cabin to recover. Gathering her strength and fed by the anger of Mike's death, Nellie grabbed her .30-40 Winchester rifle, went to a ridge above the barn and confronted the bear. It reared up to fight—a big mistake, given Nellie's shooting proficiency. She pulled the trigger, but it took six slugs, the last spiraling through the heart, before it ended the battle. The huge brown bear measured nine feet, six inches tall, nearly twice the size of Nellie. When she gutted him, her cub Mike and a porcupine were in its stomach and she found remnants of other bullets from some poor hunter who probably didn't survive the ordeal.

"Ammunition with shocking power is of vital importance for shooting this dangerous game," she wrote in her book. "Sometimes a bear riddled with bullets, any of which would cause death, keeps coming toward one—perhaps for the same reason that a chicken flops around after it has been beheaded."

Nellie took these challenges in stride as a trade-off for the privilege of living in Alaska. "After terrific encounters with huge beasts that tried to do me to death, I was always ready to apply the old remedy of courage and fearlessness and go on to the next encounter undaunted," as she put it. Indeed, deep reservoirs of icy cool seemed to course naturally through Nellie's veins

But sometimes two-legged beasts will wreak havoc too. Case in point: After noting how hard Nellie worked to keep Grandview operating at a high level, a well-heeled lodge guest with an alcohol addiction offered to partner with Nellie—he also suggested marriage on top of that. Nellie turned him down on both accounts. She eschewed partnerships with anyone in the roadhouse business, and there was no way she was going to get hitched to another drunk. The jilted man opened an opposing place of business nearby. In order to offset that competition, Nellie bought another roadhouse twenty-six miles north of Grandview in Kern Creek. Situated on the side of a mountain that overlooked Turnagain Arm, she tirelessly commuted back and forth to oversee the operations.

Her competitor subsequently disappeared from the area, most likely due to his drinking problem and the fact he was mixed up in bootlegging "white mule," an illicit whiskey distilled and sold during those Prohibition years. At first an older married couple looked after day-to-day operations at Grandview for Nellie, but they later moved to Anchorage, and her brother Homer and his wife took over that responsibility.

Nellie concentrated her main efforts at Kern Creek, but another roadhouse guest would also prove a major distraction. He managed to talk Nellie into becoming a stockholder in a gold mine operation being set up in California Creek near the town of Girdwood. Against her better instincts, Nellie spent that summer cooking at the mine while others minded the two roadhouses. She even agreed to let the mining company buy the lumber from her three-bedroom house in Kern Creek to build a storage enclosure for supplies at the prospect site. Not only did the whole operation turn out to be a scam, the gold mine owners at one point even conspired to kill Nellie. After the dishonest culprits were caught and later convicted in Seattle, Nellie sold Grandview and moved all her belongings to Kern Creek.

By that time the railroad workers had moved on after the Seward-to-Anchorage connection had been completed. Accordingly, Nellie switched her sights to the unfinished segment between Anchorage and Fairbanks and the potential roadhouse business that would be needed for the railroad. After a stint of cooking at the railroad spike camp of Mile 281 near Mount McKinley, she succeeded in obtaining another contract with the railroad to operate a large-scale roadhouse

Lawing relaxing in front of her cabin with a stuffed cub and a real dog. Photo courtesy of Doug Capra.

operation at Dead Horse Hill. It was located at Mile 248 about halfway between Seward and Fairbanks along the Susitna River. Nellie arranged for all her belongings to be transported by freight car from Kern Creek.

Dead Horse Hill hummed with activity. Travelers to the United States, Seward, or Anchorage plus scores of railroad men, gold prospectors, fishermen, and trappers accounted for the thousands of meals served each month in the 125-seat dining room, which was often filled beyond capacity. Nellie had a small staff, but she worked even harder than they did to keep up with the unending chores. During winter months when the trains weren't running due to ice and snowdrifts on the rails, Nellie would run her traplines and mush dogs.

On February 21, 1921, she even entered a dog sled race consisting of many experienced male mushers. She finished fourth, only a minute behind the third-place winner. Feats such as that embroidered further the respect and fame of Nellie Neal.

Still a divorcee (possibly twice over) facing the daunting social challenges in Alaska for a woman, she well understood the huge unbalanced ratio of males to females in Alaska during that era. It's evened out nowadays, but even so, the curious backgrounds of many woodsmen attracted to The Last Frontier still prompts the often-voiced observation by some women that "the odds are good, but the goods are odd."

Nellie's fate in that regard was about to change. While operating Dead Horse Hill, Nellie began to enjoy the companionship of a happy-go-lucky, piano-playing gentleman named Kenneth Holden. A shop foreman for the railroad, he asked Nellie for her hand in marriage before setting off on a temporary assignment to operate a steam shovel crane just north of there in Nenana. They expressed their love, and Nellie agreed that they would be married upon his return, but that was not to happen.

Holden had had a premonition that something might go wrong on this trip, and it did. As it turned out, the shovel engineer lost control and the boom swung too far, crushing Holden against the shovel's frame. Heartbroken, Nellie accompanied the coffin on the train ride to Seward.

She disembarked briefly at Grandview and again felt the overwhelmingly magnetic appeal of the area. She met Holden's mother as well as his cousin Billie Lawing, both of whom had left their home in Chattanooga, Tennessee, to travel to Seattle and await word from Holden on the proper timing for them to join him in Alaska.

Lawing stayed in touch with Nellie for the next couple of years, their correspondence evolving to a very personal and touching level that calmed her stress from the constant work at Dead Horse Hill, now renamed Curry to carry a less-negative connotation to travelers.

With her contract with the government soon to expire and key members of her staff already departed, Nellie had only one goal: Return to Roosevelt and start her own operation. The timing couldn't have been better because the owner of the roadhouse there had died and his wife didn't want to run it. Nellie made her an offer and she accepted. Nellie grabbed the next train to Roosevelt to seal the deal, during which time she envisioned turning the big log home on the lake into the perfect repository for all her game mounts.

She described in her book the joy of a lifelong dream about to come true: "This was the place that had so impressed me on my first visit—where the scenery surpassed all description, where the perfume of wild flowers sweetened every breeze—and which I had earnestly wished to call my own." Nellie returned to Curry to gather her belongings and accompanied them on the train ride back to Roosevelt. She passed Kern Creek and saw that it had burned down; the roadhouse in Grandview was being rebuilt. Finally at her new abode in Roosevelt, Nellie became excited to get the operation in gear and especially to start the museum.

"This was one of my first steps toward realization of my ambition when I first came to Alaska—to have a log home with its walls covered with heads and hides of Alaska's large and small game," Nellie wrote in her book. The museum would indeed soon house a moose head, all the bear species in various fur colors, deer, caribou, mountain goats, musk ox, Dall sheep, ptarmigans, owls, hares, foxes, otters, lynx, porcupines, bald eagles, swans, and imports from her travels to the Lower 48 of a cougar, elk, buffalo, and more. She also bought the piano that Kenneth Holden used to play, which originally came from a saloon in the Klondike Gold Rush town of Dawson City, Yukon, replete with twenty-eight bullet holes in it.

She opened her roadhouse and museum to great fanfare, for Nellie Neal was already known far and wide throughout the territory by 1923. Here she had arrived eight years before in Seward, stepping off the steamship with thirty-five dollars to her name, two suitcases, and a few keepsakes. And now, with a life already filled with adventure, misadventure, great happiness, and deep despair, she sensed that a new chapter in her life portended even greater experiences.

In July of that year, the railroad was completed from Seward to Fairbanks and President Warren G. Harding first arrived in Seward for the celebration. He and his wife deigned to meet the now-famous frontierswoman named Nellie Neal, whose signature, he knew, had also appeared on numerous expense and payroll vouchers pouring into Washington, D.C., from Dead Horse Hill. After a public address at the Seward Theatre, the Hardings and their party, which included future president Herbert Hoover and the territorial governor of Alaska, wanted to visit Nellie's museum. They stayed for over an hour, in particular commenting about the large caribou and moose heads. The next morning Nellie served all her famous sourdough pancakes before they departed to Fairbanks so that Harding could drive the golden spike that marked the completion of the $65 million railroad.

As Nellie's business at Roosevelt boomed, she continued to receive letters from Billie Lawing. In her autobiography, she admitted being totally affected: "The words he wrote might lend to my life a new and tender grace; words that sometimes add hopeful beauty to the plainest face." In one particular letter, Lawing asked her to marry him and wrote that he'd be willing to move to Alaska. She cabled him an acceptance. He soon arrived with a black Chevrolet touring car, quite a spectacle in 1923 Alaska with only sixty thousand residents and just a handful of brick-lined streets.

On September 8, 1923, they married in a ceremony at the Seward Theatre, where President Harding had spoken two months earlier. The rug on which he'd stood was later given to the bride and groom as a present. Billie and Nellie Lawing departed for Roosevelt. And for the very first time in her storied life, Nellie felt totally complete: She had a loving mate at her side and an idyllic place of her own in her cherished Alaska.

Life couldn't have been any better, and Billie indeed provided that missing element in Nellie's life, a fact she put so eloquently in *Alaska Nellie*:

> After years of loneliness and being denied the privilege of precious love, which is the foundation of happiness and without which our lives are only half lived, a kindred soul had now vibrated the hidden depths of my heart and kindled the flame of love to a glowing heat. Billie had the magic key, which would unlock the secret chamber of my heart. In the past I had allowed love to go from my heart, only to have it flung back, crushed and mutilated. Then, tenderly placing it down deep where I thought no mortal could be able to penetrate, I never expected to bring it to the surface again.

The new couple applied for a post office in Roosevelt, and it was granted, with Nellie becoming postmaster. Because other towns in the vast Territory of Alaska were also known as Roosevelt, the area was renamed Lawing. Thereafter, a letter simply addressed to "Nellie, Lawing, Alaska," would always reach her.

The Lawing roadhouse bustled during each June 1 to September 1 season. Billie later bought a thirty-six-foot boat, which he named *Nellie Neal*, for sightseeing and fishing trips on Kenai Lake and Cook Inlet. He and Nellie also bought a two-story log house near Lawing and moved it to their property, and later they installed the first windmill on the Kenai Peninsula.

Besides drawing locals and tourists for lodging, dining, and visiting the Alaska Nellie's Wildlife Museum, Lawing became a regular train stop. Everyone enjoyed the museum, and food connoisseurs raved about Nellie's superb cooking. A garden supplied all vegetables and salad greens, and fish and game couldn't have been any fresher, their kitchen jutting out directly above salmon-rich Kenai Lake. Praise always followed servings of her sourdough pancakes and strawberry pies.

Over and beyond her culinary talents, Nellie continued to be a rip-snorting storyteller. Her tales of facing dangerous attacks by bears, of saving lives in blizzards, and of acts of integrity were soon chronicled in newspapers. The legend of Nellie Lawing surged. Her guestbook swelled to fifteen thousand signatures including those of two U.S. presidents, humorist Will Rogers, a European prince, military brass, and Hollywood movie stars—in particular silent-screen star Alice Calhoun and her mother. Calhoun would later become a key figure in elevating Nellie's fame.

Billie and Nellie were absolutely inseparable until he died in March 1936 of a heart attack while removing snow from the ice near their cabin. Nellie's book describes this cataclysmic event: "My life felt empty. The face of all the world seemed changed. Twelve golden years my lovely mate and I walked the way of life together. His once noble presence had now become the guardian angel of my soul."

Nellie was sixty-three years old at the time of Billie's death and totally heartbroken. The only solution to assuage the grief: keep working. Billie had put the bug in Nellie's ear to write her autobiography, and when not tending to the lodge, she decided to do so. By 1938 she'd completed a manuscript and embarked on a bus tour all across the U.S. in search of a publisher, but none were interested. It's likely that Nellie also visited her old stomping grounds in Missouri to meet with family and old friends.

She especially liked visiting Hollywood due to her long-standing and deep friendship with Alice Calhoun. A veteran of forty-eight films, Calhoun knew everybody in Tinsel Town, and Nellie herself became a novel curiosity to the leading directors and actors of the time. As a result, in 1940 Metro-Goldwyn-Mayer produced a short movie called *In the Land of Alaska Nellie*. That same year Calhoun also encouraged Nellie to publish her autobiography with the title *Alaska Nellie*, a moniker that stuck forever after.

Frustrated at not finding a publisher willing to produce the book under her strict demand for no editorial changes, in May of 1940 she self-published it with the Seattle Printing and Publishing Company. However, in reviewing letters written by Nellie, historian Doug Capra suspects she may have been convinced by Calhoun to accept some editing help with the autobiography. "Nellie was a great storyteller, but not that good a writer," said Capra. "After her book came out, many people in Seward suspected the wording wasn't solely Nellie's work."

In any event, Nellie went on a nationwide publicity tour with book signings in many cities across the country. She even attended President Franklin Delano Roosevelt's inauguration in 1941 as a front-row guest and presented him with a signed copy.

After each venture away from home, Nellie would return with reams of memorabilia and souvenirs. Added to the collectibles and gifts from visitors along with a growing number of animal mounts from Nellie's hunting and trapping days, the museum became jammed. Being somewhat of a hoarder, Nellie didn't want to part with anything because each item reminded her of a story that would be regaled in vivid detail to her guests. Adding to the eccentricity was Nellie's pet bear cubs, which themselves spurred much attention and acclaim. One could also buy a signed copy of *Alaska Nellie* for $2.50.

Never one to retire to a mundane life, Nellie ran the roadhouse and the museum until her death in 1956. The Lawing property at Mile 23 had served as a huge attraction for many years, and at times lucky tourists could get a picture taken with Nellie and a bear cub or see her sporting the Colt pistol strapped to her waist that she'd worn for show for many years. Sometimes her spiel included fending off a grizzly attack near the lake, and pointing to her pistol, she'd exclaim that it misfired and the bear bit her on the wrist before running away. Nellie

Nellie's and Billie's lodge building and facilities on Kenai Lake in Lawing, Alaska.
Photo courtesy of Doug Capra.

would then peel back her cuff and as proof reveal a scar, and with a grin she'd add that the next day she hunted down that bear and shot it with a rifle.

The roadhouse and some of its structures were already falling apart when the most powerful earthquake ever recorded in North America struck near Anchorage on March 27, 1964. The property later became a souvenir shop and then a B&B until finally abandoned. Nonetheless, the Lawing homestead became part of the National Register of Historic Places on April 3, 1975. "Like so many before her and since, Nellie came to Alaska to reinvent herself," said Capra. "She left behind who she was and became someone else."

Nellie is buried next to Billie Lawing in the Seward Cemetery. Unfortunately, her estate and that of Billie became a probate mess. As it turned out, she and Billie had long before turned over most of their property to the Alaska Railroad and the Territory of Alaska. Nellie's latter years revealed a property in disarray, although she still joyfully entertained visitors with tales of yesteryear in her dusty museum.

Despite the squandered estate and structures lost to the ravages of time notwithstanding, the robust and colorful personality of one Nellie Lawing—like a treasured work of art—will be long preserved in the history and legends of Alaska.

2

FRANK GLASER, 1887–1974

Anchorage

A loner who enthusiastically endured forty years of living in the remote Interior Alaska, he was hired by the U.S. government to eradicate wolves. He taught many woodsmen the nuances of hunting and became an important voice in the controversial debates about predator control in Alaska.

The essence of the quintessential mountain man, Frank Glaser traversed the great Alaska wilderness repeatedly behind dog sleds and in bush planes. He hunted for subsistence and for a living, gaining perspectives about the balance of nature that one can never fully appreciate otherwise. Glaser possessed far more depth and character than merely one who dispatches animals with a rifle or traps, and yet he rose to prominence by—of all things—becoming proficient as a hired gun for a government agency.

Eradication may sound despicable nowadays, but it wasn't in the 1930s, when wolves and coyotes competed for the same meat as the burgeoning numbers of two-legged creatures arriving in Alaska to build cabins, hunt, and farm. The U.S. Fish and Wildlife Service (FWS) needed a proficient hunter both to rid certain areas of predators deemed either dangerous or a nuisance to homesteaders and to teach other hunters and trappers how to become more efficient as well.

An agent for the U.S. Fish and Wildlife Service, Glaser inspected these thirty- and forty-pound sheefish caught by Eskimos ice fishing near Kotzebue in December 1952. Photo courtesy of the Fabian Carey Collection, Elmer E. Rasmuson Library, University of Alaska, Fairbanks, UAF-1975-209-10.

That scenario would change as future generations came to recognize that all animals in the oceans, streams, and fields play important roles in their respective ecosystems. But prior to the 1960s, that wasn't the case.

Born in Boston, Massachusetts, Frank eschewed city life and, like a good many easterners then and now, wanted to see for himself if stories about the Territory of Alaska's beauty and brilliance rang true. In his late twenties, Glaser arrived in Alaska in 1915 as the winds of war were engulfing Europe. He settled in Interior Alaska around the Savage River area in what is now Denali, which Congress soon thereafter designated a national park that includes Mount McKinley. Glaser trekked between there and northeast to the Black River near Fort Yukon.

He learned the intricacies of the trapping business by trial and error and by being observant because trappers were seldom eager to tutor another competitor. Glaser set up outlets to sell furs and bartered with Natives and merchants.

After two years of learning the ropes of not only trapping but also dealing with extreme weather and animals capable of killing him,

Glaser (*right*) and Harold Ervin examining a dressed-out bison at Big Delta in 1950. Photo from the U.S. Fish and Wildlife Service National Digital Library (http://digitalmedia.fws.gov/cdm/ref/collection/natdiglib/id/413).

news came that the United States had entered World War I. As did many brave young men in the bush, Glaser enlisted. It's unclear whether he ever saw combat or was sent overseas to help France, Russia, England, and the other allies in Europe. However, it's likely that he underwent basic training as did all would-be soldiers, which would have included range time with a rifle.

In any event, after the war he returned to Alaska—a doughboy determined to become a sourdough. Perhaps needing a respite from firearms in general, for over a decade he operated a roadhouse. Situated in the town of Black Rapids on the Valdez Trail near the Delta River, the roadhouse accommodated prospectors, anglers, hunters, fur traders, and other visitors needing room and board.

But the call of the wild from his days in the Alaska Interior wilderness—hunting, setting traps, the magnificence of Alaska—evidently never escaped Glaser's heart. Pampering guests and fussing over minutiae such as bedding sheets and laundry most surely wore thin. He returned to trapping and hunting for furs, but when fur prices dropped, an acquaintance named Clarence Rhode offered him a job. Rhode, who became the regional director of the FWS in Alaska, needed a professional hunter as a predator control agent, and no one fit that job description better than Glaser.

The whole idea of being paid by the U.S. government again to shoot a rifle elated Glaser. Rhode and the FWS quickly recognized the zeal with which Glaser took to his responsibilities. He far surpassed expectations in terms of proficiency with a rifle and trapping, but as all successful people do, Glaser went beyond the boundaries of his job description.

He turned out to be an effective communicator, and his trusting nature, combined with other personal attributes, garnered greater public cooperation. He could thus extract techniques, suggestions, and ideas from trappers with whom he wasn't competing as well as from Native People to devise the most successful methods of hunting and trapping. In turn, Glaser willingly passed on his expertise to others. The FWS moved Glaser from region to region and station to station. He became respected by his bosses, his colleagues, and untold thousands with whom he came in contact in the Alaska Range.

Without question, Glaser's impact on efforts to control wolf populations became the most controversial subject associated with his name. The policy of the FWS in those days was to get rid of every wolf possible by using as many agents as possible and by applying any means possible, including aerial shooting, trapping, snaring, and even poisoning. Glaser was but one man and could hardly be accused of making much of a dent in Alaska's wolf populations on his own.

Even so, references to Glaser still regularly appear in studies and papers on that topic by game biologists and researchers. As such, his nickname, Alaska's Wolf Man, was indicative of Glaser's deep knowledge of—and affection for—his namesake species rather than a character slur or an attribution of wanton killing.

Jim Rearden, considered by many the dean of outdoor communicators in Alaska, wrote an excellent book about Glaser appropriately titled *Alaska's Wolf Man*. Rearden told me that the impetus for the book occurred by chance in a sporting goods store in Fairbanks one day. "This rather small, nearly baldheaded man came in and started telling stories to a customer," said Rearden. "I edged closer and listened, and so did other customers until a small crowd had gathered around the talkative old man. He told of adventures with grizzly bears and how

Glaser and a team of reindeer in northwest Alaska, where he controlled wolf populations as a federal predator agent. Photo courtesy of Frank Glaser and Jim Rearden.

he'd outsmarted some wolves. After a bit he broke off, bought some ammunition and left. I asked the storeowner who he was. It was Glaser, of course."

Rearden looked Glaser up, started tape-recording his stories and, years later, located diaries he'd written. In *Alaska's Wolf Man* Rearden cites numerous anecdotes demonstrating Glaser's ability to handle life-threatening challenges commonly faced by those living in the bush. In one such predicament, Glaser crashed through the ice when traversing a river, climbed out, undressed, and quickly built two fires. He then twisted and turned between the two flames to thwart hypothermia and to keep his circulation going.

Another memory involved one of Glaser's less-glamorous habits. "Like many old-timers in Alaska, Frank was addicted to snuff—'snoose,' as it was commonly called," Rearden told me. "However, it often caused him an upset stomach, to which Frank would say, 'It's not fit to put in your mouth and I'll never use it again.' However, within a week or so he'd be back with the familiar metal can in his pocket."

Glaser had no use for animal-rights groups and enjoyed showing them up whenever possible. "Frank had a naturalist's ability to identify

Glaser at his Fairbanks log cabin home in 1954. Photo courtesy of Jim Rearden.

animals," said Rearden. "He once identified a small population of trumpeter swans he'd heard from a distance while somewhere in the Puget Sound area. No one believed him until some 'expert' took a closer look and became amazed because everyone thought at the time that trumpeters were only in Montana and Oregon."

A naturalist indeed. Glaser flourished in Alaska's Interior because it reflected the interior of his soul—wild, passionate, adventuresome, intrepid. As the debilitating limitations of advancing age caught up to him, he opted to retire for the modern conveniences afforded in Anchorage. However, in his heyday Glaser preferred going it alone, living in isolation, and traveling the path one must traverse to truly comprehend animal behavior: He actually lived among the sheep, bears, wolves, moose, foxes, and caribou, and shared the challenges and hazards of their environment. By walking the same trails, eating the same foods, and breathing the same air, he gained insights that escape most others.

Living for lengthy periods of time in Alaska's Interior—in Glaser's case, for forty years—certainly can make one an expert on animal behavior. But unlike many mountain men who would rather do without civilization altogether, Glaser had no trouble adjusting to evolving improvements in wilderness gear or modes of transportation. For that reason, he easily took advantage of modernization that evolved from getting about on foot or horse to traveling by dog sled, jeep, snowmobile, and airplane. However, when first hired by the FWS, he didn't know how to drive and once missed a turn on the Steese Highway in Fairbanks, damaging the car.

Glaser took to photography, owning the newest versions of cameras whenever they became available. Many of the images he took became part of Alaska's visual archives. He also acquired numerous rifles throughout the years, his favorite purportedly being a Savage Model 99 that fired .250-3000 cartridges—perfect for taking wolves, coyotes, wolverines, and the like.

Glaser harvested an estimated five hundred wolves during his career, but his largest kill is the one that's still a legend. On July 12, 1939, Glaser trapped a 175-pound alpha male east of Fairbanks near the town of Eagle. There may have been even bigger ones shot or trapped before or after, but nearly all wolves taken back then were gutted and skinned out in the field. Since Glaser was working for the FWS at the time, he brought in the entire carcass for purposes of research.

Many of the wolves Glaser killed were quickly dispatched by rifle, but those caught in traps oftentimes played on his conscience. It upset Glaser to pry open a trap around the leg or snout of an animal he'd come to idolize for its adaptability and cunning. He realized that if dead, the wolf had struggled futilely during its ensnarement—perhaps even for days. Worse yet, if the animal were still alive when he arrived on the scene, he'd have to witness its torment before dispatching it.

In either case, inflicting death was far more merciful when instantly performed by a well-placed bullet, but trapping was to Glaser a necessary evil. Wolves are smart, instinctive survivalists; even an expert hunter like Glaser could not depend on getting a clear rifle shot very often.

As a triggerman rather than a policymaker, Glaser was not responsible for the political mechanizations so part and parcel of fish and game management. As all would come to know, decisions made by the FWS as well as by the Alaska Department of Fish & Game (formed after statehood in 1959) changed as wildlife research methods became more reliable and as evolving public opinion become more prominent as a factor. In the post–World War II era, the term *predator control* took on a negative connotation. Animal-rights groups sprang up to "save the wolf," with media exposure at times fanning the flames. From Glaser's viewpoint, however, his lifetime of admiration for wolves and appreciation for how wolves contributed to his own survival in the Interior transcended political disagreements.

Through it all—the good, the bad, and the controversies—he emerged with the distinction and respect of being known as Alaska's Wolf Man.

3

BILL PINNELL, 1898–1990
MORRIS TALIFSON, 1909–2000

Kodiak Island

After becoming close friends and business partners in Montana, these two men eventually discovered the alluring wildness of Kodiak Island in Alaska. They developed a world-famous Kodiak brown bear guiding business during the economic boom by the use of magazine advertisements and video presentations in the Lower 48.

Mention trophy brown bear hunting, and Kodiak Island will usually jump out in the same breath. So long as hunting for brownies is still excellent sport there—and should always be so with wise game management—excellent brown bear guides will also continue to step forward. That said, any discussion about the golden age of Kodiak Island brown bear hunting will include the guiding duo still commonly referred to simply as "P&T."

Bill Pinnell and Morris Talifson stand shoulder to shoulder with other pioneering Kodiak guides like Charley Madsen and Hal Waugh, all of whom staked out bear-rich territories, built rustic lodges, established spike camps, and attracted clients worldwide for the trophy brown bear hunts offered by the south portion of the island.

I became fascinated with Pinnell & Talifson both as individuals and as a working duo. While the research involving some of the characters

All hides were left for Talifson to ship after curing. Guide Scott Mileur is on the ladder to the left, and guide Dale Fisher, to the right. *Left to right standing*: Steve Howard, Harry Dodge, Bill Pinnell, Morris Talifson, packer Roger Walters, guide Ken Langlois, and packer Jim Swenor. *Front*, guide Steve Bergeron. Photo courtesy of Harry Dodge.

in this book often became tedious and difficult to organize, the numerous stories about P&T occasionally included nuggets of insight about one man or the other that helped make this chapter one of my favorites.

As pointed out later in this chapter by Harry Dodge, P&T exhibited opposite personalities and skills, yet they remained determined to ride out their frequent disagreements by staying mindful of the big picture: To maintain a very successful hunting enterprise and to keep their life-long friendship alive. From my own experiences, family and friends seldom meshed well with business pursuits. Jealousy and acrimony arise, and I still have relatives with whom I never speak after fallouts over money or power. It's ridiculous, but that's reality. However, such personal breaks never happened with P&T and my hat is off to them.

P&T also enjoyed the good fortune of opportune timing. As in all parts of Alaska, the guiding business developed significantly when air travel to Alaska became more commercialized after World War II. During the war years themselves, hunting pressure on brown bears on Kodiak Island decreased and the populations soared. The timing was perfect for guides like P&T. In addition, the increasing numbers of bush planes and pilots who could fly them converted subsistence hunters into professional guides.

Another factor that transformed guiding into a robust business pursuit is that the U.S. postwar economy boomed, providing greater disposable income and enabling more outdoors enthusiasts to visit Alaska. The upsurge in the client potential and popularity of magazines, such as *Outdoor Life, Field & Stream* and *Sports Afield*, turned seasonal guiding from a sideline into a full-time pursuit for talented and aggressive types like Pinnell and Talifson.

Their eventual success represents a true riches-to-rags-to-riches story that is quite remarkable. Pinnell, born near Sedalia, Missouri, on July 18, 1898, had a father who worked as a truck driver and coal miner. He also became something of a politician with a penchant for oratory. That gregarious, articulate trait would be passed on to his son Bill. In 1923, Pinnell started with a fellow named Bob Slowe a fur farm that proved successful, and the partners decided to relocate the business to Choteau, Montana.

The men bought and sold furs of raccoon, coyote, fox, and other animals, plus opened a second office in Browning, Montana. In 1927, eighteen-year-old Morris Talifson, a trapper in the area, entered the scene. Although at first Talifson seemed resistant to Pinnell's persistent offers to buy furs from him, he eventually went to work for Pinnell as a helper on the fur farm and in the office. Slowe decided to leave the business, and Talifson replaced him as Pinnell's partner.

Morris came into the world on August 9, 1909, in Bynum, Montana. He was one of ten children to a diligent but tender mother and a father who worked as a timber evaluator and farmer. At an early age, Morris learned to hunt out of necessity due to his father's shaky financial status, but that chore grew into a passion.

The partnership of Pinnell and Talifson thrived initially. They became fast friends, possibly because of their opposite personalities and skills. While Pinnell tended to be outgoing and garrulous, Talifson was quiet and unassuming. Pinnell could wheel and deal with the best of businessmen; Talifson, a born hunter, preferred toiling in the background. Neither man was educated, with Talifson reaching eighth grade and Pinnell never attending school at all, but both were quick to learn new skills and absolutely resilient once their minds united on a common goal.

Prices for furs continued to escalate for two years, but the crash of the stock market in 1929 immediately threw their business into a tailspin. No one was buying furs, and Pinnell and Talifson were unable to find any employment, so they took off in a 1928 Chevy for the West Coast. The men drifted for six years, returning home now and then from points out west and in Montana, but nothing clicked until they heard about a gold strike at Cow Creek near Roseburg, Oregon. They lived in an eight-foot-by-ten-foot tent and mined gold, at times taking odd jobs such as picking apples or cutting wood. Pinnell did some hunting with an old 8 mm Mauser rifle he'd acquired from a friend, and poached deer for food. Life was tough, but the men remained inseparable.

During a trip back to Montana in the winter of 1938, a friend of P&T mentioned an article about gold being found on remote beaches of Kodiak Island. That was enough for P&T to take a steamer from Seattle, Washington, to Seward, Alaska, where they arrived on July 5, 1938. They obtained a job working on a boat headed toward Kodiak, and the fate of P&T took shape into what would become two of the greatest brown bear guides in history.

But that success and fame would have to wait. Hunting brown bears would not become their profession for another eleven years. They initially mined gold on the beach at the mouth of the Red River and, three years later in 1941, became watchmen of an abandoned salmon cannery at the head of Olga Bay, about thirty-five miles north of Cape Alitak and seventy-five miles southwest of the main town of Kodiak.

Kodiak Island itself lies over 300 miles southwest of Anchorage. It's the second largest island in the United States, measuring 100 miles along a northeast-to-southwest axis and varying in width from 10 to 60 miles. The island is mountainous on the northern and eastern sides while trending toward more open and treeless to the southwest. Kodiak Island was prime brown bear habitat.

P&T knew they had hit the mother lode. Marvin H. Clark Jr.'s *Pinnell and Talifson: Last of the Great Brown Bear Men* quotes Pinnell's excitement about Olga Bay: "When we got to Olga Bay, we had it made! The beach had plenty of gold to be mined, the creeks were full of salmon. All we had to do was work out the gold and net our fish. For two hungry souls from the depression down south, that living was mighty good I must say."

Besides moving from their primitive Red River shack into the solidly built, bright-red cannery buildings, they enjoyed running water, blankets, and comfortable beds—rare luxuries for them. The men decided to do some trapping for foxes and otters in the vicinity, but a huge brown bear kept raiding their traps. Pinnell at the time was using a .30-30 rifle and figured that would be enough to get rid of the "varmint" bear. It took many shots at close range to put the big bruin down—its hide measuring an incredible eleven feet, three inches long. The massive Kodiak brown bears were unlike anything the men had even seen or heard about, with many exceeding ten feet in length and weighing far more than a thousand pounds.

Even though both were expert riflemen, P&T knew that more firepower than a .30-30 or the old Mauser would be required, or they'd be tempting death in future encounters with the massive brown bears.

Neither man served in World War II because by then Pinnell was considered too old for infantry service and Talifson had a foot injury. However, when Japan later invaded the Aleutian Islands, they were given duties as coast watchers. P&T also worked off and on for the U.S. Fish & Wildlife Service (FWS), with Talifson supervising a series of weirs (barriers placed across rivers to alter the water flow) and Pinnell serving as a fishery enforcement officer.

The latter office often pitted Pinnell against local commercial fishermen. Pinnell took the position that a future with abundant salmon resources demanded the observance of FWS regulations, but fishermen bitterly resisted and resented him. Those disputes deeply affected Pinnell and would be the root cause for his future support of stricter laws involving brown bears.

In the winter of 1947, as a change of venue from Olga Bay, P&T tried their hand at trapping and gold mining near Denali in Interior Alaska. However, the absence made their hearts grow fonder for Kodiak Island, and they went back in September of 1948. But the FWS had an interesting attractive proposition for P&T upon their return: become hunting guides. The brown bear populations had been nearly obliterated prior to World War II due to Natives having more access to rifles and commercial hunters killing them to sell the huge hides, but their numbers rebounded when in 1941 Kodiak Island was designated a National Wildlife Refuge. As a result, in the following years the brown bear population had grown immensely and pressure to thin it down had mounted from cattle farmers whose herds were being impacted by bear predation.

One problem faced Talifson and Pinnell about the FWS proposition: Neither of them possessed a guide license, which called for them to first work as apprentices to a licensed guide. However, the FWS waived the requirement based upon P&T's detailed knowledge of the southern portion of Kodiak Island and their established reputation as hunters and trappers.

P&T hastily built a hunting cabin on Fraser Lake in spring 1949. Remembering the challenges of stopping a brown bear with too little firepower, Talifson acquired a new .375 Holland & Holland (H&H) Model 70 Winchester rifle. His first kill, however, involved taking out a large brownie for a group of Aleut Natives. They'd heard about Talifson's skill as a hunter and his new bear rifle. He agreed to help them and tracked the bear to the south end of Akalura. It took eight shots to put the giant bruin down—a monster brown bear that taped out at eleven feet, four inches, and still regarded as one of the largest brownies ever taken.

P&T soon guided their first clients, taking them to Little Dog Salmon Creek, Akalura, and their Fraser Lake cabin. When back at camp, Pinnell liked to entertain them with bear stories while Talifson smoked his pipe—a ritual and role-playing that would be common for the next four decades. Their clients went on to shoot two brownies, one measuring nine feet and the other, ten feet, two-inches.

News of their success didn't sit well with the few competitors already established in the area. One guide in particular successfully challenged the waiver that had been approved by the FWS, causing demotion of P&T to assistant guides. However, they got around that obstacle by continuing to book hunts at their three camps for the 1950 season under the direction of a local Master Guide until they obtained the requisite licenses. The following season they opened a fourth camp after being tipped off by a retiring FWS manager that it would be wise to do so because of an impending law that would prohibit further cabins being built on the southern portion of Kodiak Island.

P&T's business became famous, and not just by word of mouth. On one spring hunt in 1952, three of their hunters shot enormous brown bears. The following day, the hides were hung side-by-side on an outer wall at the Olga Bay cannery and photographed with the three hunters sitting in front of them. That picture was used in a P&T ad in *Outdoor Life* for twenty-five years. It became known as "the three hides" ad, and it inspired many hunters to book trips with P&T.

P&T also produced a film in 1954 that highlighted their operation and hunting successes. Pinnell showed it during appearances in Alaska and the Lower 48. The film was hugely popular, and Pinnell loved being the center of attention at conventions, sportsman shows, charitable events, and hunting-club meetings. The events put Pinnell into contact with wealthy executives, celebrities like golf legend Sam Snead, and political figures of the day. Pinnell himself had become a celebrity and through him Talifson as well.

Besides the advertising and film, the timing couldn't have been better for Pinnell and Talifson to become hunting guides. Besides airline travel and postwar prosperity, word-of-mouth testimonials by P&T's clients brought in more clients. Even the spam sandwiches and copious cups of hot coffee served by P&T became a humorous tidbit of gossip at hunting clubs across the nation. The combination of all those elements resulted in bookings for each season selling out quickly—and then the next season and even the next in advance.

P&T weren't the only guides in the right place at the right time. Famed hunting guide Charley Madsen had already been offering guided hunts out of Kodiak Island for over a decade, but Madsen's territory was distant enough to not rub elbows. The same would be the case when soon-to-be-a-legend Hal Waugh set up his guiding business in the region in the early 1950s. The southern chunk of Kodiak Island would be plenty big enough to handle several proximate hunting operations while the northern region of the island had been mainly ceded to cattle farmers.

The meld of personalities that had brought success to P&T's fur business in Montana reached even greater heights with their guiding pursuits. Pinnell handled most of the business and public relations while Talifson ensured excellent hunts. They had a good product and it was selling well.

Harry Dodge, a biologist and guide on Kodiak Island for over thirty years, came to know Pinnell and Talifson very well. Dodge describes their relationship:

> Bill did all the hunter correspondence, usually signing 'Bill, a friend you've never met.' Morris was indeed the hunter of the two, although Bill was certainly bear-savvy himself. Though Morris usually got the biggest bear, Bill always claimed he guided the majority of hunters. They each actively guided in the field until age seventy with Bill continuing to go out to the hunting camps each season until he reached ninety. Morris was also the mechanic of the two—Bill had no mechanical abilities whatsoever. They were definitely two opposites in most ways, bickered constantly, and yet were inseparable partners.

An interesting indication of how Pinnell and Talifson marketed and explained their services can be viewed in the following wording of one of their magazine advertisements that ran in the late 1950s with "the three hides" picture.

A public relations piece that P&T included in mailings and used as a handout at sportsmen shows and for inquiries was a small booklet with the following note (spelling and grammar same as in copy):

A MESSAGE FROM YOUR GUIDES!
DEAR FRIEND,

We have done our best to tell you, and show you with the pictures what we have to offer.

Our hunting camps are located in the heart of the bear country. We live here the year around and see bear all the time. We know

This famed "three-hide ad" appeared for twenty-five years beginning in the 1950s and created a lot of notice for Pinnell and Talifson. Photo courtesy of the Pinnell family.

our hunting country like a book and know where the big old bear hang out. You will see by the pictures that most of our hunters have taken very large bear with us. We give personal guide service and don't farm our hunters out like some of the guides do.

Our fishing is fine, you can fish out of any of the camps and make good catches only a few feet from the door of the cabins.

Our ptarmigan and duck hunting in the fall of the year is the best on the Island. If you are a wing shot you will enjoy this along with your bear hunting and fishing.

Should there be any matter not covered in this booklet concerning a hunt with us, please feel free to write for information. Hunting is our business and we take great pride and pleasure in striving to honestly describe our hunting conditions, terrain, and other facts. Your success is our main interest.

We hope to have the pleasure of booking you for a hunt with us.

Yours respectfully,

BILL and MORRIS

The same booklet also suggested proper gear (spelling and punctuation as it appeared):

Bring your gun and two boxes of ammunition.
1 fishing rod with a spinning reel.

1 pair of light weight hip boots, not ankle fitting and Converse preferred.

1 light full-length raincoat. L.L. Bean sells a good one.

1 light warm coat, down preferred. This can be purchased in Seattle, Washington, at Eddie Bauer.

Light, medium weight long handle underwear.

Medium weight wool shirts.

Medium weight wool socks.

Medium weight wool pants.

A cap with ear flaps as some of the mornings will be frosty.

A flashlight and two extra batteries.

You can ship your extra gear by parcel post 30 days ahead of the time you make your hunt. Ship it to yourself in care of us, Olga Bay, Kodiak, Alaska.

Don't bring a lot of junk you will have no use for as excess air baggage is very expensive. You are allowed 66 pounds on your ticket as Alaska is considered overseas.

Don't bring Bright Red Clothes—you don't have to wear red clothes up here as no one is going to shoot at you. Bring dark colored finger gloves.

Like most guides of that era, P&T discouraged hunters from bringing along a .44-caliber magnum handgun whenever that inquiry was made. However, they couched the reply to that constant question in a humorous way. Either Pinnell or Talifson would usually just nod and say something like, "It's okay to use a .44 as long as you save the last round for yourself."

Talifson, who did most of the guiding, had two words for hunters whose first bullet hit home on a bear: "Keep shooting." Even with .375-caliber H&H magnum rounds, it usually took several shots to knock down a big brownie, and often hunters would shoot once, and stop and stare as the bear reacted. That could be a fatal error, which is why Talifson encouraged them to keep right on firing until certain the beast was a goner.

In the late 1950s, P&T took yearly trips to the Brooks Range and guided sheep, caribou, and moose hunts. This of course meant they often had to fend off grizzly bears. P&T considered grizzlies necessarily more aggressive toward humans than their coastal brown bear cousins

A successful spring hunt in 1981. *Left to right:* Bill Pinnell, Harry Dodge, Scott Mileur, Morris Talifson, hunter Chuck McKinley on the ladder, and dog Misty. Photo courtesy of Harry Dodge.

because of the availability of less forage foods such as salmon and clams, and a longer period of hibernation in the Interior. As such, they regretted having to shoot grizzlies that entered their camp and, despite warning shots, wouldn't leave.

With the problems from serving as a FWS enforcement officer still in his memory, Pinnell led efforts to stop the shooting of sow brown bears with cubs as well as to establish shorter seasons and a per-hunter seasonal bag limit. Pinnell constantly had to walk a tightrope that sometimes resulted in too little or too much regulation. He also helped put a stop to cattle ranchers using a Piper Cub to track and shoot brown bears.

While Pinnell tied the knot in 1961 with a gal named Rena, Talifson never married. Talifson, an introvert who craved the solitude of Kodiak Island, at times looked back on his life and expressed the wish to have enjoyed more personal interactions with people. When asked in

Bill Pinnell skinning a caribou in the Brooks Range in March 1971. Photo courtesy of Jim Rearden.

interviews how he and Talifson managed to get along for such a long period of time, Pinnell would jokingly refer to Talifson's disagreeable manner and that they argued constantly, but in the end he felt it was a matter of fate that the two became lifelong friends and successful partners. As I mentioned earlier in this chapter, that's quite an accomplishment in itself.

In *Pinnell and Talifson*, Marvin Clark states that no other guides in Alaska's history have matched the record-book success of these two men and "probably none ever will."

That's a pretty bold prediction. Nonetheless, Kodiak Island is still considered by many the home of the best brown bear hunting in the world. Some believe that the feats of personality opposites like Bill Pinnell and Morris Talifson will indeed stand the test of time when it comes not only to setting world records but establishing a very high bar for what makes a successful guiding partnership. Ask any knowing source to provide a list of legendary Alaska hunters and the names of P&T will almost certainly be there.

4

SAM WHITE, 1891–1976

Fairbanks

First a surveyor for the U.S. government and later a game commissioner when few hunting regulations existed, his bush plane, the Swallow, frightened poachers but became a welcome sight for remote villagers in need of food or medical help. He thus became widely known as Alaska's first flying game warden.

Some historians observe that the emergence of the United States in the twentieth century as a dominating economic power had much to do with war. While the country certainly was barreling forward on its own into the prosperous era of trains, planes, and automobiles, the United States after World War I undoubtedly became a force to be reckoned with. And following the next world war ending in 1945, the United States became the undisputedly dominant country both militarily and economically.

Given that backdrop, the Territory of Alaska took on a new perspective too. Since buying the region for a song and a dance from Russia in 1867, the vast area didn't receive official status as a U.S. territory until 1912. That's about the time that the U.S. military and economic decision makers finally recognized Alaska's strategic location in the North Pacific and the vast potential of the raw materials of what would become the forty-ninth state in 1959.

Sam White next to *Swallow*, his name for the plane he flew to become the famed "flying game warden." With an open cockpit, he could only fly for three hours at a time on cold winter days. Photo courtesy of Jim Rearden.

A six-foot, two-hundred-pound former lumberjack, Sam Otho White had the toughness and mettle to handle the extreme conditions of Alaska's north country and face down those who chose to challenge his authority. Born on a hillside farm in Eustis Ridge, Maine, on November 26, 1891, White grew up in a log home with eight siblings. He managed to get through the eighth grade before the relentless chores involved with running a farm necessitated his strong back.

The White family never had much extra money lying around, but a hundred-plus years ago it was common for farmers to trade their products for goods and services. For one, the barter system meant that farmers wouldn't go hungry or do without suitable clothing, and for another, Sam's steady aim produced plenty of deer and bear meat for the dinner table.

In addition, whenever time allowed, Sam worked odd jobs as a lumberjack, canoeist, hunting guide, and foreman for the International Boundary Survey. In 1917, World War I sent White into the U.S. Army.

Because of his robust physique, he was assigned to a special battalion of rangers to fight in France.

The rangers included a fellow from Ketchikan and another from Fairbanks. From both White heard plenty about life in southeast and Interior Alaska. Their colorful depictions of the new territory's untamed waters and forests appealed greatly to White. It was a wind song that would be carried in his consciousness for the next five years.

After the war, White returned to Maine and his former job with the International Boundary Survey. He later jumped to the U.S. Coast and Geodetic Survey (CGS) in April 1922, and that's when his Alaska dream began to take shape. White took the Civil Service exam and passed it. The following month he was assigned by the CGS to Alaska to perform reconnaissance for geodetic teams mapping the wilderness areas and later to help update the U.S. Army's maps.

White arrived in Seward and boarded the Alaska Railroad for Anchorage. "My first real taste of the north came when that first train ride stopped at Nellie Neal's cabin," White wrote as part of a series of articles for *Alaska Sportsman* magazine in the mid 1960s. "She was a frail little woman, I thought, but one could sense her driving urgency to get things done. And there at her place were laid out bigger bearskins than I had ever imagined, and moose racks like I had never seen before. Nellie had a pelt or trophy of every game animal in Alaska." Nellie, who also became a legend, later was to marry Billie Lawing and become known as Alaska Nellie, one of the subjects in this book.

Onward to Anchorage he went, which White described as a small village back then. His reconnaissance job in dense bush country north of Anchorage involved advance work for the survey crews. That meant creating trails from point A to point B, which at times entailed traversing swamps, hacking through dense alders, selecting the most practical routes, and improvising safe passage through what would be otherwise inaccessible to surveyors and trains of pack horses.

If you're frequently amid the wilds of Alaska, a dangerous rendezvous with a wild beast, particularly a bear, is inevitable. White's first bear encounter occurred when he was checking out a trail two-and-a-half hours ahead of the pack train—not a typical procedure, this type of scouting normally occurred with a much shorter time differential. At one point he walked around a bend and found himself between a sow grizzly and two cubs, exactly where one doesn't ever want to be. She let out a deafening roar and immediately charged. Despite her bounding speed, White sent a rifle bullet home directly on target between the huge bear's neck and shoulder.

The bear hit the ground momentarily, her legs kicking wildly before she righted herself to charge once more. White fired another round that landed in the same kill spot. Incredibly, the bear relentlessly dragged itself toward White while snapping and popping her jaws. It took yet a third shot to finally end the ordeal. White regretted having to kill the beautiful animal even though in self-defense he had no choice. Fortunately the cubs appeared old enough to fend for themselves.

White and the survey crews constantly sought the most advantageous and practical mode of transportation. That meant at times going by foot, horse, dog sled, canoe, riverboat, airplane, or some combination thereof. Walking was of course the slowest; horses and dogs had to be fed and cared for; boats were only useful when rivers weren't iced; and airplanes required cleared landing strips. Everything had its own complications, but White's job was to find a way for the crews to reach the desired coordinates as quickly and safely as possible and then move on.

The winter weather proved to be the most difficult challenge to overcome, particularly in the frigid interior and northern regions of Alaska. The survey crews especially disdained sleeping in tents with temperatures at times sliding to forty degrees below zero and often to sixty below or more. On those occasions, work came to a standstill, and it became a fight for life to stay warm—or at least not freezing—in the tents.

White described the tent-survival modus operandi on such occasions. Generally, two men would share an eight-foot-by-ten-foot wall tent erected low to the ground so the extension of the flaps would fold under and be weighted down. After stomping on the snow to smooth out the flooring, spruce tips would be spread about except directly under the stove. The stove was propped atop two birch logs and, when lit, melted the snow beneath it to the ground, creating a hole in which coffee grounds and other degradable refuse would be poured.

If stove oil wasn't available or it became scarce, wood was piled in whatever portions of the tent possible so ideally it wouldn't necessitate exiting. However, just in case, extra wood had to be cut and tiered around the sides of the tent for quick access. A snow wall built around the tents also aided in blocking some of the swirling blizzard winds. Stovepipe dampers were adjusted at times to create an opening for some air exchange without letting in too much cold air.

Sleep was conducted in two-hour shifts. One person always watched for errant sparks and kept the fire going. If the tent went up in flames in minus-sixty-degree weather, it meant either burning or freezing to death. When frost collected on the inside of the tent surface, it had to be knocked off after care was taken to cover the wood and belongings. One mishap could spell disaster. White became used to the tent routine, but survey crewmembers familiar only with camping trips in the Lower 48 complained endlessly about having to sleep in such severe conditions.

All the skills White had acquired while working reconnaissance in the bush couldn't have been more advantageous for his next life's adventure: becoming an agent for the Alaska Game Commission (AGC) in 1927. He was initially based out of Fort Yukon during an era when historically there had been few game laws and even fewer hunters or trappers who followed them. White mushed a dog team to patrol the area, but he could only supervise limited portions of tracts.

Considering the AGC's minuscule budget despite the enormity of the square mileage under its purview, quick access to remote areas where poaching might be occurring was impractical on foot or by dog sleds, and rails or highways were few and far between. The only reasonable solution was air travel. A single-prop plane with wheels, floats, or skis would be just the ticket.

Sam White bought with his own money a plane that he named *Swallow*. He learned to fly it at Weeks Field in Fairbanks under the tutelage of Alaska aviation pioneer Noel Wien. Noel, his mechanic-turned-pilot brother Ralph (who would die in a plane crash in 1930), and in later years mechanic-turned-pilot brother Sig operated Wien Air Alaska.

With the *Swallow* at his command, White became Alaska's first flying game warden and quite probably the first in the world. White became not only an enforcer of game laws aimed at stopping poachers and controlling game populations, but also a savior of sorts to villages large and small. White would arrive with food and other supplies, fly out the

White grimaces to drive home the need for a conservation ethic by posing next to this large pile of antlers. Photo from the Wien Collection, Anchorage Museum, B1985.027.

sick and injured to hospitals, and become an honored guest at festivals and ceremonies. He was in effect an ambassador for the territorial government, exerting fair but tough enforcement while serving as a conduit for seldom-heard voices from the bush. Many villages cleared a landing site just for White's access in his familiar airplane.

White's test as a game warden came with that first AGC assignment to Fort Yukon, a regional fur-trading center. He'd arrived there to inspect furs brought in for sale or barter. As expected, White immediately came up against contemptuous hunters and trappers, but he didn't back down an inch. He made arrests, gave stern warnings, and treated everyone with equal justice. But those who wished to fight or take flight received the full fury of White's determination and powerful will. If scofflaws went into hiding, White tracked them down; if someone wanted a fight, he got one. It didn't take long for word to spread that it wasn't wise to challenge White's authority and that paying attention to game laws led to less trouble.

However, the commerce for generations in the remote environs of Alaska involved gathering furs in winter and fishing during summer. Most did so legally. But poaching wasn't the only way that some made a living—profiteers were always looking to make an easier buck. White recalled just such an occasion when he'd been invited to a Christmas dinner at a village on the Koyukuk River. He let it be known that he'd fly in with turkey and all the fixings, but with no whiskey. Soon after White arrived and the dinner commenced, another plane landed. The pilot was selling bottles of whiskey out of his plane. The price of a fifth that normally sold for $7.50 had been inflated to $18.00. After making a pocketful of cash, the pilot took off into the night, undoubtedly with other villages on his schedule. There was nothing White could do about it.

By 1941 and after fourteen years of working for the AGC, White had had enough and resigned. Evidently this came about more as a result of internal squabbles at AGC than any trouble from civilians. White apparently had already done some spadework because he immediately signed on with Wien Air Alaska as chief pilot. By this time White's experience as a reconnaissance trailblazer and bush pilot had become legendary throughout the territory. He'd flown in all types of weather conditions, at all times of the day, and during every season on wheels, floats, and skis to fly passengers, freight, and mail to many of the bush villages he'd been visiting for years.

During World War II, White flew charter planes for the U.S. Army Air Corps and returned to Alaska when the conflict ended. He briefly became a partner in a venture called Yukon Bush Air Charter, but the company closed down in 1947.

Wayne Heimer, a noted career biologist for the Alaska Department of Fish & Game in Fairbanks, recalled meeting White in the early 1970s and becoming familiar with his reputation for impacting moose

A lumberjack in Maine before arriving in Alaska, White always carried an axe when afield; one is shown here protruding next to his rifle in 1930. Photo courtesy of Jim Rearden.

populations. "Sam's 'place in the pantheon' is most likely due to his being the first flying game warden," said Heimer. "To Sam's credit, he was generally known to be fairly good-hearted while unbending in his enforcement of the law. But we're probably mistaken if we think that Sam carting poor locals off to jail for three months for shooting a moose out of season really impacted moose expansion to a significant degree."

Some of White's often-stated observations about Alaska game populations and habits are revealing: Caribou were so numerous during that era that on one occasion it took thirty minutes for a massive herd to run by him; wolves mainly dined on caribou except when moose cows were carrying calves, making them heavier and easier to catch; Interior grizzly bears took a lot of moose; and on some meadow flyovers, he witnessed bears actually corralling moose. White also witnessed an increase in black bears over the years and therefore didn't think they were in need of protection, but felt differently about grizzlies due to their need of greater range and more forage food than black bears.

White was not without some idiosyncrasies. A reliable source (one of his neighbors in Fairbanks) reported seeing White blithely and routinely bathing outside his home while wearing nothing but red flannels. Nobody, particularly White, seemed too concerned about it.

Sam White became a key man during the formative years after World War I in helping to map the remote portions of Alaska. But beyond that, he also played a huge role in the enforcement efforts of the fledgling Territorial Department of Fisheries, which after statehood morphed into the Alaska Department of Fish & Game. White brought order where only the lawless had tread. Neither of those initiatives was to prove easy, but Sam White turned out to be equal to the tasks.

On White's seventieth birthday in 1961, about a hundred friends gathered to fete a man who spent most of his life traversing the length and width of Alaska's bush for a living. I wish I could have been there. It would have been a kick—an honor really— to raise a glass in toast to a man who had maintained his integrity and gained the respect of many fellow Alaskans. Sam White surely deserves a little corner in history for being the first flying game warden.

5

HAL WAUGH, 1909–1973

Ketchikan

A boat builder, musician, and extraordinary frontiersman, his guiding prowess helped put Kodiak Island brown bear hunting on the map. He was one of the first to strongly advocate fair-chase hunting, and even his favorite rifle, a Winchester Model 70 .375 he named Old Nan, became famous.

A lot has been said and written about Hal Waugh, and every bit of it indicates he was the perfect blend of ability, ethics, and congeniality.

One should realize that before statehood in 1959 and the advent of a far-more-formal infrastructure for state oversight of fish and game, all one needed to obtain a hunting license was a driver's license, a letter of recommendation from someone, and ten bucks. Pretty much anyone could also proclaim to be a fishing guide. The loose standards allowed a number of incompetent and unscrupulous types to operate. Compounding the problem was that national outdoors magazines did little or no vetting of advertisers that at times made exaggerated claims and promises of fishing and hunting success.

Some of the more common complaints from dissatisfied clients stemmed from ill-equipped camps, insufficient knowledge and experience, charging hidden fees, and other questionable business practices. This bad press came at a time when interest in Alaska tourism was booming.

Stricter guiding rules were put into force. These included back-ground checks, minimum standards for experience or expertise, residency requirements, proof of guide-related income, recommendations from prior clients, and more for each level of license.

A Master Guide designation required the highest levels of experience. In that regard, few could boast of more field experience than Hal Waugh, who held Master Guide License number one. And like a sports team honoring one of its legends, the State of Alaska even retired that coveted number forevermore as a tribute to Waugh.

Waugh's experience extended from a long Civil Service career that began at age sixteen in the navy yard in Bremerton, Washington, and spanned eighteen years. Waugh had mainly toiled as a boat builder and, during World War II, helped construct minesweepers. He met his wife, Julia, on March 12, 1949, at the Kodiak Naval Base. She was on leave from the Marine Corps at the time, and Waugh was an administrative assistant to the industrial manager of the Seventeenth Naval District.

At thirty-nine years of age, Waugh stood six feet, two inches tall and was in good shape. He sported wavy brown hair and could expertly play the banjo and organ while singing with unbridled enthusiasm. He also spun a good story, and the military gal from Bemidji, Minnesota, fell head over heels for him. After that, Julia and Hal considered themselves one unit. Included in the decision-making of occupational ventures, she became a constant companion even on extended hunting trips in the bush when she wasn't teaching high school. Julia's camp meals and friendly disposition became valuable assets to the family's burgeoning guiding business.

Waugh's big chance to become an Alaska guide traces back to 1950 when he received a letter from Dick Rochelle in Kodiak. Rochelle had been working as a guide for Charley Madsen during the brown bear hunting season. People referred to Madsen reverently as Brown Bear Madsen, Mr. Bear Madsen, or the Father of Kodiak Brown Bear Hunting. Madsen's ninety-two-foot boat, which served as a floating lodge to access distant bays from which hunters could go ashore to hunt, was called, appropriately, *Kodiak Bear*.

Madsen needed another packer, and Rochelle knew all about Waugh's tall-and-hardy build and familiarity with Kodiak from his years of naval service there. The terms for apprenticeship under Madsen were strict: Waugh would not get paid for his first two weeks of work. Madsen believed that a probationary period was necessary to weed out prospects who didn't have the stamina or character for extended trips with clients. Waugh instantly agreed, having already been aware of Madsen's reputation. That Waugh passed Madsen's inspection is clear—he proceeded to work seven hunts for him.

But Waugh wasn't just another packer. He was extraordinary, doing not only as told but also always more than expected. Waugh constantly solicited information, his questions never-ending about the details of guiding, the business challenges involved, where and how to set up a camp, emergency procedures, soliciting clients, and keeping them happy. Madsen was only too happy to pass on whatever possible knowledge to the young fellow because he recognized Waugh's potential as a guide and liked his easy-going manner. He also appreciated the young man's deep respect for the habitat and game animals, which Madsen knew not all guides displayed.

Waugh's character and ethics can be explained by the old saying that the acorn never falls far from the tree. Being Herman's only son, Hal had received from his father not only the enjoyment of hunting but also a profound respect for nature. He bought Hal a .22 Stevens Walnut Hill rifle for his seventh birthday plus a box of .22 shells. Each week, Herman would provide another box as long as Hal could account for small game meals or the riddance of pests.

Herman's best hunting pal was Hal, and vice versa. Hal was observant with a good memory, and he quickly learned from his dad how to travel trails and mountains without getting lost, how to group shots into the bull's-eye and notice the subtle characteristics of how waterfowl, deer, and elk behave. Herman hunted with a .270 Model 54 rifle and took many elk, deer, and moose with it; soon enough, Hal was borrowing his dad's rifle to do the same.

By the time he was a teenager, Hal could spot movement from astounding distances, hear telltale sounds that others didn't perceive, creep through the thick bush without making a sound, and decipher the slightest scent, track, or swatch of hair with flawless accuracy. One special skill that would be forever useful was learning how far away an animal stood.

"My dad taught me to guess a distance through the brush or across a flat when I was just a kid, and then pace it off to see how far off I was," he would later write.

But talent alone wasn't enough. Herman ingrained into his son a reverence for game. Sure, he was shooting it, but he also owed it to the animal to ensure it didn't suffer. A one-shot kill was always the objective, and shooting from too far a distance or when a shot wasn't clear tended to wound animals, causing them to run away and die slowly. Herman instructed Hal to take as close a shot as possible. If an animal did run away, it must be tracked until found.

Another important lesson from his dad was to always follow the letter of the law. That credo became an integral part of Hal's heritage and later established his enduring reputation as an honest hunting guide in Alaska who insisted on observing all game regulations at all times.

Waugh became popular due to a non-pressuring, amiable manner. He always wore a friendly smile and maintained a level of enthusiasm even when weather or conditions became bleak. For those reasons, Waugh preferred the company of "fun" hunters to "award" hunters. Hunters out for world-record bears were often impatient or their expectations, unreasonable. Even so, all clients received a notice that— despite claims by some guides—trophy brown bears, even on Kodiak Island, were not common.

Waugh also obtained the age and physical condition of his hunters before a trip and chose camps accordingly. There was no point in putting someone into an area requiring a lot of walking or into steep terrain if he or she wasn't fit. This consideration earned Waugh a high percentage of repeat clients.

Though his skill set was uncommon even for a Master Guide, he never flaunted his abilities with other guides or hunters. Always unassuming, Waugh didn't need to brag or blow his own horn; he let his vast talent speak for itself. Assistant guides were treated as equal colleagues, not ordered around contemptuously or yelled at if a mistake was made. Hunters became more than clients in many cases, with lifelong friendships established.

No matter how bad the weather might be or what equipment may have broken down, Waugh never lost his cool or yelled at anyone. His was an infectious attitude that kept spirits high even under the gloomiest circumstances. Another remarkable aspect of Waugh's personality is that while many hunters and guides liberally sprinkled their conversations with cuss words, Waugh refrained from doing so. If upset, Waugh would usually utter "plague-take it," a rather unusual expression in itself. After a week in the wilderness with Waugh, even the most flagrant vulgarians usually cleaned up their act.

Waugh also loved practical jokes. Dale Miller, a neighbor of Julia and Hal when they lived in Skagway in 1957, became good friends with Waugh and later guided for him. On one occasion, Miller bounded out of bed early one morning only to find his shoes nailed to the floor. He also once returned to camp at the end of a long day of hiking and discovered a large rock had been added to his pack board.

But Waugh could appreciate that turnabout was fair play. Miller got him back on one occasion when Waugh charged him with making sandwiches at camp for a hunting party. Miller lathered a thick layer of horseradish to Waugh's moose-meat sandwich. When Waugh and the hunters later returned to camp, Waugh the Master Guide mumbled something about how good his sandwich tasted, but Miller noted that he was not asked to fix Waugh's lunch again during that hunt.

After his fruitful apprenticeship with Charley Madsen, Waugh was ready to begin his own guiding service. He noted that no one was guiding on Deadman Bay on the southeast end of Kodiak Island about ninety air miles from Kodiak City. Fred Henton, a mining engineer, had put up a cabin there in the mid 1930s, and he made it available to Waugh for hunting throughout the 1940s. That location wouldn't elbow into anyone else's operation because Madsen was on the opposite side of Kodiak Island and almost all other guides worked the other side too.

Waugh obtained a twenty-two-foot dory to haul supplies to the camp at the headwaters of Deadman Bay. In April 1951, the Hal Waugh Deadman Bay Camp featuring several cabins became a reality. Besides specializing in the famed Kodiak brown bears, hunters could also expect good opportunities for bagging mountain goats and blacktail deer. Sightseers enjoyed the plethora of wildlife viewing that included whales, otters, beavers, and bald eagles.

In 1952, Waugh established another site called the Post Lake Camp on the Kenai Peninsula near Homer. That camp enabled him to offer mixed-bag hunts for black bears and moose in a different area. While Hal and Julia would live in many different towns scattered throughout Alaska over the years, Hal's favorite quarry—and that for which he became most famous—always remained the Kodiak brown bear.

But Waugh's legend extended beyond his considerable guiding reputation. His name is even more inexorably connected to the ethics of fair-chase hunting and in 1972 he co-authored with Charles J. Keim *Fair Chase with Alaskan Guides*. The essence of the book is that a guide should work hard to put his clients onto game but make no guarantees of a shot or game. Waugh only guaranteed an honest effort to make each hunt a success. That included getting hunters into decent range and giving the go-ahead to shoot only when satisfied that a one-shot success was almost assured. If the animal was wounded, every effort would be made to find it.

In contrast, some guides advertised a "no shot, no pay" policy, often resulting in clients being encouraged to take difficult or impossible shots to collect the fee. Waugh referred to these types as "bandit guides" who provided low-grade hunts.

In a frequently cited letter dated November 30, 1972, to Frank Jones, then the director of the Division of Game based in Juneau, Alaska, Waugh wrote:

> I believe I sincerely feel that the proper and better way to save our game and worldwide reputation is to educate and train people to "fair chase" and ethics rather than a change in legislation. Legislation has never been able to curb drugs, excessive drinking on the job, illegal and unsporting acts in the game fields. Rather, it just builds up a hodgepodge of legal maneuvering that leaves us startled, short of cash—and the legal profession wealthy.

Although Waugh learned to fly in 1963 and banked heavily on his bush-piloting capabilities, he strongly objected to the use of airplanes to spot game and call in hunters. While vehicles were also becoming common in the wilderness in the 1940s and 1950s, Waugh preferred hunting on foot once reaching the preferred area—vehicles were never to be used for stalking game. He also objected to pictures taken of hunters next to a kill that denigrated the animal, insisting instead that

Hal Waugh built this above-ground cache to store supplies in his remote spike camp near Iniakuk Lake. Photo courtesy of the James Edwin Morrow Photographs, Elmer E. Rasmuson Library, University of Alaska, Fairbanks, UAF-1977-0059-00009.

hunters wipe away any blood from gunshot wounds before a picture was taken and to not pose with cigarettes dangling from their lips.

Waugh would never overhunt an area. He had a specific idea of what the game population should be for various species, both prey and predators. That's why Waugh created so many spike camps and cabins. If game were thinning out in one area, he'd leave it alone for a few years and hunt elsewhere.

Soft-spoken and gentle, Waugh was nonetheless firm in his views of the need to protect Alaska's wilderness. He remained passionately involved in conservation. He attended endless meetings and was a consultant to fish and game managers both before and after statehood.

Some of Waugh's perspective on conservation methods that were realistic and those that were not arose from trips outside Alaska. Bud Helmericks, who obtained Master Guide License number four, hunted the arctic and central sections of Alaska during the same time frame as Waugh did in his southern and central sections, so at times they overlapped. In *Alaska Game Trails with a Master Guide*, Helmericks writes:

> We both traveled about all of Alaska and studied the wilderness and conservation in Africa, Asia, Australia, Europe, New Zealand and Hawaii, always to return to our Alaska, which we loved. It was by seeing the other wilderness areas of the world that we were better able to evaluate and understand what a really priceless heritage we have here in Alaska's wilderness. Hal felt that the future and hope of all mankind lay in our understanding and preservation of the earth's wilderness.

Waugh became a huge vocal critic of the oil companies, believing that the exploration and pipeline would be tantamount to exploitation and ruinous to Alaska's game populations. Not everyone concurred, and some would postulate that game management actually improved despite drilling and pipeline activities.

Waugh didn't spare his tongue or pen regarding the encroachment of civilization, either. Helmericks wrote of a campfire chat when Waugh voiced the opinion that it wasn't hunters who wiped out buffalo from the plains of the Old West but that it was instead railroads, fences, farms, and tourists until no habitat was left. Waugh worried that the same thing was happening to Alaska's bear populations. In a letter to Bernd Gaedeke on August 2, 1971, Waugh wrote: "Some time between the years 1949 and 1951 we once counted 188 bears during a single twelve-day hunt off Charley Madsen's ninety-foot boat. Later we were to count up to 148 on a three-day season at Deadman Bay, but since about 1960 we have never run over 90 to 110 during a three-hunt season."

Waugh of course confronted many brownies during his hunting and guiding days. He suggested that if a brown bear is deciding whether to fight or take flight, a good tactic is to stand your ground and talk calmly and softly to it. The idea is to convince the animal that you're not a threat and just passing through. If the bear still appears agitated and looks like it might attack, have a piece of garment in your pocket with your scent on it and toss it toward the bear. During the few seconds when the bear is destroying the garment, it gives added time to get off a kill shot. Waugh also advised to keep firing if being charged—more than a few hunters who shoot once and look to see if that was enough pay dearly for it.

Some of Waugh's other bear-related advice:

Be patient when hunting brown bears.
Find a good traffic location and sit and wait as bears are always on the move.
Don't wear brightly colored clothing, instead going with gray, tan, brown, green, and the like.
Never act frightened—instead appear confident.
Be quiet and observant. Too many hunters scare off bears by their own movement and don't vigilantly watch for bear movement.

Waugh's favorite—and famous—brown bear rifle was a Winchester Model 70 .375 modified to chamber the .375 Weatherby magnum cartridge. He affectionately named the rifle Old Nan and kept it in a sealskin scabbard. Waugh did not believe that a less powerful rifle such as the popular .338 was sufficient for brown bears because he said that in his experience not many single shots from a .338 put them down for good. When pursuing smaller game such as caribou, Waugh carried a .270 rifle with a Leupold 4x scope.

He was often asked by hunters whether they should bring along a .44 magnum handgun as a backup, but his answer was always no. Waugh didn't think it was powerful enough to stop a large brown bear. To that everyone would agree, but big handguns now on the market such as the .500 Smith & Wesson Magnum (which I own) can take out even a huge brownie.

Waugh once said, "I would rather be caught without trousers than without binoculars." He never ventured into the woods without his favorite optics that included 9 x 35 Bausch & Lomb lightweight binoculars, 10 x 50 Bushnell binoculars, and a Bausch & Lomb 30x spotting scope.

Hal Waugh passed away from complications associated with the flu on January 9, 1973, in Ketchikan. The following year, the Alaska Professional Hunters Association started the annual Simons-Waugh Guide Award to recognize a guide who distinguished himself or herself by practicing ethical, fair-chase hunting. Waugh was a man who always considered his presence in the wilderness to be a treasured privilege, and those who honor fair-chase hunting will likewise always treasure his memory.

6

RAY PETERSEN, 1912–2008

Anchorage

Initially swayed to flying as a teenager in Chicago, he became a bush pilot and one of the most successful early airline entrepreneurs. He was the first pilot to establish air service to a remote region in Alaska that accessed fishing lodges he developed and the first hunting outfitter to sign an operating agreement with the National Park Service.

We all know that life is more about quality than quantity. Ray Petersen lived to ninety-six and, during that long life, distinguished himself as a pioneering bush pilot. At one time he ran the largest airline in Alaska, introducing turbo-prop service to many remote towns in 1958. Eight years earlier, Petersen had also founded the first sport fishing lodges in southwest Alaska's Bristol Bay by receiving the only lodging concessions sanctioned by the National Park Service inside Katmai National Park and Preserve.

In 2001 at age eighty-nine, Petersen attended his induction into the Alaska Aviation Heritage Museum Hall of Fame in Anchorage with over two hundred present for the ceremony. Luminaries expressing their admiration for Petersen included former Alaska governor Jay Hammond, Regional Administrator Pat Poe of the Federal Aviation Administration, numerous airline officials, fellow bush pilots, family, and friends. The Alaska Legislature also recognized Petersen as the "Father of Alaska's Sportfishing Lodges."

A fly rod, a float-plane, and waders were all Ray Petersen needed to explore and catch fish. Photo courtesy of Sonny Petersen.

Born August 10, 1912, in York, Nebraska, his dad, John, was a Danish immigrant. His mom was the daughter of German immigrants. The family moved to Wyoming when Ray was a young boy, and he grew up on a ranch, learning how to handle horses, build fences, and perform other such chores.

The next move by the Petersens was to Chicago, where Ray attended high school but didn't graduate. His father worked as a painter during the days of Prohibition and Mafia turf wars in the Windy City.

"Dad liked to tell the story about when he and his father painted Roger Touhy's house, who was a leader of the Irish mob competing against Al Capone," said Sonny Petersen, Ray's son.

"My dad got a job working on a nearby farm running a team of plow horses," said Sonny. "One day a barnstormer—a trick pilot—landed in the field and asked the farmer if he could give rides there. The farmer agreed, but only if he'd give my dad a free ride first. That field is now the site of O'Hare International Airport and Dad used to jokingly say that he was the first passenger to take off from O'Hare."

That single flying event elated sixteen-year-old Ray Petersen, instilling in his mind and heart a commitment to become a pilot and own an airplane. Petersen learned to fly in the Chicago area and obtained his pilot's license in 1930. At one point he likely heard about the burgeoning logging and mining businesses in expansive Alaska and that air travel was becoming a practical necessity. When just twenty-one, he stowed away on a steamship and arrived in Anchorage on April 1, 1934.

The streets were unpaved, and the census showed fewer than three thousand residents. Most commerce in Anchorage centered on the railroad, but with about three hundred dollars in his pocket—a decent bankroll in post-Depression years—Petersen landed a job in only four days with Star Air to help fulfill a contract for a mining operation.

The following year he moved to Bethel, about four hundred miles west of Anchorage on the Kuskokwim River. Even now, it's only accessible by boat or plane. Petersen lived in Bethel for six years, but in 1935, he made a trip to Chicago to buy a six-passenger airplane. He flew it back to Bethel, no doubt reminiscing about his first air flight as a kid. Petersen then started a new airline called Bethel Airways and then acquired another. However, one source reports that both of his planes ultimately crashed and the company bit the dust. Not one to quit easily, he got right back into the game in 1937 with Ray Petersen's Flying Service. Even though Bethel's population at the time was only about four hundred and included mostly Yup'ik Eskimos, the family got by thanks to providing air service for mining camps as well as ferrying residents between Anchorage and McGrath.

Navigation was tricky, very tricky, particularly flying through the passes such as Merrill, Rainy, and Clark. Petersen often navigated in winter by following established dog sled tracks. A Signal Corps was based at several cities and kept in touch by phone to provide weather reports, but pilots were essentially on their own back then with no radio communications or instrument flying. If a plane went down and wasn't sighted, chances were that the passengers didn't survive.

As war broke out in Europe and the United States became a grudging participant after the surprise attack on Pearl Harbor, Petersen did not enter the military. "His civilian flying service was considered essential to the war effort," Sonny Petersen recalled. "Most of the Alaska pilots had travel priority because the top brass preferred to ride with local pilots as they didn't tend to get killed in bad weather like the military pilots often did."

Ray Petersen helping two clients hoist a nice moose rack. Photo courtesy of Sonny Petersen.

Petersen flew supplies for the military during the war, but he used his own planes and mainly serviced his regular customers, the chief of which was the Platinum Mine at Goodnews Bay. Petersen became a very popular man in Anchorage. Just as someone with a boat soon attracts new friends, a pilot with a plane does likewise. With fishing a popular Alaska avocation, it didn't take long before business leaders, military bigwigs, and others who enjoyed wetting a line befriended Petersen. That suited him just fine since he was also passionate about fishing. Many of the ensuing fishing excursions occurred in the pristine Bristol Bay watershed southwest of Anchorage, and Petersen took great interest in the beautiful geography.

In particular, the areas surrounding Brooks River were breathtakingly alluring, and they soon became encompassed within Katmai National Park and Preserve. The streams teemed with spawning sockeye salmon, trout, and other species. Word quickly spread about the outstanding fishing prospects and the wondrous wildlife just waiting to be experienced in the region. Repeat visitors wanted to return; new visitors wanted to check it out.

Ray Petersen in his younger days,
donned in a tie and leather jacket.
Photo courtesy of Sonny Petersen.

Petersen pondered the idea of taking anglers and tourists into
the Brooks River on a regular basis and not just on a day's fly-in and
-out. He recognized that with such a marketable product, a tourism
business could be developed and expanded with the right promotion.
Furthermore, tourists with the money to stay a few days and to pay
for guided trips and sleepovers in fish camps could make for a lucrative
business.

But first, he needed to make a steady income, particularly since
he'd wedded Toni Schodde and started a family while in Anchorage.
To maximize revenue, Petersen surmised that bringing all the small
airlines that had popped up here and there under one umbrella would
be a wise financial move. He acted on it, adding Bristol Bay Air Service
and Jim Dodson Air Service to Ray Petersen Flying Service. With his
appetite for expansion whetted, in 1945 Petersen bought out Northern
Airways and two smaller carriers to include mail routes along with the
passenger service.

The boy who worked a farm behind plow horses had become a
mogul.

With final approval of the mergers from the Civil Aeronautics Board in 1947, Petersen created Northern Consolidated Airlines. The next big move occurred in 1968 when Northern Consolidated itself merged with Wien Air Alaska, which provided jet service in addition to the regular turboprops. As chief executive officer, Petersen was a mover and shaker, leveraging local-connection needs and becoming a part of one of the state's largest and most-lucrative industries—tourism.

Prior to 1950, Petersen entered into negotiations with the U.S. Department of the Interior's National Park Service (NPS) for the mutually beneficial purpose of opening greater enjoyment of hundreds of miles of remote portions of the Bristol Bay watershed to fly fishermen. The NPS fully embraced the idea, and Petersen—with fellow aviation pioneer John Walatka—started the first fly-in lodge concession in the region.

The earliest facilities were five tent camps collectively designated as Angler's Paradise Lodges: Battle Camp, Nonvianuk Camp, Kulik Camp, Grosvenor Camp, and Brooks Camp. Northern Consolidated Airlines built them in the spring of 1950, after the park concession had been secured. Petersen at first tried to convince developers and investors to build commercial-grade lodges, but they couldn't perceive the potential, and his sales pitch fell on deaf ears. So Petersen developed the lodges himself.

Petersen had finally fit together the pieces of his puzzle. He'd paired air access to remote regions with a fly-in fishing lodge operation. As the wilderness-lodging concept caught fire along with his expanding aviation empire, Petersen increased routes to Alaska towns and villages. Those wearing a business hat saw the advantages of lengthening airstrips previously built for only single-prop planes, so DC-3s and other larger planes could land.

By the late 1960s, Petersen had moved out of the cockpit as a commercial pilot to become more of an aviation administrator. That move in turn allocated more time to vigorously promote and oversee the lodge operations. To say the least, he was a very busy man. Sonny Petersen followed in his dad's footprints; in 1974, Sonny purchased a Cessna 180 from his dad and started Katmai Air.

Over six decades later, his Brooks, Grosvenor, and Kulik lodges are still going strong. Ray and Sonny operated the Angler's Paradise Lodges

Sonny Petersen gets a ride on his dad's shoulders. Sonny now runs the Angler's Paradise Lodges established in 1950 in Katmai National Park. Photo courtesy of Sonny Petersen.

until Ray's passing. Sonny took over the reins, and the lodges continue to flourish by offering comfortable accommodations amid an outdoorsman's dream playground. Another attraction that's been a big hit is the volcanic Valley of Ten Thousand Smokes reached with a twenty-three-mile bus ride. Once one visits the area, it's easy to appreciate why Ray Petersen knew that all the outdoor amenities would provide great promotional fodder to attract fly-in lodge guests.

Plus, a new attraction brought a different kind of tourism element to the Brooks Falls area. Bears started showing up in large numbers in the 1970s, and organized bear-viewing tours opened in the 1980s in the region and for that matter throughout Alaska. Articles about stupendous Alaska bear-viewing trips began appearing in newspapers and magazines everywhere. Rated as one of the best bear-viewing locations in the world is Brooks River Falls, where oglers can safely observe wild bears from the "Falls" and "Riffles" platforms and at other portions of the river. July is the peak bear time at Brooks River.

Live bear cams here can be accessed on the Internet. At times as many as a dozen brown bears are present during the summer salmon runs, snatching leaping fish in their jaws. Other options Ray and Sonny developed at Brooks River included bear viewing from boats or in small, guided groups with nothing separating tourists from bears in the wild.

Collaborating with Sonny Petersen for this book was a rewarding experience. Besides sharing details about his father's history, Sonny provided images and background material that greatly enhanced this chapter. I look forward to visiting one of the Angler's Paradise Lodges in Brooks Falls and sipping a brew with Sonny. We will most certainly reminisce about many renowned Alaskans, not the least of which is his dad's fabulous career as an aviation pioneer and fame as the father of Alaska's sport-fishing lodges.

7

SIDNEY HUNTINGTON, 1915–PRESENT

Galena

Half Athabascan Indian, at age five he saved his sister from a bear attack and witnessed his mother's death. He is the father of twenty children and now one hundred years old. His adventurous life remains a model for young men and women growing up in Interior Alaska.

One person's path to legendary status may be totally different than that of other legends. In the case of Sidney Huntington, the manner in which he handled extraordinary adversity positioned him to become an iconic Alaska figure.

Let me start Huntington's story this way: What were you doing at the age of five? A good guess would be those things typical of a young child: playing "Duck, Duck, Goose"; attending birthday parties; climbing monkey bars with schoolmates; and feeling the security of a family unit. Not Huntington. He watched his mother's dead body decompose before his eyes, took command of the care and feeding of his younger siblings, and even fended off a bear intent on dragging away his diapered sister. Meanwhile, his dad was long gone on a hunting trip.

As if all that wasn't enough to handle at five, Huntington endured a lifetime of taunts and rejection as a "half-breed" due to his heritage of a white father and an Athabascan Indian mother. But he not only persevered, he rose to become an inspirational figure, a symbol of endurance and integrity.

His father, James Huntington, familiarly known as "Old Man Huntington," was born in 1867 in Buffalo, New York. Thirty years later, he heard about the Klondike gold-rush boom centered in Dawson City in Canada's Yukon Territory. Gold fever proved to be an infectious disease for tens of thousands of young men from all points of the globe, but the reality was that only a small percentage ever actually hit the mother lode.

James's gold pan never showed enough color, so he turned to hauling mail and passengers on dog sleds, hunting, fishing, trapping and selling furs, and even operating trading posts. He got arrested for trying to hustle illegal furs, but he escaped and made his way back to New York. But once gold permeates a person's consciousness, it never evaporates. James came back to Alaska in less than two years, ready again to hunt, set traps, run dog sleds, and pan a stream in which a fortune in nuggets surely awaited.

In 1908, James married Anna, an Athabascan woman, and they lived in a village called Cutoff. Sidney was born in 1915 in the small town of Hughes along the Koyukuk River. The family uprooted to the town of Hogatzakaket (now known as Hogatza) about 90 miles downstream from Hughes at the confluence of the Koyukuk and Hog Rivers, where James organized a busy trading business.

As parents usually do, James and Anna had a profound influence on Sidney's future, each for different reasons. Anna gave birth to Sidney's brother Jimmy nearly two years later and shortly after that sister Marion. Anna dutifully took care of the young family while James was away hunting for gold and trapping. She taught the kids her culture and the rudiments of hunting, fishing, and survival as soon as they could walk and converse.

At first they perceived nothing different about being half white and half Athabascan. That would come when first entering their teens with taunts of being a "half-breed Siwash." But for now, their lifeline—figuratively and literally—was their mother. Anna wanted to pass on to her kids how the Athabascan culture had survived for centuries, which meant quickly acquiring the skills to hunt, trap, plant, and handle the myriad seasonal challenges necessary for living near the Arctic Circle in Interior Alaska.

Anna came from a hearty lineage, a trait that she passed on to Sidney and that would become important throughout his life. One example of Anna's tenacity occurred in 1906 after she was called as a witness for the trial of a man who murdered her first husband, a Finn by the name of Victor Bifelt. As the ravages of another harsh winter were about to set in, she was taken by two deputies from her village on the Koyukuk River to Nome to provide testimony in the trial set for February. After doing her duty, Anna was told she should remain in Nome until spring when the iced-over river thawed enough to transport her the four hundred or so miles back home by boat.

Not willing to be apart from her family that long—she had two children with Bifelt and was herself the oldest of fifteen kids—the ninety-pound Anna set out on foot by herself. Not only was the trek treacherous in terms of personal survival, but there was the likelihood of being killed if encountered by archenemies of Athabascans. Against all odds and despite dire warnings by those in Nome of chancing such a journey, Anna emerged after months in the bitter cold into the joyous and astonished arms of one of her brothers.

Along the way, Anna had even received help from a sympathetic Eskimo, who had been a trading partner of her father. Without his help Anna would have likely been killed or abducted as a wife. Anna's trek is still a legendary tale in the region.

In June 1920, while taking her three kids on a hunting and fishing trip while James was away, Anna ingested the guts of a whitefish at dinner. She became violently ill and died, leaving Sidney, Jimmy, and Marion to discover her body the next morning. Days later, her body was enveloped in blowflies and maggots, which caused Sidney great angst and painful memories. But he didn't panic.

At the time, Sidney was five, Jimmy three, and Marion one and a half. Two older sisters, Elsie and Alda, lived elsewhere at an Episcopal mission. The three kids built a shelter, a tarp covered with mosquito netting outside, and they slept under it to avoid the decomposing smell of their mother while fending off swarms of mosquitos. On the second day, Sidney was awakened by screams from Marion as a mama black bear pulled her away by her diaper. Sidney grabbed Marion's arms and saved her, the bear ambling off with only the diaper.

For the next two weeks they survived off canned milk, crackers, candy, and other items from their dad's trading store next to the cabin, which was locked to customers in James' absence. Suffering from insect bites, filthy all over, and depressed after several failed attempts to summon help, the kids were found by the crew of a passing steamer called the *Teddy H.* Taken downstream, they were reunited with their father and two older sisters.

The ordeal left Sidney with a profound feeling of abandonment and distrust of adults. He didn't comprehend why his mother had to die and why his father wasn't there to help. It would take years for that feeling to dissipate.

The rigors of running a trading business didn't leave much time for child rearing, even with the help of Elsie and Ada. James eventually turned all five kids over to the Anvik Mission, which was run by the Episcopal Reverend John Chapman and his wife, five hundred miles away. An Episcopal bishop, Peter Trimble Rowe, delivered the Huntington kids to the mission.

From local Natives, Sidney found out how to build wooden fish traps, which would nourish him when hunting or trapping was unproductive; from the reverends, he learned not to look down upon those in need and to help people whenever possible. It was a legacy that would be the pillar of his future legend.

At the age of six, Sidney returned to live with his father in a cabin in a village called Alatna and attended the St. John's-in-the-Wilderness Episcopal Mission. He was able to gain a rapport with James and understand him better, but the trading business became more difficult and his dad's health took a bad turn. James had to be transported to the United States for medical treatment but returned months later. Sidney was sent back to Anvik to rejoin his brother and sisters for several years, but in 1925 his father put Sidney and Jimmy into the Eklutna Vocational School near Anchorage, which was run by the Bureau of Indian Affairs.

Sidney completed the third grade and never progressed further in school, but he did learn the basic skills of reading, arithmetic, and writing. He also learned how to defend himself. Bullies didn't intimidate him, and he got into more than a few fistfights. During the second year at Eklutna, Sidney experienced his first ride in a car while

A moment of levity as Huntington pretends to strain while lifting a beaver. Alaska State Library, Juneau, Connie and Rev. Pat Keller Slide Collection, ASL-P303-054.

in Anchorage. He and Jimmy also soon got their first tastes of the explosion of modernization with steam engines on railroads and the overhead buzz of airplanes.

When Sidney reached the age of twelve, James wanted the boys back in Koyukuk to help him. It would serve as another transition in Sidney's maturation and in his ability to accept the good and bad of being both white and Athabascan. They took a barge to the Batza River where Sidney helped his father tend to a trap line along the Hog River.

With the valuable early teachings of his mother Anna about how the Athabascans hunted and survived still fresh in his mind, Sidney continued to learn little-known intricacies about hunting, fishing, and trapping from his father. Sidney soaked up all of James's tales about how he learned to live and avoid dangers in the wilderness by being self-dependent. The boy became successful at stalking game, catching fish, preserving and preparing food, skinning and selling furs, building a dog sled and a boat, and overcoming temperatures that at times dropped to seventy-eight degrees below zero.

In his richly informative autobiography, *Shadows on the Koyukuk: An Alaskan Native's Life along the River*, Huntington describes how he dressed in extreme cold:

> Over my wool union suit I wore a pair of heavy wool pants and a heavy wool shirt. Over the shirt I put on a wool jacket, and on top of that I wore a cloth parka with a hood with a wolverine fur ruff. I pulled wolf fur socks over my wool socks, and packed a clean innersole of dry local sweet-grass in my moccasins before putting them on, then pulled on a pair of Alaska Indian-type moosehide moccasins, which folded and tied at the ankle. My mittens were the moosehide ones made by my Aunt Eliza, lined with Hudson Bay five-star blanket wool. Beaver fur was sewed to the inside of the gauntlets, which kept the heat in yet allowed enough circulation to prevent sweating. Beaver fur was also attached to the outside of the gauntlets, giving me a place to wipe my nose, the inescapable nose drips one gets in the extreme cold.

Huntington learned much about dealing with the weather from Koyukon elders, who said not to fight the cold but to be cautious. That starts with knowing how to forecast weather and of course to always be prepared for the worst. But conditions such as floods cannot always be predicted, and a flood was about to swamp the family's cabin, forcing the three Huntingtons and a friend, Charlie Swanson, to retreat downriver to the old Hog River cabin.

The Huntingtons persisted, banking on their survival skills to plant vegetables and catch salmon because fur prices were down. However, in 1931 James told Sidney and Jimmy that he was leaving the trap line to them. He left to take a job as a guard at the jail in Nulato. Despite Sidney's sixteen years of age and Jimmy's fourteen, their father wasn't worried about their ability to handle the hunting, fishing, trapping, farming and surviving.

The boys did so, building a thirty-four-foot barge they called the *Ark* to live aboard when traveling to fishing or hunting sites along the Koyukuk River. Sidney and Jimmy were inseparable, enjoying the life

Huntington gets a little shut-eye in his sled before heading back into the wilderness to hunt, trap, and fish. Alaska State Library, Juneau, Connie and Rev. Pat Keller Slide Collection, ASL-P303-055.

of frontiersmen and surviving dangerous pursuits such as shooting hibernating black bears, whose fat and meat were delicious.

Without power tools, Sidney made a guitar and fiddle, and taught himself to play them. He also messed around with trying to make a perpetual motion machine. A major flood would swamp the *Ark* in 1945, but not before the Huntington brothers got plenty of use out of it.

In 1934, with his health deteriorating further, James entered the Alaska Pioneer's Home in Sitka, leaving the nineteen-year-old Sidney even more necessary to face life on his own. James would quickly tire of the retirement lifestyle, however, and his sons would help build him a cabin at Bear Creek in 1935 so he could again prospect for gold, at the age of sixty-eight. But as his father departed the scene, Sidney married a woman named Jenny Luke, and they lived in a cabin on the Hog River.

James died a few months after getting back into prospecting, but he failed to reach bedrock—the level at which gold often settles—in his diggings at the claim site. Ironically, Sidney would later work the Bear Creek claim for a mining company and find a fortune in gold. But Sidney, realizing that the gold—an estimated $20 million worth—should have been his father's, walked off the job. Who could blame him?

By December 7, 1941, Sidney and Jenny had six children. As news of the Pearl Harbor attack reached them and President Roosevelt declared war on Japan and later Germany, Huntington went to Anchorage and enlisted. However, the authorities wanted him to instead remain a civilian and do sheet metal work at Fort Richardson near Anchorage. He made a lot of money, but the family didn't much care for city living. Huntington asked to be transferred to Galena Air Force Base at the edge of the wilderness he knew, and the family moved there in 1943.

In 1944, Sidney and Jenny divorced. They remained close friends thereafter. Now aged twenty-nine, he married Angela Pitka later that same year, an eighteen-year-old who had no qualms about chopping wood or running traplines. After the war, Huntington moved with Angela from Galena to Hog River. There he hunted fish and game, set up a trapline, and started making babies every year.

Back to Galena he and Angela went in 1963 as he got into the fish-processing business in a big way. At one point he employed ninety-two people, working for the Whitney-Fidalgo Packing Company in Anchorage. However, due to new government regulations, he switched to his own smoked fish business.

Huntington grew to believe, as did his ancestors, that eating the meat of an animal represented a spiritual communion with the dead. He felt awed by the wild toughness of a bear, wolverine, moose, wolf, or beaver. He never trapped, fished, or shot an animal without the intent of eating it, selling the fur or hide, or trading the product with others for necessities.

But an epiphany hit Huntington during a moonlit hunt. A huge bull moose walked calmly to within twenty-five feet of him, and he raised his rifle. But the combination of the moose's magnificent yellow-gold antlers reflected by the moonlight mesmerized him. "The moose's yellowish eyes met his and Huntington lowered the barrel of his .30-30." The moose seemed aware that it wasn't in any danger and casually meandered off.

Sometimes, however, protecting one's property or life necessitates taking action. A rampaging grizzly started raiding the Huntington family's fish drying racks at their Hog River cabin. It so happened that sometime prior to that, famed bush pilot Sam White had given Huntington some steel control cable to lighten his plane for a takeoff.

Huntington took the cable and fashioned a snare out of it. Early one morning, Huntington saw the grizzly fighting the snare. He raised and fired his .30/40 rifle and the bear threatened the family no more.

An even more incredible extraordinary bear encounter occurred one October day when his brother Jimmy located a black bear den. Jimmy crawled atop the den and probed into it with his .30-30 rifle, but didn't stir up anything. So Jimmy instead crawled into the front entrance of the den, and a bear growled, slammed his rifle with a paw swipe, and knocked it out of his hands.

Most people would consider that risky enough and make a quit exit. Not Jimmy. With his rifle still in the den entrance, he decided to chop an opening at the den's top, hoping the bear would stick his head through it so he could kill it with an axe. After climbing down to release his four sled-dogs for added security, he remounted the den and swung the axe into the hole, striking a bear. Enraged but not dead, it charged out of the den growling while spewing dirt and blood. Jimmy let the bear have it in the head again with the axe.

Meanwhile, the dogs weren't much help as a second bear emerged and attacked one of the dogs. Seconds later, a third bear ran from the den. Jimmy disabled the first bear he'd struck in the head with an axe blow through its backbone. He disemboweled the third bear with the axe as its claws raked his arm. The second bear then knocked the axe out of Jimmy's hands.

All of this was happening, mind you, in a matter of seconds. Jimmy, now weaponless, leaped into the den opening with the bear in pursuit clawing his boots and blocking the entrance. Fortunately Jimmy felt the rifle in the darkness, did a half turn and killed the bear with one shot. The first bear, paralyzed yet still growling, was finished off. Blood and guts were spewed in a thirty-foot diameter around the den. Jimmy miraculously survived, although one of his dogs was badly injured and had to be put down.

While subsistence and dire emergencies are understandable when living in the presence of wildlife, it upset Sidney greatly that white hunters often showed contempt for wildlife. Mistreatment of an animal brings bad luck, according to Koyukon lore. However, Sidney managed to straddle both the white and Athabascan worlds despite seeing the good and bad in each. To disdain one side would be a denial of the whole. That realization propelled Sidney to bridge those differences, not only internally but with others as well.

Life in Interior Alaska centered on survival. Not just making an every-day living but flourishing and attaining fulfillment while co-existing with other two-legged animals. That danger was not just a white-Indian or Athabascan-Eskimo conflict, but it also involved transcending cultural, racial, or ethnic differences. Territorial disputes, it seems, have reigned supreme as the source of conflict ever since the Stone Age.

Who better than Sidney Huntington, a multicultural Native Alaskan, to turn hostility into cooperation? He recognized the beauty of Alaska and also had witnessed death, the imprudence of prejudice, and the impracticality of belligerence.

Huntington mentioned during a taped interview at age ninety-eight that he could only walk about a quarter of a mile now due to a bad hip. "I still live now like I did in my earlier years," he said. "I've changed some to keep up with the times, but my diet is much the same except I don't eat as much beef because of a triple-bypass operation way back in '82."

Huntington grew up bush-smart, thanks to a head start from his father, James. He also possessed an innate intellectual perceptivity and resilient personality, thanks to his mother, Anna. Through it all, Huntington could see the big picture. He extended his hand in friendship to all those with whom the Athabascans had long warred.

Sidney Huntington rose above counterproductive politics and attitudes, in turn elevating himself and those around him to the virtues of that big picture: individual dignity and the advantages of cooperation and collaboration. This Huntington accomplished by example, not lecturing. Slowly, sometimes painfully, his example was embraced. Not by everyone, but by everyone enough.

And, would you believe that Huntington was to father twenty children from marriages to Jenny Luke, whom he married at the age of nineteen, and later to his present wife, Angela? But he had nearly gotten married at fourteen in 1929. "An old custom among Sidney's people was that when a man killed a grizzly, he was entitled to have a wife," writes Alaska historian and journalist Jim Rearden, who helped Huntington write his autobiography.

"When Sidney's uncle—a traditional Koyukon native named Weasel-heart—learned that the boy had killed a grizzly, he paid a family five dollars for their twelve-year-old daughter to marry Sidney. His father vehemently opposed it and Sidney made it clear to Weaselheart that he wasn't yet prepared to support a wife."

As with all those eking out a life in the Interior, Huntington succumbed at times to illness, injury, and self-abuse. At one point he lost an eye while chopping wood, necessitating a glass eye. He and Jimmy ran a moonshine still to make extra money, selling to Indians and white men. That access led to Huntington's becoming an alcoholic. He finally quit drinking when his wife Angela, battling tuberculosis, had to be hospitalized for six months, while Huntington took care of their fourteen children.

But challenges and hardships faced everyone in that era growing up in Interior Alaska. However, the soulful times more than made up for the difficulties. In his book, Huntington writes about just such a magical moment: "The aurora lights many winter nights, and so does the moon. The beauty of a full moon on a sparkling snowy landscape is difficult to describe: it can seem almost like full daylight, with tree shadows. Even the stars provide plenty of light for traveling on clear nights. Alaska's crystal air seems to magnify the millions of diamond-bright stars in the northern skies, and there is no background of city lights to dim their brilliance."

But Huntington didn't always live in the wilderness, being forced at times into the "real world." He took on a variety of jobs that included working on a gold mine, providing carpentry for the U.S. Air Force and, during World War II, working as a roofing foreman on military bases in Galena and Anchorage. By the 1970s, Huntington started a fish-processing business. He also served on the Alaska State Board of Game for seventeen years starting in 1972 and received an honorary doctorate from the University of Alaska in 1989.

Sidney and Jimmy remained close for the rest of their lives. Jimmy passed away in 1987 after a series of heart attacks. As of this writing, Sidney is nearly one hundred years old and still going strong.

Until he draws his last breath, Huntington will fight to preserve the old cultures handed down to him from Native elders, which in turn he

Huntington wearing winter clothing in his elder years. Photo courtesy of Jim Rearden.

passes on to new generations. While many changes in Alaska excited him during his formative years, not all made him happy. As more white settlers arrived, they sometimes imposed too much of their lifestyle and methods on Natives.

"It's important to keep the Koyukon traditions," said Huntington. "Children in rural Alaska also need a bush education about subsistence living. We lived with nature and respected nature. Things are deteriorating because we see a lot of problems on TV and the Internet in this fast-moving world, and there are too many people who don't support themselves and looking for an easy way out."

Unfortunately, three of Huntington's sons ended up committing suicide. It inspired a school play written about his life with the main story surrounding his life-saving mentoring of a young man considering suicide. His daughter Agnes helps him take care of everyday matters in their hometown of Galena.

In Galena, Huntington helped found a community school that's named after him. "I consider myself well paid when I see those kids get their education and graduate," he said.

Among Sidney's many recognitions:

- in 1980, the Galena city school system names him its founding father;
- in 1986, the Alaska Outdoor Council awards him its prestigious Conservationist of the Year;
- in 1987, he is named Trapper of the Year by the Fairbanks Trappers' Association;
- in 1988, the Alaska State Legislature honors him as the Trapper and Conservationist of the Year; in 1989, the University of Alaska at Fairbanks confers an honorary degree of Doctor of Public Service.

Nothing says more about Huntington than an episode witnessed by Jim Rearden in 1975 when Huntington met a young man from Galena. Huntington asked him about progress at school, but the reply was that he had to drop out for lack of money. Huntington asked how much he needed to go back to school, and when told $800, he gave him eight $100 bills, which the man promised to repay one day.

Years later, Rearden asked Huntington if he'd ever been repaid that $800. "He paid me back after he got an education," he replied. "He now has a family, a home and a job. He's doing well."

I'd say Sidney Huntington is doing well too, and he's done well. After a century of living, that will hopefully continue for a long time.

8

DICK MCINTYRE, 1917–2009

Fairbanks

A mill worker, World War II bomber pilot, successful businessman, and flying-service pioneer, he became an expert skeet shooter and archer. For decades, many thousands of outdoors enthusiasts traveling to Interior Alaska and residents frequented his sporting goods store to stock up on supplies.

Though known by some to be a tough businessman with a sharp tongue, family and friends considered Dick McIntyre a big-hearted teddy bear, the proof of which is the fact that he was married to the same woman for seventy years.

Few would deny McIntyre's impact on hunting and fishing in Interior Alaska for the latter half of the twentieth century. But let's first take a look at his history and the experiences that brought him to Alaska.

Born in the rural coal-mining district of Hazard in eastern Kentucky on April 14, 1917, Dick was one of eight children to Alex and Cordelia McIntyre. Money became particularly scarce in the early 1930s after the stock market crash of 1929, but Dick took to his studies during his adolescent and teen years with vigor at the Pine Mountain Boarding School. He knew that the only ticket out of becoming a coal miner like his dad was to combine his inherent intelligence with book smarts.

While attending high school, McIntyre worked at a local lumber mill to help the family keep afloat. He eventually ascended to the position of

Dick McIntyre at the register of Frontier Sporting Goods, which for decades served as a popular supply store and gathering place for anglers and hunters visiting Interior Alaska. Photo courtesy of John McIntyre.

manager at another mill, but more momentous was meeting a young lady named Irene. They'd marry on December 23, 1939, have two sons and stay together until McIntyre died exactly seventy years later on December 23, 2009.

McIntyre would accomplish many things throughout his life, but getting a huge raise as a young man in Kentucky ranked right up there as one of the best. "He told me the biggest moment of his career until then was, while working in a lumber mill, getting a raise from a dollar to a dollar-and-a-half a day," wrote his son Edward. "With this new-found wealth he went to a local car dealer, but found he couldn't afford anything there."

As for many young men his age, World War II presented both danger and opportunity. McIntyre decided to enlist but applied to take the entrance test to be an officer. He passed the exam in June 1942, and, months later, began flight training. By the following spring, he performed his solo flight and in May 1944, he was attached to the Sixteenth Bomber Group for the Eighth Air Force of the new U.S. Army Air Corps (AAC).

A B-17 bomber pilot, Alaska bush pilot, hunter, fisherman, and retail entrepreneur, Dick McIntyre became an institution all to himself in Fairbanks. Photo courtesy of John McIntyre.

McIntyre was shipped overseas to England to coordinate missions with the Royal Air Force. Quickly moving up in rank from a lieutenant to captain, he logged thirty missions over Germany and Poland in a B-17 Flying Fortress that he named the *Hazard Express* because it flew as the lead plane in bomber formations.

Surviving that many bombing raids through antiaircraft fire and dodging attacking Messerschmitt fighters was daunting. Many American and British bomber crews died, became seriously injured, or wound up POWs. His plane often returned riddled with bullets and flying on only two of the four engines.

After the war, Dick and Irene McIntyre moved to Fairbanks as he decided flying without being shot at would be a nice change and an honorable career. By this time, the AAC had developed the Strategic Air Command (SAC) in bases around the world as a hedge against the growing military threat of the Soviet Union. With the Soviet Union a hop, skip, and jump from Alaska's Aleutian Islands, it was imperative to counter any sign of vulnerability.

McIntyre served at Ladd Field in Fairbanks from 1946 to 1948, and thus began his introduction not only to Alaska but also this growing frontier city deep in Interior Alaska. He flew B-29s for the SAC's Forty-Sixth Reconnaissance Squadron—in essence, these were spy missions code-named "Project Nanook" and "Floodlight"—to identify previously unchartered regions and to see if the Soviets were creating any naval or air bases near Alaska's borders.

Fortunately, it turned out that the Soviets were focused elsewhere in challenging the West, so no confrontations occurred. Nonetheless, the new charting of various polar sectors provided valuable data. McIntyre stayed with the AAC for another assignment in the Lower 48, but in summer of 1950, he decided to return to Fairbanks and make a new life with Irene and sons Edward and John.

McIntyre already knew the potential of Fairbanks, a remote city with gravel roads. Founded in 1901, it mainly consisted of farms around the Tanana Valley, gold prospectors, trappers, hunters, and trading posts. Although agricultural goods drove the local economy, it never quite met the needs of residents or served as a reliable trading capacity. Not helping matters were periods of bitter cold and occasional floods; what did help matters was Ladd Army Airfield (which became Fort Wain-wright in 1960) and three other military installations in the vicinity: Mile 26 Satellite Field (later becoming Eielson Air Force Base) in 1943; Big Delta Army Air Base in 1942 (now Fort Greely, one hundred miles to the southeast of Fairbanks); and the Alaska Air Command's Clear Air Force Auxiliary Field in 1949 (now an intercontinental ballistic missile early-warning station).

That military presence provided jobs and infrastructure, two key components for growth. McIntyre recognized the pluses and minuses of those dynamics. Banking on his piloting prowess and the limitations of local fishing and hunting guides having fast access only to areas close to Fairbanks, he started Frontier Flying Service. He'd previously scouted remote areas to determine which would be prime fishing and hunting sites for clients.

He could fly to Anchorage or other locales to pick up clients, gaining himself additional advantages as a guide. This also engendered "flight-seeing" tours of the Alaska Range and Denali–Mount McKinley areas for tourists, photographers, and hikers.

As a respite from his flight-service company and successful store, McIntyre loved exploring The Last Frontier by motorcycle. Photo courtesy of John McIntyre.

But the cost of maintaining a plane and the stretches of time when weather prevented flights and kept clients at home meant the necessity of another revenue stream. Fairbanks had trading posts that carried provisions for frontier living, but fishing and hunting supplies were an afterthought. McIntyre therefore launched Frontier Sporting Goods in downtown Fairbanks in conjunction with Frontier Flying Service.

Anglers and hunters, hikers and tourists, and outdoor enthusiasts of all stripes could find under one roof all the clothing, tents, camping gear, rifles, rods, ammunition, targets, archery supplies, and other accouterments needed. Trophy fish and game could be sent for mounting. With the simple slogan, "Everything for your hunting and fishing needs," Frontier Sporting Goods became popular and famous, a must-stop for any outdoors enthusiast traveling to Fairbanks. The store's customer base led to additional guiding clients, and the guiding clients patronized the store—a very successful commercial symbiosis.

McIntyre guided numerous celebrities, politicians, and military brass including World War II hero General Curtis Lemay. The flying service is still operational, although the store property was eventually sold and now houses a restaurant. But many Fairbanks residents still vividly recall Frontier Sporting Goods and Dick McIntyre.

Dick Bishop, a Fairbanks resident and a longtime manager with the Alaska Department of Fish & Game, visited McIntyre's shop often over the years. But it was McIntyre's piloting skills and hunting ethics that left the deepest impression on him. "He was my pilot for many hours of aerial counts of moose during the late 1960s," said Bishop. "He was a superb pilot and a man of great principal. Dick did not suffer fools lightly because he took fair-chase hunting seriously and was not impressed by braggadocio."

His son Edward died in 2011 in Fairbanks at the age of sixty-six. Irene McIntyre lives near her son John in an assisted-living facility in Terre Haute, Indiana. John is a music professor and his wife, Patricia, a theology professor, both at St. Mary-of-the-Woods College.

"Dad spent a lot of time standing near the store's entrance to greet each visitor," said John. "He imparted information to fishermen and hunters that no one else in our region could possibly give, details that he had amassed as a pilot, guide and sportsman. As a result, over the years thousands of people benefited from his advice. That knowledge not only improved their outdoors experiences but also made trips into the wilderness safer."

No one doubted McIntyre's ability and to challenge him in skeet shooting was a losing proposition. Interestingly, he became renowned with a bow rather than a firearm based on a trip in 1958 when hunting for polar bears. After flying into an Arctic region in his Piper Cub, McIntyre and an assistant guide found bear tracks. They stalked them until McIntyre was in range and let loose his broadhead. The polar bear turned out to be the largest ever taken by bow and became a Pope and Young record.

More than anything, Dick McIntyre loved Alaska. Humans there often had disagreeable attitudes, but the harmony and perfection of Alaska never let him down. He saw most of the state from the air, traversed it on long motorcycle trips, and skied innumerable slopes. His heart and soul never left the mountains, and some say he's up there still.

9

RENE "FRENCHY" LAMOUREUX, 1921–1990

Anchorage

He was a horse wrangler and later a longshoreman. As a guide, he popularized float-fishing trips long before they became widely known. Though basing his main hunting camps around the Chugach and Talkeetna Mountains for moose, sheep, and caribou, he became one of the first full-time guides to also operate hunts in multiple locations such as Kodiak Island for brown bear and the Arctic for polar bear.

One of the most notable Alaska hunting guides was Rene "Frenchy" Lamoureux (pronounced LAM-uh-row). Upon first meeting Frenchy Lamoureux, one might wonder if he had the strength and stamina to be a big game Alaska guide. Though he was a slight man who never weighed more than 140 pounds, clients were nonetheless always amazed by his ability to pack out the entire hindquarter of a moose.

Born in Saint Paul, Alberta, Canada, on June 15, 1921, he actually had dual citizenship because both of his parents were Americans. His mother, Rose Emma Bouffard, was born in Central Falls, Rhode Island, and his father, George Norbert Lamoureux, was born in Woonsocket, Rhode Island. Both parents grew up in Rhode Island but lived in Vancouver, British Columbia, on Canada's Pacific west coast when Frenchy was born. When not attending school, he spent many days bird hunting in the fields around Vancouver, which undoubtedly became

One of the great brown bear hunters of his time, Lamoureux stands next to a trophy taken by one of his clients on Kodiak Island. Photo courtesy of the Lamoureux family.

the seedling of what was to sprout as a lifelong love for hunting by the young Rene.

At age twelve, Lamoureux experienced his first big game hunt. He and a friend enjoyed biking the outskirts of Vancouver at every opportunity, and one day they happened upon a black bear and Lamoureux shot it.

"Dad had to get his brother Tiny—real name Clarence—to bring a truck so they could pick up the carcass," said his son Gus Lamoureux of Anchorage. "The family would not eat bear meat so they buried it in the back yard. A neighbor once asked his mother when dad was going to bring home an elephant and she replied, 'When he finds one.'"

Lamoureux had an aviary at the family home. He once took a pet squirrel to school, and as the teacher petted it, the animal pooped on her dress, much to the delight of the class. He became infatuated with horses and, as a teenager, worked for horse wranglers in the more-remote and -wild portions of British Columbia.

In 1943, Lamoureux crossed the border into Seattle and enlisted in the U.S. Army Air Corps as an airman. He was assigned to Sheppard Field in Texas near the border of Oklahoma for basic training. Thereafter he went to Tonopah, Nevada, as part of the 402 Service Squadron and became a staff sergeant right away. Because of his name and the fact he could speak French fluently, Frenchy became his nickname in the service and it stuck.

After completing his training in Nevada, he joined his squadron aboard a troop train to Edmonton, Alberta, Canada. Lamoureux met his future wife, Lorraine, in September 1943 when she was a senior in high school. They married the following September when he was twenty-three and she, eighteen. Their union would last forty-six years until Lamoureux's death in 1990.

"Not many people know that Edmonton had a large U.S. airbase to facilitate the building of the Alaska Canada Highway during World War II," said Lorraine. In 1946, the base closed down and the Lamoureuxs were transferred to Great Falls Army Air Base in Montana. The base was later named the Great Falls Air Force Base and again changed to its present name of Malmstrom Air Force Base.

"Frenchy became a flight engineer and flew from Great Falls to all the U.S. outposts along the Alaska Highway as well as to Anchorage," Lorraine said. "He liked Anchorage a lot and asked for a transfer there, which the Army Air Corps granted."

By that time the couple had two daughters. Upon arriving in Anchorage, Lamoureux received the rank of congressional master sergeant, which means it would literally take an act of Congress to demote him. His assigned job was as a line chief at the Military Air Transport Service terminal at Elmendorf Army Air Corps Base. Lorraine and the children joined him in Anchorage in March 1950. The family obtained quarters on base and enrolled the eldest daughter in school.

Lamoureux immediately took great interest in the bush country around Anchorage, which ignited his passion for hunting and fishing. He soon became the top source of fellow servicemen and friends on the best places to fish or hunt. Lamoureux befriended local sportsmen, like taxidermists Lonnie and Brad Temple, who increased his knowledge about Alaska game animals and fish.

After ten years and six months of military service, Lamoureux jumped into the vocational interest he'd gravitated toward his entire life: guiding. Lamoureux's intense craving for the fabulous Alaska wilderness could only be satisfied by making a profession out of hunting. In 1952 he worked for guide Lee Hancock, who had just returned from Canada with a herd of horses in need of breaking, and

HUNT ALASKA
Now booking SPRING 1959 HUNTS
—for KODIAK, BROWN BEAR, GRIZZLY, POLAR BEAR
and WALRUS. ALSO—Fall 1958 hunts for BEAR, DALL
SHEEP, GOAT, GIANT MOOSE and CARIBOU.
Summer Fishing & Photo trips.
For the ultimate in guide service, contact: (Wire or Air-mail)
NABESNA GUIDES
Guides & Outfitters
FRENCHY LAMOUREUX
P.O. Box 4444   SPENARD, ALASKA
Phone: Anchorage 77344. References and Brochures on request

This is a June 1958 magazine advertisement for the guiding services of Lamoureux and lifelong friend Andy Runyan. Image courtesy of the Lamoureux family.

he knew of Lamoureux's experience as a wrangler in British Columbia. Also working for Hancock at that time was Andy Runyan, and he and Lamoureux became fast friends and hunting buddies.

He and Runyan went about working with the horses to make them sociable enough to be saddled and ridden. Hancock utilized the horses on guided trips not only as transportation to camps but also for packing out game meat.

After learning the ropes about the guiding business from Hancock, Lamoureux and Runyan branched off on their own. They named themselves the "Nabesna Guides" because Nabesna was the area of Alaska where they planned to hunt. However, that arrangement lasted only one season as the pair decided to split up. Runyan (see chap. 26) chose to move to Juneau to guide and later formed a very successful business called Exclusive Alaskan Hunts, which specialized in Kodiak and Alaska Peninsula trips.

Lamoureux remained based in the Anchorage area as a sheep guide in the Chugach Mountains and targeted moose, caribou, grizzly, and black bear at Cache Lake in the Talkeetna Mountains. He also guided hunts for brown bear at Kaiugnak Bay on Kodiak Island, moose, caribou, and brown bear on the Alaska Peninsula, and polar bear in the Arctic. Even before river float-fishing trips became widely known and popular, Lamoureux had already been guiding many such trips for trout and salmon.

Over the years, Lamoureux established permanent camps at Cache Lake and Kaiugnak Bay. He also opened a camp named after Lorraine at a lake on the Alaska Peninsula off the southeast side of Upper Ugashik Lake. The family still owns the camps, and Gus, the only Lamoureux child interested in following in his father's footsteps as a guide, still operates a successful guiding business on Kodiak and the Alaska Peninsula at the Ugashik Lake and Kodiak bear camps. Besides Gus, the Lamoureux children include Paul from Anchorage, Linda from Anchorage, and Lana from Homer.

Lamoureux was a collector of items he found in the wilderness such as rocks, which became a hobby for his family. "One summer my mom, Georgie, and stepfather Earl Samis from Edmonton came along for a five-day rock-hunting expedition to Billy Creek near Sheep Mountain," said Lorraine.

I found a large ammonite fossil and spent three days chipping away at it. As it turned out, we all found a lot of fossils that are now prized possessions for our granddaughter, especially the 20-inch ammonite I found.

Meanwhile, on that same trip Frenchy took our son Paul, then nine years old, to where caribou were grazing. He told Paul to catch a baby caribou, which in fact turned out to be a lesson in stalking prey and learning how to get close to them without scaring them off.

Lamoureux exposed his children at an early age to fishing and hunting. He once took Gus, who at the time was nine, to the Kodiak camp after the clients were gone so Gus could shoot his first brown bear. Guide Mike Molchan and Frenchy stalked a brownie and got Gus set up for a shot. However, Gus delayed and wouldn't pull the trigger, and the bear meandered away. When asked why he didn't shoot, Gus replied, "I didn't have a good shot and I just couldn't shoot him in the butt." However, a few days later Gus did bag his first brown bear. When he turned eleven, Gus also took a Dall sheep and caribou.

Linda, Lamoureux's daughter who lives in Anchorage, said that an indication of her dad's true character could be appreciated by his frequent interactions with the family. "My first memory of dad took place when I was about three years old," she said.

It was wintertime and we went ice fishing. I remember sitting in a sleeping bag inside a cardboard box to keep warm and sipping coffee while we fished together—that began my lifelong love of fishing.

Another favorite memory occurred when my children and I went to Deep Creek fishing with the whole Lamoureux family.

While my brothers, husband and others went out halibut fishing in a big boat, dad and I left together in a twelve-foot Zodiac. I
caught the largest salmon of my life—a seventy-four-pounder—
that day and the next day lost an even bigger one.

Also, dad loved animals, the outdoors, hunting and fishing, but
most of all his family, children and grandchildren. I fondly remember him on the floor, crawling around on hands and knees, playing with the grandkids, just as he did with all of us when we were
young.

Of the enormous number of hunts guided by Lamoureux, a very
memorable one involved World War II–ace pilot Joe Foss, then governor
of South Dakota. Although Foss did not get a brown bear, the Kodiak
trip was televised. A writer from the old *True* magazine named Norbert
Darga stayed on after Foss left and later wrote an article that appeared
in *True* called, "The Bear That TV Left Me." The title referred to the fact
that Darga took a nice bear in Foss's absence.

Another client of renown was noted big game hunter Herb Klein.
Lamoureux led him on hunts all around Alaska for sheep, moose, caribou, brown bear, polar bear, and walrus. Lamoureux also helped many
hunters achieve game that won tournaments and notched high-point
rankings with the Boone & Crockett Club.

But no matter how many world records or tournament wins that can
be claimed by even top guides like Lamoureux, sometimes trips don't
always go as planned despite the best of intentions and preparations.
Such occurred with Lamoureux during a hunt in the Chugach
Mountains during the sheep season, which is often a time of windy
and rainy weather. Shelter in a spike camp is usually composed of tents,
which can get very damp and cold after a week or so of constant rain.
Lamoureux came up with the idea of flying an aluminum garden shed
to the sheep camp. At first, it was ideal—warm, pleasant and dry—for
two clients from Mexico. But one day, the wind blew really hard and
suddenly it lifted the shed upwards and sent it tumbling down the
mountain, leaving it in a twisted ball at the bottom. The hunters were
left in their bunks completely unharmed and staring at the sky.

The guiding business is very competitive, but close bonds often
develop among guides. Lamoureux and Andy Runyan remained close

Lamoureux also guided in the Arctic for polar bear hunts. Photo courtesy of the Lamoureux family.

friends throughout their lives. (Runyan was killed in a car accident in 2004 long after Lamoureux had passed away in 1990.) The two men were instrumental in establishing a guide board after statehood, working closely with then-State Senator Howard Pollock and the Alaska Department of Fish & Game (ADF&G) to push it through the legislature to become state law.

Lamoureux and Runyan also believed firmly in fair chase, meaning that all game regulations should be followed and animals taken only in an ethical manner. They also eschewed the practice of using airplanes to spot or herd game and were pleased with the passage of a law that disallowed hunting until twenty-four hours had passed after a plane landed.

At about age fifty-five, Lamoureux decided to utilize the free time on his hands when not guiding. He became a longshoreman and ultimately retired from the Anchorage Independent Longshore Union, Local No. 1.

One interesting note is that Lamoureux despised porcupines and would go into high gear to great lengths to get rid of them. Lorraine explained:

> He had an ongoing war with any that came near camp. He once had to kill an abandoned small bear that was blind and could not eat because of a mouthful of quills from a porcupine. One of the funniest instances happened when Gus and Frenchy were coming back to camp in the boat. As soon as Frenchy touched the boat to the shore he suddenly jumped out saying nothing and ran to the cabin. When Gus caught up to him all you could see were two legs sticking out from under the cabin. Boom! A porcupine finally came out and a bullet from his .375 bear rifle finished it off. It all happened so fast that Gus exclaimed, 'I didn't know the old man could move that fast.'

Lamoureux had obtained Registered Guide License number thirty-eight and chose not to become a Master Guide even though he could easily qualify. His reasoning: It required divulging all his financial information, which he did not believe the state was entitled to know. ADF&G discontinued issuing the Master Guide License for a while and reinstituted it when personal financial data would not be required. By that time Lamoureux was too close to retirement to bother with it.

In putting together his chapter, it delighted me that Lorraine, Linda, Gus, and his wife, Koreen, enthusiastically pitched in to provide images, and bits and pieces about Frenchy. It further drove home how closely he related to his family and they, to him.

Rene "Frenchy" Lamoureux took out his last hunting party at age sixty-five in Kaiugnak Bay on Kodiak Island. His health started to fail soon thereafter; four years later he passed away on October 16, 1990. His ashes were scattered over Cache Lake in the Talkeetna Mountains, a special place in his heart and a fitting tribute for a special character in Alaska's hunting history.

10

JAY HAMMOND, 1922–2005

Lake Clark

His diverse background included stints as a fighter pilot, dog musher, fur trapper, laborer, wildlife agent, and book author. As president of Alaska's state senate and later its chief executive, he promoted fishing and hunting as an important component of tourism and increased land and water access for outdoors enthusiasts.

Plenty of state governors in our nation's history liked to fish and hunt, but very few if any actually worked as a hunting guide, commercial trapper, and bush pilot. Jay Sterner Hammond's term as Alaska's governor took place from 1974 to 1982, a crucial period of expansion and commerce.

In 1977, the eight-hundred-mile Trans-Alaska Pipeline from the oil-rich North Slope was completed. Hammond helped establish the Alaska Permanent Fund that to this day pays each resident an annual dividend from oil revenues that typically totals between $800 and $1,500.

Hammond served as Alaska's fourth state governor, mixing political conservatism with a passion for environmental conservation. He often referred to himself as a "bush rat governor" and "reluctant politician," but he talked the language of hunters and anglers, both recreational and commercial. He had walked the walk and made sure everyone

Jay and Bella under lines of drying salmon fillets. Alaska State Library, Juneau, Alaska Office of the Governor Photograph Collection, ASL-P213-4-035.

knew it. But ego aside, the practical instincts that go with being a successful outdoorsman enabled him to sniff out biased positions and seek sensible paths that benefited both the resources and resource users.

Hammond fought hard to establish land reserves without denying recreational access. He strongly supported the work of the Alaska Department of Fish & Game (ADF&G), giving state researchers added autonomy to conduct studies on how best to revive fish and game stocks. Hammond knew that without healthy ecosystems, the economy would suffer—he knew that tourism would explode as long as Alaska's magnificent resources were properly managed.

The governor's informality at times caught people off guard. He'd often show up unannounced at a festival, convention, or sporting event in his trademark flannel shirt and black beret. His beard, stocky frame, and gregarious manner were disarming and well received. He was a hardy character in the mold of Ernest Hemingway.

Jay Hammond was born in Troy, New York. His dad was a minister and the family moved to several towns in New England when new church assignments arose. In 1940, he graduated from Scotia High School. For the following two years, he attended Penn State University and studied engineering, which gave him an understanding of the petroleum business—a considerable advantage when he later became governor of the largest oil-rich state in the nation.

But the call of duty in World War II interrupted his life as it did everyone else's. Hammond enlisted in the U.S. Navy and flew Corsair fighters in the South Pacific for three years with the famed Black Sheep Squadron. Thereafter, he went on reconnaissance and sortie missions over China as the war came to a close. (We'll revisit this China connection a little later.)

After the war, Hammond headed for Alaska. The story goes that he got an earful from a fellow pilot during the war about the unimaginable beautify of Alaska's wilderness. The whole vision of flying single-prop planes on pontoons into remote areas of Alaska played to Hammond's sense of adventure, so that's where he went in 1946.

He homesteaded property near Lake Clark, about 185 miles southwest of Anchorage. Alaska was still thirteen years from statehood, and talk of joining the Lower 48 flowed passionately from the lips of just about everyone. Hammond took interest in the pros and cons of such a momentous choice as well as in other issues affecting what was then Alaska Territory, a federal jurisdiction.

But this was no time for politics; he needed to earn an income. The lucrative fur business drove Hammond to become a trapper, and he learned how to mush a dog team, set a trapline, and sell furs to wholesalers. He also took on odd jobs as a laborer when the traps ran bare, with one such assignment resulting in a serious back injury that threatened any future career involving heavy physical duties.

Hammond decided to go back to college and finally get his degree. He enrolled at the University of Alaska, majored in biology, and graduated with a bachelor of science in 1949. In deciding what to do next, the U.S. Fish and Wildlife Service (FWS) came calling with an offer to serve as a wildlife agent due to his hunting skills. It's likely his duties entailed

The future governor in his younger days as a bush pilot and hunting guide. Alaska State Library, Juneau, Alaska State Library Place File, ASL-P01-4735.

thinning game populations where needed and playing backup with a rifle for FWS employees in the field should a moose or bear show displeasure at their presence. Hammond's experience in the fields and streams also allowed him to take on clients now and then as a hunting and fishing guide.

His political prospects appeared to be a long shot at first. Raised in a conservative Republican family, he couldn't bring himself to change parties and become a Democrat, even though after statehood in 1959, the bicameral legislature was composed predominately of Democrats. He instead served in the first Alaska state legislature as an Independent, having won a seat in 1959 in the state house and continuing through 1965. He became a state senator from 1967 to 1973, but eventually re-registered as a Republican and became president of the Senate.

Hammond enjoyed politics, his persuasiveness and congeniality more often than not winning over constituents and fellow legislators. His infectious passion about issues put him at the center of numerous debates. But it was time to move on from the state legislature. After a short stint as mayor of his hometown in Bristol Bay Borough and doing some commercial fishing, he threw his hat into the ring for the race for governor in 1974.

A photo op as Governor Hammond walks atop the Trans-Alaska Pipeline. Alaska State Library, Juneau, Alaska Office of the Governor Photograph Collection, ASL-P213-4-190.

It wouldn't be an easy campaign. Hammond was up against incumbent governor William Egan. But Hammond's strong credentials as a conservationist and his background as a sportsman dug into Egan's support. Another major factor was the presence in the race of a third-party candidate who further split Egan's vote. Hammond—the ex-marine, New Yorker, and son of a minister—won the election. He also won reelection in 1978. He'd scaled to the highest political office in the still-fledgling state of Alaska.

By virtue of fortuitous timing and, as Hammond would likely say, his leadership, Alaska experienced an enormous economic boom during his eight-year tenure as governor. Fishery stocks revived and a flourishing tourism industry sprouted. While those accomplishments alone make for an interesting story, for this book's purpose the significance of Hammond's experiences with a rifle, fishing rod, and traps, and as a bush pilot makes him truly unique in the annals of Alaska's fishing and hunting personalities.

Rather than the push and pull of political influences that often stunts the development of workable fish and wildlife management, Hammond nurtured and tended to the success of ADF&G with unbridled enthusiasm. Along the way, he cemented many close alliances and friendships with state biologists and managers as well as with leading outdoors journalists of his day.

One such bond formed with a man who went on to become the dean of Alaska's fishing and hunting writers—Jim Rearden. Unbeknown to Hammond and Rearden initially, it was both of their wives who first crossed paths. In 1952, Hammond got hitched to Bella Gardiner. Bella had grown up with a close friend named Audrey, who would later marry Jim Rearden.

During his career as a magazine writer and editor, Rearden often interviewed Hammond regarding issues of interest to fishing and hunting enthusiasts. The ready access to the governor of Alaska helped Rearden get the inside track on significant issues. In turn, Hammond had found a key media contact to spell out the government's positions. Combined with their wives' childhood connection, the collaboration glued both couples to a lifelong friendship.

The Reardens recalled a story about Hammond traveling to China in the early 1980s on one of the first official visits by a U.S. politician in many decades. His visa easily received clearance from Chinese authorities because they knew of Hammond's history as a fighter pilot against the Japanese in World War II.

"The leader of the People's Republic of China at the time was Deng Xiaoping," Rearden said. "Jay spent forty-five minutes in a private chat with Deng, during which he was asked through a translator, 'Governor, you have seen the old China and the new. What do you think of our progress?'"

"Hammond replied, 'Well, any regime that has done away with the necktie can't be all bad.' Hammond, in keeping with his wry sense of humor, remained expressionless. The interpreter relayed it to Deng, who instantly broke into laughter and slapped his own thighs with both hands. Deng uttered a response and the interpreter deadpanned: 'The Chairman said you crack him up.' This took guts and a sense of humor, and a politician's shrewdness. Hammond was, of course, a Republican, and he wasn't about to fall into the trap of publicly admiring any progress by the Communists."

Audrey Rearden offered some insights into Hammond's better half. "Bella left the politics behind in Juneau each summer and returned home to Bristol Bay to fish commercially for salmon," said Audrey. "Seeing this pretty, diminutive lady in hip boots and rain gear wading in mud and pulling salmon out of a net is not the picture most people would expect of the First Lady of any state. She was very popular and much admired."

As governor, Hammond opened huge acreages of state-owned lands for agriculture as well as allowing access for lawful fishing and hunting practices. He showed no fear of engaging in legislative power struggles and proposed a number of controversial measures, including changing the state's constitution to six-year terms for governors (which was handily defeated by voters). The controversial and complex state corporate-income-tax law of 1981 also put him in the forefront of both applause and derision, with opponents saying it favored the big oil companies. In 1982, he oversaw the passage of a constitutional amendment to limit state spending.

I was amazed in 1982, Hammond's last year in office, when I attempted to reach ADF&G for comment on a *Boating News* article I was working on about salmon regulations. I spoke with a secretary and fully expected to be passed to an aide as she transferred the call. The man answering said on a speaker phone, "Hit me with your best shot, buddy, this is Hammond at your service." I heard laughter in the room and didn't know what to think. After a pause, the same voice said, "I'm Governor Jay Hammond, friend, paying a visit to the fish and game boys. What info do you need about salmon issues?"

I provided the angle, and without hesitation Hammond spoke for a solid five minutes, offering up statistics and data he couldn't possibly have been reading. Before the call concluded, he spoke of looking forward to retirement and getting back onto the water and into the woods more. His spontaneity and command of details specific to my article impressed me. When I told this story to Jim Rearden, he nodded and said that that was typical from the gregarious governor.

Hammond maintained a high public profile even after his second term ended. He wrote three memoirs with garrulous titles that themselves drew derision from detractors who considered him a self-aggrandizer: *Tales of Alaska's Bush Rat Governor: The Extraordinary Autobiography of Jay Hammond, Wilderness Guide and Reluctant Politician*; *Chips from the Chopping Block: More Tales from Alaska's Bush*

A gregarious and imposing figure, Hammond strikes a pose framed by a mountain. Alaska State Archives, #00869, Office of the Governor, RG 348, Ser. 612, Box 7464.

Rat Governor; and *"Diapering The Devil: How Alaska Helped Staunch Befouling by Mismanaged Oil Wealth; A Lesson for Other Rich Nations.*

Hammond penned articles for various newspapers extolling his philosophy on fiscal conservatism. His state budgets, he proudly reminded readers, always showed a surplus, even topping a billion dollars one year. He hosted "Jay Hammond's Alaska" from 1985 to 1992, one of the first TV series showcasing the state's magnificent natural beauty. This also gave him a pulpit from which to preach the fragility of nature and humankind's responsibility to manage it wisely while enjoying the beauty and bounty.

A terrible accident occurred in 1988 during an episode being filmed for the TV series while rafting on an extremely turbulent river. Hammond and three others managed to survive, but a cameraman, the executive producer, and his daughter were killed. Hammond considered folding the series, but viewers strongly urged him to continue on, and he did so for another four years.

Hammond's controversial nature didn't wane after office. He stayed active while serving on the Alaska Humanities Forum, Alaska Land Use

Council, Alaska Airmen's Association, and Veterans of Foreign Wars, to name just a few. He advocated reinstating a state income tax, which the sitting governor, Frank Murkowski, opposed, and pushed to double the dividends paid to citizens from the Alaska Permanent Fund. Neither of those suggestions passed the state legislature.

Hammond was nonetheless revered in the state. In 1994, he was named Alaskan of the Year and received the University of Alaska's Medal of Merit. In 2013, the Alaska Legislature honored him by designating July 21 of each year to be known thereafter as Jay Hammond Day.

He didn't spend all the years after his governorship embroiled in political issues or basking in the limelight, however. In addition to the stint as a TV-series host, Hammond could often be found fishing and hunting with friends in what he cherished the most—the Alaska bush.

Jay Hammond loved Alaska and the outdoors, and his public service coincided with some of the most economically robust decades since statehood in 1959. He will always be remembered as the bush rat governor with a lion of a personality.

11

JIM BROOKS, 1922–2006

Juneau

~~~~~~

He was never one to dodge controversy during his long professional career. As commissioner of the Alaska Department of Fish & Game (ADF&G), he put an end to a program eradicating harbor seals and pioneered studies involving polar bears, beluga whales, walruses, and sea lions. He was also instrumental in the protection of salmon spawning areas and in the prohibition of hunting wolves on the same day they're spotted from the air.

~~~~~~

James Washington Brooks was an unassuming man who sought no accolades but deserves many. For fifty years he served Alaska with his involvement in conservation issues, particularly during the formative decades of the 1950s and 1960s when fish and game policies were being framed. In fact, Brooks drafted the original blueprint for game regulations even before statehood came in 1959.

Brooks's legend and impact on Alaska's resources has largely faded. That's not due to his lack of stature but instead is a result of memories fading decades after a career ends. Just as few of us can recall many names of Hollywood actors from the silent movie era, such is the fate of many fish and game biologists.

Brooks became a biologist but not a bookworm. He became a leader but not a loudmouth. He received a doctorate but wasn't an egghead.

Jim Brooks with a beluga whale harpooned for research. Photo courtesy of Beatrice Brooks.

Not that any of those terms are associative or mutually exclusive, but the point is that Brooks carried himself as a regular guy while effectively using his influence to better Alaska's wildlife.

His memoir, *North to Wolf Country: My Life among the Creatures of Alaska,* chronicles Brooks's arrival in The Last Frontier in 1940 and how he came to embody his adopted home's quintessence. As was typical of Brooks, he humbly recounted his contributions to the cause of improved research methods and doing what's best for fish and game as well as anglers and hunters. But as the title of his book suggests, he much more treasured living amid four-legged creatures—wolves, in particular—than bipeds.

Born August 6, 1922, in Erie, Pennsylvania, he and three sisters spent their youth in Detroit, first living on the west side of the city and then on the east side. It was a special era bookended by the First and Second World Wars: Joe Louis, Babe Ruth, Douglas Fairbanks Jr., Bette Davis, Charles Lindbergh, the Four Horsemen, Al Capone, Franklin D. Roosevelt, and the incongruous yet simultaneous moral tug-of-wars between restraint (Prohibition) and living it up (Roaring Twenties).

His father, Lewis Knox Polk Brooks, decided he'd continue the family tradition of a son's middle name carrying a presidential designation. A navy veteran, Lewis worked for General Electric Company as an engineer while his wife, Mattie, took care of the household—the typical husband-wife roles of the time.

Jim was entranced by his father's skill in catching perch and sunfish along with his tales about hunting with dogs and shooting ducks. With his canine companion Pal, young Jim paddled a small rowboat given to him by his father up and down the Detroit River and Lake Saint Clair. He caught stringers of fish and learned basic navigation and how to deal with inclement weather while on the water. At age fourteen, Lewis bought a 1.5-horsepower Evinrude engine for the boat, and the greater access became a springboard for even more fishing adventures. Jim also began plinking ducks with a single-shot .22 rifle.

By then, Lewis was occasionally taking his son along on hunting trips for rabbits, upland game, and deer. When Jim came home one day with a hawk and owl he'd shot, Lewis took them to a taxidermist. The mounts hung over the parlor mantle, but Lewis cautioned his son that there was no more room for such trophies and thereafter that he shouldn't shoot any other birds or animals unless meant for consumption. This respect for living things would stay with Jim Brooks for the rest of his life, producing a disturbing conflict at times within him between being a predatory hunter and a protector of nature's creations.

Brooks attended Foch Intermediate School in 1937 but did not obtain a high school diploma at that time. His mind wandered in class, the only subject of interest being biology. Instead, Brooks dreamed of independence and adventure. In the spring of 1939 at age sixteen, Brooks, his dog Pal, and a friend left Detroit and went west on a series of stowaway boxcar sagas across the northern states to California. In a couple of months, he ended up back in Detroit, but despite the hardships of hanging out with hobos and dodging railroad security, the experience ignited a wanderlust in need of satisfying. He'd also heard that many people who visited the Territory of Alaska for the first time decided right then and there to make it their home.

The following spring, Brooks at last set out for Alaska. He reached Seattle and boarded the SS *Yukon* headed for Ketchikan. The other men on the ship likely spoke of unexplored streams strewn with nuggets, of red light districts, hunting, fishing, bears, and other adventurous topics. In Ketchikan, Brooks secured a job as a dishwasher and cleaner at a hotel. He even worked up the nerve at one point to pay three dollars for an interlude with a lady of the night on Creek Street—the first time he'd ever seen a woman naked.

Brooks later found employment in the Civilian Conservation Corps (CCC), a federal public works program designed to help employ young men during the Great Depression. He lived aboard a houseboat, learned to cast a fly rod, and observed the huge population of black bears around Southeast Alaska. Brooks also witnessed the unwise practices of Alaska's fisheries management that often did more to exploit and negatively impact salmon stocks than help. He also became aware of how Japanese gill nets were decimating fish populations just off the shorelines. That skepticism and concern in Brooks's initial time in Alaska would be influential years later when just after statehood, he became the preeminent overseer of the state's fish and game.

After four months in Alaska, Brooks became homesick and returned to the Lower 48 in October 1940. He spent November in a cabin in central Michigan, where he learned how to trap skunks, raccoons, muskrats, and other critters, a skill that he would soon reapply upon his return to Alaska. But in early December, Brooks finally realized that his future could only be fulfilled in Alaska, not in the Lower 48. He returned to Ketchikan and employment with the CCC, adding to his skills by driving trucks and bulldozers.

Helicopters were used to transport or relocate large animals, as Jim Brooks is doing with this polar bear. Photo courtesy of Beatrice Brooks.

In April 1941, Brooks agreed to go to work for a fellow whom he'd met at CCC and who owned a commercial-fishing trolling boat. However, it wasn't long before the fickle fisherman decided to take a job offer in Seattle, so Brooks bought a steamer ticket to Seward on the Kenai Peninsula. Lying at the southern terminus of the Alaska Railroad, Brooks became a gandy dancer, a railroad crewmember that levels the track. The railroad cut through incredibly beautiful hills, mountains, forests, streams, and fields. Brooks marveled at the frequent sightings of wildlife such as moose and Dall sheep. However, bored with railroad work, he headed for Anchorage and was hired at a mill for the Lucky Shot Mine in the Willow Creek district north of Palmer. Brooks enjoyed the work and the after-hours poker games, but in August 1941, the mill closed and Brooks decided to take the train to Fairbanks.

Partway to Fairbanks, the train stopped at a roadhouse in Curry. While there, Brooks learned of a job about fifty miles southwest of Fairbanks in Nenana, where a new airfield was being constructed. He became a grease monkey and tasked with keeping the tractors fueled and greased. Just nineteen years old and already listing a wide variety of jobs on his résumé, Brooks considered his sundry skills to be a blessing. To be sure, that repertoire of capabilities would catapult Brooks into bigger and better things.

Not surprisingly to Brooks, the Nenana job also folded in less than two months. At this juncture, Brooks decided to do what he wanted to do and not what he had to do: spend the upcoming winter as a trapper in Interior Alaska. He knew it would be a formidable challenge. Brooks went about picking the brains of pals whom he'd made in Nenana and who were experienced trappers. They showed him a map depicting trails with vacant cabins and traplines marked in the Kantishna River area.

Brooks absorbed advice on where to locate the purest layer of snow for drinking water (near the bottom, not the top), the best clothing and tools for trapping, coordinating a dog team, and numerous requisite skills for survival and not freezing in the subzero climes. He was told of those poor souls who never returned alive after falling into an icy river, breaking a leg, getting lost, or being attacked by a bear. Brooks bought four male sled-dogs named Mutt, Tony, Patty, and Seagram, and practiced with them (shouting "gee" means turn right, "haw" left) while the Nenana River was still too slushy to cross.

In early November 1941, it was now or never. Into the wilderness he went, learning more each day about crossing frozen rivers, optimizing sled runs with the dogs, finding kindling even under wet conditions, setting traps, skinning hides, identifying animal tracks, and navigating after snowfalls hid the trails. A recurring toothache meant he had to pull it out himself; the result was accidentally yanking out two more teeth than needed. This time was to be an education and experience in Interior Alaska that cannot be fully grasped by reading books, magazines, or listening to storytellers.

Brooks quickly grew to appreciate the practice and practicality of mushers sharing cabin space. He complied hospitably in kind when he occupied a cabin, welcoming passing mushers at any hour of the day or night to spend as long as necessary near the wood-burning stove. Brooks, though a quick study, was still very young and inexperienced, and trappers with whom he conversed would never guess that this young man would one day become such an important Alaska muckety-muck. For that matter, Brooks didn't visualize that either.

It wasn't long before Brooks experienced the ambivalence of his prior hunting days near Detroit and trapping in Michigan. He came upon a wolf caught in one of his traps and shot the animal to end its misery. In his book *North to Wolf Country*, Brooks mentions the mental anguish it caused: "It was puzzling that I could be motivated to kill something and then suffer a sense of remorse. Looking into the eyes of an animal whose life I was about to extinguish was somehow unsettling, though these feelings passed once the animal was dead."

After that first galvanizing winter season around the Kantishna River, Brooks moved to Fairbanks. It was 1942, and Brooks liked the available conveniences compared to the austere nature of the bush. He got a dental bridge for his mouth to cover the toothless gap; he liked the people at local bars creating mirth while nickelodeons provided music; whites and Natives mixed easily; silver dollars rather than fur hides or hindquarters served as currency.

Brooks found a job at Weeks Field through Frank Pollack, the owner of an air service. Brooks didn't particularly care for his duty of cleaning and wiping down airplane engines and interiors, but he did become intrigued with the crafts themselves as well as with the swagger of the pilots. He always accepted any offer to ride along on mail flights to out-lying villages. The aerial views were invigorating, and the whole practical advantage of bush plane transportation became obvious.

Although Brooks remained spellbound by all aspects of flight, he needed to make more money. He found a better-paying job driving trucks, heavy equipment, and Caterpillars (duties known as being a "cat skinner") for the Alaska Road Commission. His leisure time centered on fly-fishing for grayling and hunting caribou and moose, with leftover hours spent playing poker at the Elks Club.

With World War II already months in progress since the Japanese raid on Pearl Harbor, Brooks joined the Territorial Guard unit in Fairbanks and participated in drills that later led to his enlistment in the U.S. Army Air Corps. He went through basic training at Ladd Field in

Fairbanks and then was assigned to the 439th Squadron. Brooks helped with kitchen duties and the transfer of planes to Russia, particularly P-39s and A-20 Havocs. He wanted to do more, however, and succeeded in becoming an aviation cadet. He ended up at Albuquerque's Kirtland Field for training as a B-24 Liberator bomber pilot. Two years later on December 22, 1944, after rigorous trial runs at a variety of bases in the United States, Brooks took off in a new B-24. He and the nine crew-members eventually landed in Italy and joined the bomber group based at Spinazzola.

Brooks participated in bombing raids over targets in Vienna both as a pilot and copilot. With the war winding down, he test-flew combat planes while still in Italy to ensure they could be safely flown back to the United States. Brooks and his original crew returned to Savannah, Georgia, in September 1945. He visited his family in Detroit briefly and thereafter arrived in Fairbanks eager to take up where he left off. Only now, his pilot experience would mean greater pay, prestige and—more importantly—the freedom to explore more of Alaska.

While beginning his studies at the University of Alaska in Fairbanks (UAF), Brooks met another student who set his heart aglow. Bertha Mae Jane Schaeffer, a part white, part Inupiat Eskimo coed, from Kotzebue, Alaska, also was attending UAF. They married and moved to Dillingham so Brooks could fly for Dillingham Air Service in Bristol Bay. After a couple of years on the job and the air service facing stiff competition, Brooks and Bertha left for the Inupiat village of Wales on the Bering Strait in March 1947 to run the weather station. The Bering Strait had taken on greater strategic significance due to the Cold War with the Soviet Union. The station aided pilots and fishermen, and served as an early-warning scout for the U.S. military.

Brooks eventually bought a Piper J-5 Cub, using it to explore the surrounding areas of Bristol Bay. He and Bertha especially enjoyed touching down on beaches without any human footprints to beachcomb. However, a man with a plane becomes a sought-after asset. Brooks was talked into using the plane to shoot wolves, the man in the co-pilot seat leaning out the window with a 12-gauge shotgun. He also voluntarily participated in seal hunts and learned much about Eskimo customs relating to whales, polar bears, and walruses. But after two years of extreme remote living, the couple returned to Fairbanks, and Brooks resumed his studies at the University of Alaska.

Jim Brooks was a trailblazer in studies involving walruses. Photo courtesy of Beatrice Brooks.

He was delighted when in 1950, UAF added a new academic unit, the Department of Wildlife Management headed by Jim Rearden. In 1951, Brooks was hired by the U.S. Fish and Wildlife Service (FWS) to provide flight support for a project involving the banding of waterfowl on the Yukon River Delta.

On March 17, 1952, the Brooks's family became three. They had a son they named Lewis after Jim's father but didn't continue the presidential-middle-name-for-a-boy tradition. However, they decided to give him the middle name of Patrick since he was born on Saint Patrick's Day. The added responsibility of a son propelled Brooks to start taking classes for a master's degree with a thesis on walruses. He, Bertha, and Lewis returned to Wales. The nearby walrus-rich island of Little Diomede in the Bering Strait was the scene of a full spring migration of the marine mammals.

The biggest challenge to Brooks wasn't the walruses. It involved flying in the area's notoriously unpredictable and harsh weather conditions. Pilots who chanced whiteouts and heavy turbulence with little or no visibility often paid the ultimate price with their lives. Fortunately for Brooks, he always preferred to delay a departure or return to the airport in turbulent weather, instead of pressing his luck.

Brooks also traveled to Barrow on Alaska's northern coast to study walruses. He observed Eskimos as they hunted while he conducted experiments on the carcasses. Brooks also encountered polar bears and on one occasion decided to shoot one and turn the meat over to the Eskimos. However, Brooks felt awful afterward and vowed to never kill another polar bear unless in self-defense.

After two summers studying walruses, Brooks's papers on the vulnerability of the animals helped push through the U.S. Congress a law allowing walrus hunting by whites rather than solely Alaska Natives. This made way for whites to hire Eskimos as guides, which in turn provided hard currency for the struggling villages. Brooks also obtained legislation that limited the killing of walrus cows and calves.

In spring 1954, Brooks obtained his master of science degree at UAF and chose to work for the Alaska Territory instead of the federal government. Brooks stated in *North to Wolf Country* his reasoning for opting to go with the Territorial Department of Fisheries:

Talk of statehood was everywhere in the air. Fish and Wildlife Service biologists seemed uniformly opposed to statehood, and I realized I might not fit in well with this group. Besides, I still harbored a generalized sourness at the treatment of Alaskans by the federal government. I strongly resented the paternalistic, abusive, or misguided treatment of Natives. I was disgusted with the fiasco of the reindeer program and with the federal default of jurisdiction over salmon fisheries to the politically powerful Alaska Packers Association. My heart was with the Territory and aspirations for statehood.

Brooks's first assignment was to ascertain if beluga whales were impacting populations of red salmon in Bristol Bay and thereby impeding the efforts of commercial fishermen. He reluctantly left Lewis and Bertha in Fairbanks, gathered harpooning gear, and brought along his Winchester Model 70 .30-06 rifle. Brooks worked around Dillingham and the lower Kvichak River, which connected to Bristol Bay via Kvichak Bay. His work, much to the initial discontent of commercial fishermen, was to prove that belugas only consumed a miniscule fraction of the salmon in Bristol Bay and therefore were not adversely impacting red salmon resources.

Not to repudiate his work, one observation regarding the beluga study didn't corroborate Brooks's conclusion. "I recall seeing Brooks standing on the deck of a ship with a strung-up beluga whale which had a bulging belly," said ADF&G biologist Wayne Heimer. "When Brooks slashed the whale open, bushels of salmon smolts spewed out onto the deck. I always thought Brooks felt a little guilty that he'd killed too many whales and wolves."

When back in Fairbanks, Brooks enjoyed hunts for moose and goats with friends like Jim Rearden. On one occasion while hunting with Burt Libby, another UAF friend, Brooks shot a Dall sheep ram, his favorite quarry, and had to shoo away a pack of wolves from the carcass. But as they ran off after Brooks fired a warning shot, a sow grizzly and three cubs came onto the kill. She ignored Brooks's attempts to scare her off and only finally scampered away when the chance passing of a helicopter caused a blast of noise and turbulence.

Brooks always enjoyed hunting, but the old ambivalence between the thrill of the hunt and killing an animal gnawed at his conscience constantly. To assuage those concerns some, he took a hiatus from hunting. He started to spend more time trapshooting and fishing, evidently rejecting arguments from some quarters that fishing posed a similar dilemma.

But speaking of dilemmas, his next assignment proved to be far more controversial and not just within his conscience but also in the public consciousness. Brooks was put in charge of a new division of predator investigation and control for the Territorial Department of Fisheries—specifically, harbor seals. Commercial fishermen despised the animals because they tended to rob salmon from nets, trolling gear, and longlines.

At the Copper River Delta, in particular near Cordova, dynamite depth charges were being employed by fisherman to wipe out seals. Brooks arrived in Cordova with the expectation from locals that the Territory would agree with this extreme program. It became a delicate balancing act at first for Brooks to gain their trust and then to try and convince them to put an end to the needless slaughtering of thousands of seals. One blast would kill two hundred or more seals, the injured gruesomely finished off with shotgun blasts.

Sickened at the wanton destruction but realizing fishermen needed a scapegoat other than overfishing or environmental factors, Brooks eventually succeeded in putting an end to the eradication program that the Territory had been supporting. He accomplished this by claiming that the program had been a success and the thinning of the seal population was no longer necessary. Also, the advent of monofilament nylon gill nets became available at that time. That meant that commercial nets could be set without ringing a visual dinner gong for the seals.

Another mammal receiving Brooks's attention was sea lions. After months of studying the species in late summer of 1956 in Prince William Sound, he proposed that the Territorial Fisheries Department delve deeper into the species, something he would take on in addition to graduate studies at UAF. With his masters complete, Brooks enrolled as a doctoral student at the University of British Columbia (UBC) in Vancouver, Canada, with Lewis and Bertha accompanying him.

By 1958 he'd passed his oral exam at UBC and looked forward to writing his dissertation about sea lions. However, he'd already been notified that the Territorial Legislature had created the new Department of Fish and Game (DFG), the predecessor of the Alaska Department of Fish & Game. Brooks learned that he was being touted to become head of the Game Division and told to start thinking about creating the infrastructure of the division if statehood came to pass.

Brooks was in Dillingham when news flashed that Congress had passed the Alaska Statehood Act on June 30, 1958. A week later, President Dwight D. Eisenhower signed it into law. Brooks went to Cordova again to pick up on the study of sea lions, later drafting legislation for game management and even the fees to be charged. He also helped torpedo a proposal being pushed by noted nuclear physicist Edward Teller to create a harbor in northwestern Alaska by detonating a nuclear bomb.

Unfortunately, at the beginning of 1960, Brooks's new DFG duties as head of the Game Division based in Juneau left him in the disheartening role of a desk-bound bureaucrat. He belonged in the field, he believed, and not corralled in conference rooms and mired in endless meetings. The circuitous discussions about legislation and political backbiting wore heavily on Brooks. It was exactly this sort of bickering with underlying agendas that he'd naively hoped to avoid in the DFG decision-making processes.

However, there were some pluses. Initial expectations by some that the new ADF&G would start churning out restrictive measures on anglers and hunters proved not to be the case. In fact, some regulations such as the taking of cow moose in selected areas and liberalized beaver trapping rules were more permissive than the federal guidelines. Some restrictions proved beneficial for the resources, however, such as a seasonal bag limit on cow walruses.

Brooks especially bristled at the nonsense tolerated and even perpetrated at times by DFG. The main example was the state's approval of poisons to control wolf populations and a bounty system for "nuisance" species such as eagles, coyotes, and wolverines. While the bounty systems eventually fell out of favor by 1970, the intense criticism from all sides of the issue weighed heavily on the quiet, unassuming man from Detroit.

But Brooks managed to set off fireworks himself in 1965 when he issued an emergency regulation that put an end to aerial hunting of polar bears. He became the target of bitter and loud opposition from hunters and some legislators.

Even more embarrassing to the DFG was the uncovering by Jim Rearden in a national magazine article that one of DFG's own employees, a former fighter pilot, decided to aid Kodiak cattle ranchers by shooting brown bears from a Piper Cub. Brooks appreciated Rearden exposing a glaring inconsistency so it could be fixed, but such inconsistencies didn't always go over well with politicians swayed by the wrath of voters. That made it all the more difficult at times for DFG to set regulations based on sound scientific evidence rather than on who shouted the loudest at public hearings or who wrote the most letters to political leaders.

By 1967, Brooks became thoroughly frustrated when Walter Hickel beat William Egan in the 1966 gubernatorial election. Alaska's first governor in statehood, Egan had supported Brooks since the late 1950s. Hickel exercised his privilege of patronage and terminated Brooks and other DFG heads. In a way, Brooks was relieved. For a while he enjoyed the lack of pressure he'd been living under. His love of dogs steered him into the unlikely profession of training Labrador retrievers as hunting dogs. He visited states in the Lower 48 for the field trials of dogs he trained.

But his marriage to Bertha ran out of gas after twenty-one years together. She and Lewis moved out after an amicable divorce. Brooks's father also died that year, making 1967 the most disappointing and upsetting year of his life.

However, he received an offer to head a research project on polar bears for the FWS. Brooks left Juneau for Anchorage and soon arrived in Cape Lisburne on the Chukchi Sea. For four years, he oversaw the capturing of polar bears via tranquilizing darts shot from a helicopter. He conducted biological tests and measurements, and would be airborne again before the animals revived. The bears would be ear-tagged, a molar tooth removed and a tag inserted under a lip. Numbers drawn on the bears' sides with indelible ink deterred recapturing the same bears. The act understandably infuriated hunters because the marks left the bears undesirable as trophy specimens for clients. Brooks's work with polar bears helped in the passage of the Marine Mammal Protection Act by the U.S. Congress in 1992, legislation that placed the hunting of polar bears off limits except by Natives.

Another topical issue during Brooks's FWS employment occurred in 1968. Oil had been discovered near Prudhoe Bay. In the ensuing year, Brooks performed a study of the exploration techniques being employed by the oil companies. He found that exploratory detonations were pockmarking the region, track treads from heavy equipment caused irreparable damage to the tundra, and liquid waste was being stored openly in ponds. Even his old nemesis, Walter Hickel, who had resigned as governor to be President Richard Nixon's secretary of the interior, commended Brooks's report. As a result, oil companies refined their techniques to make them more ecofriendly.

William Egan retook the Alaska governorship in the 1968 election following Hickel's resignation. Four years later, Brooks was offered the job of commissioner of the Alaska Department of Fish & Game—the head honcho of the state organization. Back to Juneau he went, and while his last tenure in the state's capital saw him getting divorced, this visit would ironically result in getting remarried. He met Christa Bading from Freiburg, Germany. Fourteen years younger than Brooks, she was divorced with a young daughter named Beatrice. They married and Brooks adopted Beatrice. Christa pursued a medical career—she'd been a physician in Germany—and after a residency in North Dakota, she soon was running a general-practice clinic in Juneau.

Beatrice Brooks, who lives in Juneau, would go on to attend medical school and serve as an emergency room nurse. She idolized her adopted father as much as he did her. "I cherish the memories of flying and exploring Southeast Alaska with him in his beloved Cessna 185F plane with yellow and white floats," she said. "We'd enjoy day trips such as flying up to Skagway or Petersburg or Gustavus to explore and have lunch, then view Glacier Bay or the ice fields before heading back. He never could get enough of the glorious beauty of Alaska."

As I wrote in the introduction, Beatrice became extremely interested in my book project and was eager to share details about her father's legacy. "My dad's generation is gone and their exploits and feats will not be replicated or remembered by new generations without books like yours," she wrote. "Your correspondence served as a catalyst for me to go through the souvenirs of my dad's life, and it brought back to life that fabulous era to me."

Indeed, it was an era wrought with growing pains. As commissioner, Brooks became an even greater lightning rod for criticism than when he only oversaw the Game Division. But that conflict comes with the job. Brooks didn't shy away from being an activist, and during his first year as commissioner, he halted aerial shooting of wolves. The department backtracked a bit in 1975 by issuing permits for aerial shooting in a large region south of Fairbanks, but Brooks's face was now on the bull's-eye of those sportsmen intransigent about believing that wolves remained one of the main culprits for any declining populations of big game.

The same emotional intensity arose with fisheries when tight restrictions went into place to protect salmon spawning grounds. Yet another controversial issue during Brooks's tenure as commissioner involved the sale to Japanese buyers of roe from subsistence-caught Alaska salmon, which wasn't helped by ADF&G at first allowing such sales and then turning around and banning them. On another front in

1974, battle lines formed over regulations on catches of king crabs that resulted in a revolt staged by Bering Sea commercial crabbers: They devised their own regulations and ignored those of the state.

Other issues large and small kept Brooks dodging political bullets. As with anyone in the arena, he was soundly booed and applauded from the opening bell to the last round on every single issue. When his five-year term as commissioner ended in 1977, Brooks retired from state government for good. But he felt there was unfinished business relating to fisheries beyond state jurisdiction that he still wanted to influence. So Brooks switched over to the National Marine Fisheries Service. By then, the federal government had established a two-hundred-mile buffer zone off all U.S. coastal states, which wasn't always recognized as sacred by foreign fishing vessels.

Brooks retired from public service in 1991, a pioneer with many arrows in his back, but still standing. On occasion Brooks agreed to volunteer on various state and federal game and fish panels and committees. One example was the still-raging debates and battles over wolf control, or lack thereof. The ADF&G, it seems, became embroiled in controversy over a plan to kill several hundred wolves over five years in three areas of the Interior. However, it also leaked out that radio collars had been emplaced by the agency on twenty-five wolves to identify their packs and that ensnaring devices set by ADF&G agents caught not only wolves but also moose and caribou.

In 1996, Brooks and others such as former governor Jay Hammond pushed through a law that prohibited killing wolves the same day a person has been airborne. That rule would eliminate spotting a wolf from a plane or chopper and then landing to shoot it. Brooks was not against shooting wolves from helicopters, but he believed that they should be taken only by game officials, not by hunters, and only when necessary.

In 1989, UAF awarded Brooks an honorary doctor of science degree. As Brooks stood to receive it with Christa at his side in Fairbanks, he thought of the irony of his humble beginnings as a boxcar stowaway and trapper, and his initial biology work with the FWS way back in 1951.

He and Christa bought a cabin in Farragut Bay about ninety miles southeast of Juneau, accessible only by floatplane. Other than cleaning up messes caused by mice, birds, and occasional bears during periods when the cabin was unoccupied, the couple fished, hunted waterfowl, and picked berries.

A wolf pack would often howl at night, and to Christa's amazement, Brooks once called one to within a hundred yards of the cabin. And on a memorable day in April 1991, Christa perfected wolf howls of her own, resulting in being answered with howling and yipping as a pack came right up to their property. Other close encounters and distant howling back and forth with wolves over the years never ceased to thrill them.

But as development and new residents began filtering into Farragut Bay, Brooks and Christa wanted to regain their solitude. They sold their land-based property and bought a three-cabin diesel trawler named *Wonderon*. They leisurely floated to remote villages in Southeast Alaska with their two Chesapeake dogs and still hopped around in Brooks's plane when the notion hit them to explore—always explore— more of their adopted homeland.

When age became a factor and required the decision to again live on terra firma, they bought a house just north of Juneau. Christa died at home in 2004 and Jim, two years later. But on those precious days together when sitting alone on their porch and holding hands, they enjoyed the serene vistas of whales, eagles, otters, and, of course, that recurrent sound that forever resonated in Jim Brooks's soul—the howling of wolves.

12

LINDLEY "KETCH" KETCHUM, 1923–PRESENT

Anchorage

～～～～～～～～～～～～～～～～～～～～～～～～～～～～～～～～～～～

Parlaying his Air Force flying experience into good use, he supported oil-industry crews on the North Slope and cleanup logistics for the Valdez tragedy. Through thousands of hours of reconnaissance over some of the most remote regions of Alaska's wilderness, he introduced generations of anglers and hunters to areas only accessible by bush plane.

～～～～～～～～～～～～～～～～～～～～～～～～～～～～～～～～～～～

I start this chapter—the twelfth, you might note—with a rather unscholarly observation about Ketch Ketchum: He can't be all that bad, having the same birthday as me (March 12). The scholarly view isn't so bad either: His prowess as a bush pilot and visionary resulted in introducing thousands of anglers and hunters to previously inaccessible regions of the state.

Ketchum, a lad during the Depression of the 1930s, in one way at least looks back fondly on those years. Fate would bring together a Texas City girl (Marguerite Andrews) and an Idaho homesteader, knitting a blissful marriage to rival any fairy tale.

Much of Ketch's flair for forging his own path stemmed from his dad, Clyde. In 1917, the teenage Clyde headed west "as the sun sets" from his native Pennsylvania to carve out a life of his own. He ended up the

Marguerite and Ketch show off two king salmon after flying into Lake Hood in Anchorage in their Cessna C-85. Photo courtesy of Ketch Ketchum.

first summer on a homesteaded farm in Readyville, a farm community in the Marsh Valley region of southern Idaho. Clyde worked as a grain bagger on a wood-sided combine pulled by eight horses.

While Clyde didn't have much farming experience, he possessed excellent mechanical, electrical, and carpentry skills—valuable attributes all. He soon met Charlotte Harris, a young lady woman with flaming red hair. She set the eighteen-year-old farmer's heart aflame too, and the couple soon eloped and homesteaded their own forty acres a mile north of the old Readyville schoolhouse.

Managing a new marriage on a dry homestead was tough. In 1934, Clyde and his boys picked-and-shoveled a forty-foot well to hit water, and Clyde and Charlotte kept things under control. Charlotte bore four sons over the next eight years: Edwin, Oakley, Northrop and Lindley (Ketch), the youngest boy. Their sister, Julia, came along in 1934, but fate did not smile upon her as she later died in an auto accident. By 1980, Ketch's parents and three brothers had all passed away from natural causes.

At age twelve, Ketch and his brothers earned some extra dollars toiling for neighboring farmers. No one in the area could afford tractors during the Depression era, so the boys utilized teams of horses to plow and mow hay and performed numerous other typical farming duties such as repairing fences, hand-milking cows, and pitching hay.

Many of the original homestead cabins were built from logs pulled out of the surrounding mountains, but the one-room schoolhouse was built from lumber. Ketch's grandfather, Joseph R. Harris, organized volunteers, and they completed the structure in less than two weeks. Ketch and his siblings walked the mile to the schoolhouse, which also held church services. By the time Ketch started high school, Clyde was driving a Lincoln car as a school bus six miles to the little cowboy town of McCammon.

Ketch's free time was spent fishing with his constant canine companion, Bruce. Ketch would cut a section of willow for a pole and tie on a string and hook. He'd catch grasshoppers for bait and brought home plenty of fish for his mother's frying pan. On the occasions when his family could afford .22 cartridges, Ketch would also grab the rifle and bag jackrabbits and squirrels along Marsh Creek because the critters often destroyed their kitchen garden.

In 1938, with no visible means of support left, the Ketchum's were forced off their homestead. Clyde sold their lone Jersey cow for five dollars, closed the doors, and departed for Compton, California. A few years later during World War II, Clyde sold the family's forty-acre property for only $150. Clyde got into the used auto and parts business with his brother-in-law, and Ketch worked there after school and on Saturdays.

"Back then, prices for used car parts were rock bottom: fifty cents for starters, generators one dollar, engines—take your pick—for five bucks," Ketch recalled. Even though only fifteen years old, Ketch slept at the business as a night watchman, running home in the morning to grab breakfast before going to school. The job was a grind, but that's what people did in those difficult years to contribute to the family unit.

Ketch finished his senior year at Compton High School in the spring of 1941. The rendezvous with Marguerite jumped off by chance on a day when Ketch walked by the school's tennis courts and he spotted

The Ketchums in Lynwood, California, in 1945 just before Ketch flew a Curtiss C-46 to New Guinea to haul bombs, ammo, and troops throughout the Philippines. Photo courtesy of Ketch Ketchum.

her playing tennis. "My eye lingered for a moment or two—or was it longer?" said Ketch with a laugh. They later exchanged flirtatious glances when passing in the hallway.

The next day, two of Ketch's macho high school buddies, who knew Marguerite, told Ketch that he'd be wasting his time pursing her because of over-protective parents. One of the boys had tried to ask Marguerite out on a date, but her mom and dad nixed the invitation by saying it was a school night and offering up other excuses.

"In spite of my cohorts' sage advice, I conjured up my courage and called on Marguerite Andrews on the evening of my eighteenth birthday," Ketch said. "I was pleasantly surprised when Mister and Missus Andrews welcomed me into their home. Even though it was a school night, with her parents' permission, Marguerite and I walked the few blocks into the little town of Lynwood. There we stopped at the drugstore for a milkshake and then went into the movies. I held her hand. She was sixteen and my cup runneth over."

World War II prompted the four Ketchum boys to go on military duty. Edwin and Northrop joined the U.S. Navy, Oakley the U.S. Army, and

Ketch the U.S. Army Air Corps (AAC). Clyde helped out the war effort by building cargo Liberty ships while Charlotte worked through the church to aid the ill and unfortunate.

Marguerite and Ketch married in 1942 and soon after he was accepted into the AAC as a cadet in the pilot-training program. He trained in a variety of aircraft, graduating in May 1944 as a second lieutenant. Like most young men of that era, he was anxious to get overseas and was assigned to the Fifth Air Force in the Pacific Theater of the war under General Douglas MacArthur. Ketch's C-46 "Commando Squadron" was on Okinawa when the "Little Boy" and "Fat Man" atomic bombs were dropped on Japan. He flew into Japan for Occupation Day.

In 1946 and with his occupation duties fulfilled, Ketch jumped aboard a slow boat bound for California, where he was discharged to reserve officer duty. Ketch built a house in Compton for himself and Marguerite while earning his civilian Airline Transport Pilot license. During 1947–1948 he flew DC-3s, transporting sailors and soldiers from coast to coast and was ordered to fly Mexicans who had entered the United States illegally back to Mexico.

But the Air Force wanted him back, this time flying four-engine DC-4s between California and Hawaii. But that duty soon changed because of the Cold War ratcheting higher with the Soviet Union. In summer 1948, the Soviets blockaded Berlin and cut off the city from access by the Western powers. Ketch flew the Berlin Airlift day and night from June 24 of that year to May 12, 1949, oftentimes carrying twenty-thousand-pound loads of bagged coal, oatmeal, or flour. It required many hours of flying by instruments to follow the required Berlin air corridors due to ice, snow, and fog. The flying experience significantly added to Ketch's aviation skills, which would serve him well in Alaska.

From 1949 to 1964, Ketch was assigned to the Strategic Air Command. His service in Air Force intelligence took him to bases in New Mexico, Louisiana, and North Africa. One overseas tour posted him to the Joint Intelligence Bureau at the Royal Air Force Base in Whitehall near London. By then, he and Marguerite had three kids: Steven, Craig, and Nancy. Ketch retired from the Air Force in 1964 as a major after serving twenty-two years. Afterward, he bought a used Airstream travel trailer and drove the Alcan Highway from California to Alaska, the trailer serving as their home for the next two years.

This portrait shows Ketchum as an Air Force major in 1963. The picture is signed with a note to his wife, Marguerite. Photo courtesy of Ketch Ketchum.

Alaska. At last. And with his background in flying, it was only natural that Ketch put all that extensive experience into play. He flew single-engine de Havilland and Cessna aircraft, on wheels, skis, and floats, for a charter flight service from 1965–1968 out of Lake Hood in Anchorage. The air charters supported seismic crews exploring for oil on the North Slope and in the Cold Bay Area on the Alaska Peninsula.

Ketch parlayed his military background and experience working for the oil exploration projects when he and Marguerite began their own flying-service company in 1969. Ketchum Air Service (KAS) opened at Lake Hood, where more floatplane activity takes place than anywhere in Alaska or Canada. KAS initially offered flights aboard a single Cessna C-185, but Ketch entertained bigger horizons. Eventually he created a fleet of ten single-engine aircraft. He also bought a Pratt and Whitney turbine-powered Fairchild-Pilatus with a whopping bank loan of $125,000. There would be many more such big loans he'd handle going forward in the aviation business.

Just like his dad, Clyde, Ketch wasn't afraid of rolling the dice. That nerve saved his bacon when he picked up a sizable contract supporting seismography crews on the Arctic Slope area of Prudhoe Bay. The arrangement entailed a lot of work, and sometimes it was easy to lose track of time, even days, when constantly flying in and out of the wilderness. Here's how Ketch jokingly remembers one such occasion:

When overnighting at Deadhorse in the pilot's quarters, I was one popular guy. Starting at 6 P.M., we practiced a small ritual. I'd line up paper cups, splash in some Jack Daniels and top it off with Coke. But I was the boss and adamant that it couldn't be poured prior to six o'clock. It was only one splash per night and I couldn't be talked into pouring earlier—well, most of the time, that is.

On this particular night I had just pulled off my flying gear and we were sitting around discussing the day's activities when fellow pilot Bob Rice brightened up. 'Ketch, isn't it about time?' he asked. I glanced at my watch and replied, 'Nope, it's 30 minutes to countdown, ladies and gentlemen.'

At that moment I turned around and my eye fell upon a 1970 Fairbanks Auto Parts calendar pinned to the wall. It was open to March and was graced with a pretty lady standing by a 1931 yellow Model A Ford Coupe. Then my eye somehow landed on day number 12. 'Hey,' I announced with genuine surprise, 'It's the twelfth, my forty-seventh birthday!'

Bob Rice, never one to stand back, jumped to his feet, rapped a paper cup with a spoon while click-clicking his tongue. 'Hear ye, hear ye, I proclaim all clocks in my kingdom shall be set ahead by thirty minutes and the pub is now open.'

Having let the cat out of the bag, I could no longer play lord and master over the only libation north of the Arctic Circle. The cups were accordingly lined up and with loving hands Jack Daniels splashed in. Paper cups came together when voices sang songs in unison, including 'Happy Birthday to Ketch.'

Ketch made profitable use of summer seasons too—remember those bank loans? With his deep knowledge of Alaska's wilderness gained by thousands of flying hours over all portions of the state, Ketch and his pilots knew up-to-date migration habits of big game animals as well as the best salmon streams. His fly-in, drop-off, and pick-up fishing and hunting operation gave experienced outdoorsmen and -women a true wilderness backcountry adventure. KAS could also outfit those needing gear. Favorable word of mouth spread, and the public took notice in articles about Ketch and his air service deep into Alaska's bush country.

Ketchum spoke of a notable drop-off–pick-up trip for a fellow named Lieutenant Colonel Wallet stationed at Elmendorf Air Force Base in Anchorage and his two teenage sons:

> This would be their first outing into the Alaska Wilderness and they were raring to go on a three-day float-fishing trip to Alexander Creek, less than a thirty-minute flight from Anchorage. It was early June and by now the king salmon were well upstream and heading for their spawning grounds. Flying them upriver that morning to the headwaters of Alexander Creek, I pointed out special gravel bars for camping and gave them a good overview of the river's twists and turns. The creek's gravel bars and deadfalls provide great hideaways for salmon and trout that scarf up salmon roe.
>
> We landed at Kenny Clark's old lodge on Alexander Lake. Kenny's wife Vie had moose jerky strips ready and the coffee pot on. After a short visit I left the party in good hands. Three days later I flew the three back to Anchorage where the Colonel's wife greeted her family. At one point the Colonel explained to her that a king had struck his lure while sitting on the back of the raft. As he played the fish, one of the boys shouted that his dad's wallet had fallen into the water. Despite their best efforts, it disappeared into the swirling waters and was lost—with all of the Colonel's ID, credit cards and a wad of cash.
>
> He looked at his wife and spread his hands palms up. All the while as the Colonel was relating his tale of woe, Marguerite and I stood there with smiles while nodding our understanding. It appeared to the Colonel and his family that we actually enjoyed hearing about his misadventure with no sympathetic platitudes. He glanced at us a little perplexed as if we didn't quite understand the gravity of the situation and started to re-explain it with more passion.

Right at that moment, Marguerite pulled something from under the counter and said with a smile, 'Does this look familiar?' The Colonel's jaw dropped. He was in absolute disbelief as he examined his now dry wallet with everything in it accounted for. His wife and boys watched in amused disbelief as they examined the wallet. But how? Where? He again had his hands spread palms up.

Marguerite explained that another float party had found the wallet snagged on a deadfall and turned it into our office yesterday. They wondered if by chance we knew some Colonel with an address at Elmendorf! We all got a big laugh out of that, particularly considering the irony of his last name."

As the years rolled on, Ketch bought properties and built cabins as he and Marguerite expanded the business. But while the state's economy boomed during the 1970s with the building of the Trans-Alaska Pipeline, it nose-dived in the next decade due to oil prices dropping from over $100 a barrel to as low as $15.

The royalties paid by the companies extracting oil from Alaska supported a huge proportion of the state's income. In turn, this especially affected real-estate prices. As home mortgages went upside down, many families all over Alaska handed over their keys to the bank, loaded up their cars and reassimilated into the Lower 48. It was hard on businesses like Ketch's that depended on oil and tourism.

Even so, Ketch looks back fondly on three events that he believes jump-started Alaska's economy after the gold rushes dried up. "World War II poured federal dollars into what was then the Territory of Alaska, and the federal government is still Alaska's largest employer," he said. "Even better was the pipeline with oil revenues supporting 85 percent of Alaska's general fund. And best yet for many businesses such as mine, the Valdez Oil Spill. That involved Exxon paying billions of dollars for damages—with some environmentalists and their attorneys still crying for more."

In wake of the Valdez calamity, KAS dedicated four float-equipped aircraft to aid in the oil-spill cleanup. To support that, Ketch and Marguerite and their son Craig bought properties in the small town of Valdez and set up support facilities. They brought in trailers in which their pilots and families could live. Suffice it to say that Exxon paid the Ketchum's promptly and very well for services rendered.

His only daughter, Nancy Ketchum Smith of Anchorage, spoke about Ketch's most-enduring trait:

> When I look at my dad, the main ingredient I see in him is his abso-lute perseverance. He has an ability to look beyond what's going on around him and to move forward even when things are hard. I believe that grit came from growing up during the Depression and having to overcome many obstacles to push forward.
>
> In building his business, he didn't usually rely on others to iden-tify prime fishing and hunting locations, preferring instead to spend the time finding them himself. It's that kind of focus and dedication that made him such a favorite to clients. Even when I worked on the dock for his air service as a kid, dad wanted to be sure windows were always clean, seat belts working and ready, the floats pumped out, the planes roped off and tied down prop-erly, and whatever else to make sure not just for safety reasons but also for the comfort and favorable impressions of his hunters and anglers.

Ketch and Marguerite retired in 1995 but not before directly help-ing thousands of anglers and hunters access the Alaska bush in many areas where roads still don't exist. They sold KAS to son Craig and his wife, Bertsie, who have grown the company by keeping the home base in Lake Hood and adding satellite bases in Valdez and Cordova. The seaplane fleet now includes de Havilland Otters and Beavers as well as Cessna 206s for flightseeing, fishing, and hunting.

Retirement has been just as adventurous as a flying career in the military and running KAS. Ketch and Marguerite enjoy frequent trips in their Airstream to states in the southwest as well as Mexico. "And best of all, we're still riding—two up—on our Road King motorcycle," said Ketch.

That dedication to spending time in the great outdoors often made it difficult to reach Ketch on the telephone or get him to answer emails when I was working on his chapter. He much prefers talking to typing, and on the occasions we did connect by phone, I was entertained by his effusive nature and engaging personality. We discovered a number of mutual interests when meandering to personal chit-chat such as World

The Ketchums's cabin in 1985 on Bulchitna Lake up the Yentna River west of Anchorage. Photo courtesy of Ketch Ketchum.

War II history and a shared fascination for fighter aircraft. My father, a former P-51 pilot who flew sorties over German-occupied France and Belgium prior to D-Day, related plenty of colorful stories about his wartime experiences. Ketch hung on every word about my father's exploits and my recent trip to Germany retracing military history. Likewise, I became intrigued hearing about Ketch's harrowing adventures during the Berlin Airlift and work with the intelligence sector in the Air Force.

Quite fittingly, Ketch is now writing his memoirs, and his spell-checker is Marguerite, the same beautiful young woman who answered the birthday boy's door knock on March 12, 1941. The story of Ketch's life promises to be an adventurous and fascinating story.

13

JIM REARDEN, 1925–PRESENT

Homer

His prolific journalistic career includes originating and teaching courses for the first wildlife department at the University of Alaska. For decades his articles in state and national publications have focused attention on the state's great outdoors, plus he has advocated effective conservation methods while exposing harmful management practices.

If anyone can be bestowed the title of dean of Alaska outdoor writers, it's Jim Rearden. Do a Google search and you'll swim through a sea of articles by him and about him, not to mention the twenty-eight books he's authored.

Born in California during the Roaring Twenties and living through the tumultuous Great Depression and World War II eras, Rearden always knew that his body and mind belonged in a much quieter place. While that peaceful pathway to Alaska isn't novel, considering the thousands of others seeking the same, a curious capability made Rearden something special: wordsmithing.

Even in grade school, Rearden excelled in writing. His expressions and depictions were so colorful and entertaining that the boy's name often became the subject of banter in the teachers' lounge. With a family heritage centered on farming, Rearden at first envisioned

Jim Rearden on assignment for *National Geographic* magazine. Photo courtesy of Jim Rearden.

himself a cattle rancher. But his love for fishing and hunting trumped all other interests. So, why not turn the obsession into a career path, he pondered?

And so he did. "I decided that I simply had to figure out how to make a living based on the greatness of the outdoors," he told me. "It was an ambitious goal back then because those types of careers were few and far between."

Rearden compared curriculum listings of various colleges to see which ones offered a wildlife management track. He finally selected Oregon State College (OSC), which is now a university. A stint in the navy at age seventeen during World War II on a destroyer escort in the Pacific interrupted his studies, but he returned to OSC fully committed to obtaining his degree.

"The college wanted us to have actual field experience," he said, "so during the summer of 1947 I ran a thirty-foot patrol boat with a sixteen-horsepower Regal engine manufactured around 1920 for the U.S. Fish & Wildlife Service out of Chignik, Alaska. We enforced salmon regulations in the area, and it was during that time that I knew Alaska

A certificate of commission signed in 1975 by Governor Jay Hammond and Lieutenant Governor Lowell Thomas Jr., appointing Rearden to Alaska's Board of Game. Photo courtesy of Jim Rearden.

was the only place for me. It was like heaven for any sportsman because you could hunt, fish or hike anywhere in search of food or solitude."

Rearden returned to school and received his undergraduate degree at OSC in 1948 and then went on to earn a master of science at the University of Maine. His educational credentials set, the young fellow wanted to return to the best area on earth to combine classroom knowledge with experiences in the wilderness: the Territory of Alaska. In 1950, he applied for a rare open teaching position at the University of Alaska in Fairbanks (UAF) and, to his surprise, got it.

Rearden organized a new Department of Wildlife Management and for the ensuing four years taught the courses at UAF. Eager to learn more about his homeland's history and culture, Rearden also began a private collection of books, magazine articles, and newspaper clippings about all aspects of hunting and fishing as well as wildlife management in Alaska, both recreationally and commercially. He still has all of them in voluminous file cabinets at his home office in Homer.

But teaching proved to be too clinical and mundane for the young professor. "I got sick and tired of the same classroom routine," said

Rearden. "It was a prestigious job with a pretty good income, but my heart just wasn't in it."

"Two of my students, Jim Brooks and Ron Skoog, were appointed commissioners of the Alaska Department of Fish & Game—one at a time as they last only so long as the governor is pleased," he said. "Many other students worked in various levels of management for the U.S. Fish & Wildlife Service."

Rearden packed his bags and left UAF in 1955, moving to Homer in the Kenai Peninsula to become a big-game guide and freelance writer. "Being a guide myself, I knew the right questions to ask bush pilots, hunters and anglers for my articles," he recalled.

Homer is also where he decided to build his home. Rearden constructed from top to bottom a two-story log home that he named Sprucewood. He used his own architectural rendering without any construction contractors. Rearden cut every log and board, made every measurement, and hammered every nail. He moved into the house in 1960, and it still stands today as sturdy as ever. I marveled at its beauty when visiting him and mused that the construction looked very professional. Rearden smiled: "It didn't happen overnight or without some trial and error, but eventually I figured it out and redid whatever necessary to make it right."

To help make ends meet in the late 1950s while penning articles and books, Rearden worked at a log mill and did some construction. In 1959, he leaped feet first into fisheries management by taking a job as the assistant area biologist for Cook Inlet for the Territorial Department of Fisheries, the forerunner to the Alaska Department of Fish & Game (ADF&G) that took over management from the federal government in 1960. Rearden eventually became the lead biologist.

During his stint at Cook Inlet, Rearden hosted a daily radio show called "Fishermen's Corner" during the summer months. He'd report on everything he saw that day from the air and pass along reports by others. In time, he earned the trust and respect of fishermen to the point that they even began turning in to the authorities "creek robbers" trying to circumvent regulations.

Rearden also showed a knack for innovation that paved the way for fish-counting techniques still in use today. "In some of the milky streams with poor visibility like the Kenai and Kasilof, we couldn't get

Rearden at the log house he built from scratch in Homer, Alaska, in 1973. Photo courtesy of Jim Rearden.

an accurate census of the salmon populations," he said. "How can you set realistic fishing limits and regulations if there's no reliable data?"

He remembered techniques employed while serving as the lead sonar operator on the USS *Lovering*. He figured that with some experimentation it could become a valuable census tool in his line of work. After writing to every sonar manufacturer in the nation and getting nowhere, Rearden finally got a favorable response from Bendix Corporation. The ensuing collaboration with Al Menin, the engineer who designed the first salmon sonar counter, proved to be a huge success. Today there are sixteen sonar centers operating in Alaska.

Rearden kept up his freelance writing for various publications and, in 1968, became the outdoors editor for *Alaska Magazine*, remaining in that office for twenty years. He simultaneously served as a field editor for *Outdoor Life*. Rearden also took on the additional volunteer duty of serving for five years on the Alaska Board of Fish & Game, which was established in 1960 and dissolved in 1974 as the following year, the Board of Fisheries and the Board of Game were formed. When that occurred, he chose to serve on the Board of Game for seven years.

It is important to note that members of the two boards are still appointed by the governor and must be approved by the state legislature. It's considered a high honor to be appointed and presumably only qualified citizens who have some knowledge of the subject get the nod. These boards pass more laws than does the legislature because each hunting or fishing regulation is a law—any of which are subject to change at every board meeting.

Some might surmise that the dual roles of journalist and regulator would invite criticism of a conflict of interest, and yet that never was the case from Rearden's peers or readers. That objective image likely came about because he was known to do what he thought right for both sportsmen and wildlife and let the cards fall where they may.

"Politics and conservation don't mix, but I understand the dynamics of how decisions affect a resource and people's livelihoods," he said. "I always try to put the resource first and the let the cards fall where they may because a public that knows the facts is much better than a public you try to fool. Quite understandably, fishermen and hunters aren't easy to deal with if being treated unfairly."

Perhaps his most notable accomplishment involved the removal of a bounty on wolves while the state was still reducing wolf populations. That fight sometimes put him at odds with extreme environmental groups. In a letter to the editor that appeared in the *Anchorage Daily News* in April 2000, Rearden wrote: "Animal rightists have discovered the ballot box biology. Using the initiative process, they have attempted to buy Alaska's policies and wildlife management programs. When they don't agree with an Alaska wildlife program, letters to their members bring in hundreds of thousands of dollars. They then buy slick media programs in Alaska to advance their agenda. Sound science and proven wildlife management techniques are ignored."

Rearden's field experience combined with his ability to reach the masses with honest reporting became widely recognized by sportsmen. In July 1978, the Real Alaska Coalition stated in a letter to Rearden at *Alaska Magazine*: "Your ability to 'tell it as it is' hits home with the majority of Alaskans and other subscribers."

In another letter to *Alaska Magazine* in February 1987, Ken Fanning, a registered guide, put it this way: "I'm compelled to write and offer

Considered by many the dean of
Alaska's outdoor writers, Rearden
is the author of twenty-eight
books and working on another.
Photo courtesy of Jim Rearden.

congratulations, first to Jim Rearden for having both the intimate
knowledge of our current fish and game resource management
problems (fiasco) and the courage to say it as he sees it; and secondly, to
you for having the courage to print the truth."

After the long stint at *Alaska Magazine*, Rearden took on the position
as a field editor for *Outdoor Life,* which lasted twenty years. Throughout his long career, Rearden's byline has appeared in over forty state
and national magazines; he's written more than five hundred articles
and twenty-eight books. Many of the books became best sellers, including the novel *Castner's Cutthroats* and biographies such as *Shadows
on the Koyubuk* and *Alaska's Wolf Man.* The latter earned Rearden the
honor of being named "Historian of the Year" by the Alaska Historical
Society in 1999.

Governors of Alaska (Miller, Egan, Hammond, Parnell) and even
a president of the United States (Gerald Ford) conferred titles and
appointments on Rearden. His alma maters recognized his many
achievements in conservation and journalism, culminating in 2005
when he was presented with the honorary degree of doctor of science
at UAF. In 2011, Rearden received the Humanities Award at the Alaska
State Council on the Arts from Governor Sean Parnell. Rearden's wife,

Audrey, was at his side for that award and many others since they married 1966. Always kind and gracious, Audrey has been an active partner in Jim's career, keeping him organized and on target.

But through it all, Rearden has always kept his ego in check. He's humble, never blowing his own horn. "All the awards over the years are great, and I'm honored. But I let my writings and books do all the talking," he said. "I simply try to educate and entertain, and if that's accomplished to the reader, I'm satisfied enough."

Age hasn't held him back, either. Rearden obtained a pilot's license at the age of sixty. And despite a paralyzing fall on his icy front porch in 2010, he's still churning out articles and working on his twenty-ninth book, thanks to computer dictation software and the forever-helpful Audrey.

After five decades and still counting, Jim Rearden's work as a conservationist and articulator of Alaska's splendor has unquestionably been a huge contribution to the betterment of the state's residents and visitors.

Before my last visit with him and Audrey, I asked if The Last Frontier is getting better or worse. He laughed. "When I first came to Alaska, a friend told me that we'd arrived too late to enjoy the real Alaska," said Rearden. "He was wrong; it's still the greatest place in the world."

14

SAM MCDOWELL, 1927–2013

Anchorage

~~~~~~

Many groups and individuals are opposed to fishing and hunting practices for whatever the reasons, and they're entitled to their opinions. On the other side of the coin, some men and women advocate for public access to recreational areas and subsistence rights to fish and hunt. In the latter category, few in Alaska's history have ever stood taller than Sam McDowell. He demonstrated in deed and proclaimed in word that those wishing to unreasonably restrict hunters and anglers should not force their will upon Alaskans. McDowell was also unafraid to challenge the state or federal government in court if necessary.

~~~~~~

While his life encompassed a great deal more than being a pioneer in the political arena of conservation in the formative decades before and after statehood in 1959, McDowell's articulate representation of public access rights for recreational hunting and fishing will always be his enduring legacy.

I never met Sam McDowell, but the book project put me directly in touch with his son Dan. Dan's admiration for his dad is inspiring to me, not the least of which is shown in the regular images he posts on Facebook of family outings during his childhood and youth. People with a strong affinity for family ties—particularly for their parents—always appeal to me because I was extremely close to my mom and dad.

McDowell was in the forefront of conservation issues and rightly proud of it. Photo courtesy of Dan McDowell.

Born on September 21, 1927 in Fortescue, Missouri, Sam McDowell arrived in Alaska in a literal jalopy at nineteen. He'd already served in the U.S. Army Air Corps during World War II in the European Theater. With the war over, he and brother Claude had somehow traversed the tire-busting Alaska-Canadian (ALCAN) Highway that was seventeen hundred miles in length at the time. Considering the scarcity and undependability of post-World War II gas stations and facilities along the way, just reaching Alaska with any money left in the piggybank was no small challenge.

At first, McDowell homesteaded some property in Anchorage, eking out a living that first winter with what veggies he could grow or meat he could harvest for the grill. In spring 1946, he moved south to Seward in the Kenai Peninsula, where fish and game were more plentiful.

McDowell signed up for flying lessons and, in 1948, received his license. The mobility of flying to various portions of Alaska gave McDowell an intimate knowledge of the population centers, large and small. In ever more magazine and newspaper accounts, those in the Lower 48 learned about Alaska's phenomenal resources for anglers and hunters. That would in turn attract more residents and tourists, and a need for additional business properties and home sites.

He set to work constructing buildings for Anchorage businesses, many of which still exist today. McDowell also converted some property he owned into a park for Anchorage residents. In Chugiak, he and Claude along with another brother Bill built a clubhouse and

As do all good fathers, they pass on their sporting traditions to their children. McDowell beams as son Dan catches one in a creek during a trip together. Photo courtesy of Dan McDowell.

shooting range, from which Sam co-founded the Alaska Sportsmen's Association.

McDowell's word was his bond, even long after the handshake. According to his son Dan, a good example was after he'd negotiated a price for 127 acres that his dad owned in Anchorage with the State of Alaska. It was years later before the deal was finalized, and though by then the property had doubled in value, McDowell stuck to his original quote. The Kulis Air National Guard Base was built there for the 176th Wing of the Alaska National Guard until relocated in 2011. The property is still owned by the state.

Remembering how World War II left many families without husbands and fathers, McDowell helped descendants of killed, wounded, or missing military personnel during the Vietnam War in the 1960s and early 1970s. He'd treat the families to vacations at campgrounds and lead them, especially the children, on rafting trips on rivers.

To ensure recreational access to many of Alaska's best camping areas, McDowell founded sixteen campgrounds around Alaska. He ran them until the state could budget the funds to take them over, thus assuring those areas wouldn't be closed off.

The voice of Sam McDowell became a familiar one at public hearings held by the Alaska Department of Fish & Game, the U.S. Fish and Wildlife Service and the National Oceanic and Atmospheric Association. He wrote letters, encouraged support for issues he deemed important, and led campaigns to advocate rights for subsistence fishing

Dan McDowell pays respect to the gravesite of his dad, Sam, in a cemetery that honors military veterans. Photo courtesy of Dan McDowell.

and hunting. He fought those seeking to push what he perceived as Draconian measures to enact unreasonable regulations or to restrict access to formerly public waters and lands.

When his opinions were brushed aside by government regulators or bureaucrats, McDowell fought through the court system. He didn't always win, but one particular victory proved to be crucial. In 1988 in *McDowell v. Alaska*, in which McDowell was backed by the Alaska Fish and Wildlife Conservation Fund, McDowell battled against a state law that allowed a rural priority for subsistence. The Alaska Supreme Court ruled in McDowell's favor, stating that such a law was unconstitutional because it violated the state constitution. That meant that all Alaskans would be entitled to the right of common use of and equal access for fish and wildlife. Neither the legislature nor the state could privilege the access of one group while restricting that of another.

McDowell didn't fare as well in a battle with the U.S. Department of the Interior (DOI)—a fight enjoined by the State of Alaska until later withdrawn by then-Alaska Governor Tony Knowles. At the time in the mid-1990s, Bruce Babbitt was the DOI secretary. In essence, the lawsuit challenged the federal authority of the Alaska National Interest Lands Conservation Act (ANILCA), which was based on a 1971 law enacted to settle aboriginal land claims in Alaska.

The basis for ANILCA came about during the 1970s, especially in the presidency of Jimmy Carter from 1976 to 1980, when Congress couldn't agree on legislation granting "special protections" being pushed by the DOI and National Park Service. These measures would eliminate state control over much of Alaska's public lands. Accordingly, Carter did an end run in 1980, just weeks prior to leaving office after one term. Utilizing the Antiquities Act, he issued an Executive Order that removed 157 million acres of Alaska lands from state control and made them federally controlled forests, parks, refuges, monuments, and the like. It also meant that Alaska Natives and residents in some rural areas were given special fishing and hunting privileges not extended to non-Native, nonrural Alaskans.

The court sided with the federal government on two attempts by McDowell and others to stop ANILCA. In fact, the issue is still a sore point—a major fracture even—to many Alaskans who feel every citizen of the state should have equal access and rights. However, no matter whether Alaskans now favor or still oppose the issue, there was no doubt that Sam McDowell played a significant role in bringing the matter to a head.

Hunters and anglers in Alaska in particular owe a huge debt of gratitude to Sam McDowell for his indefatigable efforts to push for greater state control over fish and game management in Alaska.

15

KEITH JOHNSON, 1932–PRESENT

Anchorage

Most Master Guides become respected conservationists who read-
ily impart knowledge to fellow hunters, but it's uncommon to also
become a bush pilot, a successful lodge owner, and the author of a
still-popular autobiography. In addition to possessing the extraordi-
nary strength and stamina required for guiding Kodiak bear hunts,
he possessed the rare skill to take skittish mountain sheep with a
bow—all adding to a reputation that made the trips he donated to
auctions at major hunting conventions the most prized items of all.

Just about anyone who's spent time in Alaska has a bear story or two. After all, bears outnumber humans in many portions of Alaska. When it comes to hunting in the bush, odds are high for running into a bear because moose, caribou, and many other targeted game animals inhabit the same territory.

However, those brave souls who actually seek out bears in the wild for viewing or hunting are even more likely to come face to face with an *Ursus*, the genus name for bears. Taking the likelihood of a bear encounter even further, imagine the tales one would have by spending forty years as a Master Guide in Alaska hunting and guiding for brown bears.

Master Guide
Keith Johnson
with pelts of a
wolf and many
foxes at his
Wildman Lake
Lodge. Photo
courtesy of the
Johnson family.

Keith Johnson survived some three hundred bear encounters spanning four decades, and not surprisingly a good many of them were terrifying experiences, some of them actually humorous. Johnson details the most memorable confrontations in his book, *Unpredictable Giants: 40 Years of Alaskan Brown Bear Tales*, published in 2001. When the fact that most brown bear hunts involve flying deeply into remote areas to go after the really huge trophy specimens, the risk ratchets up to the extreme.

One such bear story unfolded when Johnson was hunting in the Wrangell Mountains. He'd been flying clients in and out of camps all day and felt exhausted. He stopped at one of his cabins on Glacier Creek to rest overnight before continuing to fly. All alone and in bed, he heard something banging around outside. In order to get a bit of fresh air, he'd anchored the door with a string so it opened fully.

Johnson at first thought the noise was caused by a black bear and yelled, "Get out of here" to scare it off. But then a huge brown head appeared. He leaped out of bed and grabbed his rifle, shucking a shell into it. The brownie was only one rifle length away from him as it broke the string and the entire door swung open.

Johnson knew that the bear should have been scared off by the human scent and his shouting, so he realized this wasn't a good situation. However, Johnson didn't want to shoot it right there because it would block the only entrance in and out of the cabin. He stuck out his rifle barrel and jabbed the bear in the nose. Luckily it backed up and finally ran off. Johnson fired a shot over its head to be sure it would keep on going.

Reta Johnson, Keith's wife who lives with him in Anchorage, spoke of another bizarre series of incidents that took place on the Alaska Peninsula. Johnson was a bush pilot in addition to being a hunting guide, and a bear kept acting like a car-chasing dog.

"Keith dropped hunting clients off in this one particular area and in a few days would fly in for the pick up," Reta said. "An angry female grizzly would run after the plane each time he'd take off and leap at the airplane. It happened multiple times and came really close, narrowly missing as the plane went airborne. It really scared Keith and the hunters."

Johnson was born in Hugo, Colorado. He was the fifth of ten children—eight boys and two girls—in the family of James and Minnie Johnson. While growing up in Hugo, James allowed his boys to tag along with him on hunting trips throughout Colorado. However, none of the boys was allowed to carry a rifle until the age of twelve. He must have figured that by then, the boys would be old enough to adhere to safety rules and to respect nature.

Keith graduated high school, during which he met a young woman named Reta Orrell. The relationship would result in marriage during Johnson's senior year in college, but it never would have blossomed if Reta, who came from a large family composed mainly of girls, had listened to her parents.

"Us girls were told not to date the Johnson boys as they were too wild," she laughed.

Johnson and Reta went to the same high school and knew each other. He would say hi to her in the school hallways and she would turn bashfully away and wouldn't answer. Johnson would always laugh when that occurred because he was outgoing and knew she was really shy. As you might guess, this flirtation sparked a love leading to matrimony.

After high school, Johnson enlisted in the U.S. Army. For that two-year period during the Korean War, he worked as a prison guard in South Korea. Once back home, in 1954, he attended the University of Northern Colorado in Greeley, earning a degree in education. Johnson put his degree to work immediately by taking a job at a high school in Glendive, Montana. Besides teaching classes in industrial arts, he started the wrestling team and served as the coach. Robert, his first child, was born in Glendive.

In his free time, Johnson took to the woods with a bow or rifle, picking up his hunting interest fostered in Colorado. He especially enjoyed tracking deer around the Yellowstone River region. However, as bountiful as the hunting for deer, antelope, elk and moose could be at times in the American West, most hunters jabbered a lot about Alaska's reputation as a hunter's heaven. Johnson decided he'd take Reta on a trip to The Last Frontier in August 1961.

"I convinced my wife that we would just stay in Alaska until I was done hunting," he would write forty years later in his book *Unpredictable Giants.* "She still occasionally reminds me of that."

"Yes, I sure did remind him," laughed Reta. I had the opportunity to chat with her and daughter Joni (who pronounces her name "Johnny") about Keith's life. (Unfortunately, health issues prevented Keith from joining the conversation.)

All it took was that first hunting trip to Alaska to convince Johnson to uproot the family and move to Anchorage. He taught in the Anchorage school district until retiring in 1977. During that tenure, Johnson started the high school wrestling team just as he'd done in Montana. Soon he was instrumental in getting teams started in other Alaska schools, which originated organized wrestling competition in the state.

Keith and Reta welcomed three more children into the household, all born in Anchorage: Linda, Jerry, and Joni. And in only his second year as a resident of his adopted home state, Johnson obtained Registered Guide License number 35. He signed on as an Assistant Guide in the Wrangell Mountains to Master Guide Kenny Oldham and later in the Alaska Range under Master Guide Denny Thompson. The apprenticeships helped Johnson learn protocols between guides and hunters, how to choose and set up camps, fees and tipping, and needed supplies. He could only guide part time due to his teaching career, but on weekends and during summer breaks, he was in the bush learning everything he could about the guiding biz.

As it is for all newcomers to the forty-ninth state, at first it seemed a daunting task for Johnson to wrap his arms around the many challenges of providing a successful hunt for clients. But as he watched

A brown bear hunt with Johnson (*front center*) was an extremely popular auction item at the annual Safari Club International conventions.
Photo courtesy of the Johnson family.

Oldham's and Thompson's operations grow, he felt confident that he
would be able to make a living at it too.

"When I made my first trip out to the Alaska Peninsula, my knowledge of brown bear was very limited," wrote Johnson. "A lot of what
I learned about bear hunting over the years was from firsthand, trial-
and-error experiences."

Johnson's knack for keen observation and a memory for details
would serve him well in becoming a better hunter and later a Master
Guide. He took quickly to being a student of the Alaska bush and
mountains: He noted when and where bears, caribou, moose, sheep,
wolves, and other species congregated; he observed seasonal and
weather influences; and he studied predator-prey relationships, and so
much more. Johnson could soon instantly recognize patterns that led
him to the bigger trophy specimens that hunters prize.

After retiring from teaching in 1977, what Johnson would do next
was a no-brainer. According to his wife Reta, he enjoyed only three hob-
bies: hunting, hunting, and hunting. While he loved going after moose,
caribou, bear, and other species, he was totally obsessed with sheep. All
the mounts in Johnson's home—then and now—are of sheep.

Anyone who's experienced hunting for Dall sheep in the mountains
knows full well of its extreme challenges. For one thing, sheep are

extremely elusive and prefer steep mountainsides to discourage predators. They are also constantly wary of possible attacks and forever jit-
tery. In particular, the sound of a tumbling rock or the slightest misstep
of a stalking animal sends sheep bounding away.

Because of their precarious habitat and skittish nature, not many
hunters have the physical conditioning and unending patience to stalk
sheep. Johnson, on the other hand, could outwalk and outclimb just
about any human alive. He possessed abundant stamina and a willingness to dedicate not only hours but, if necessary, days to ease into
the optimum position—perhaps on the opposite side of the mountain
from where he first crouched with a spotting scope—to get that coveted, one-shot opportunity.

Fooling mountain sheep with a flat-shooting rifle from 200 or 300
yards away from one ridge to another is one thing, but taking an animal with a bow—a recurve bow at that, not a more powerful com-
pound model—is quite an uncommon feat.

"I found this old archery magazine from the 1960s that had an article about dad being only the seventh white man on record to take a
Dall sheep with a bow," said Joni Kiser. "He went on to take six more
over the years, some with a bow and some with a gun."

Early on in his guiding tutelage, Johnson recognized the advantages
of an airplane for the guiding business. In 1965, he obtained a pilot's
license. He preferred smaller planes such as Super Cubs because the
larger Otters and Beavers were slower and couldn't land in some of the
ultra most-remote locations he wanted to access for hunting and fishing parties.

Johnson ended up logging over twenty thousand flight hours—a
large total even by bush-pilot standards—and never crashed. He had
a few minor mishaps, but a tendency to play it safe had much to do
with his outstanding safety record. If weather was questionable or the
weight was too heavy for takeoff, Johnson would postpone a trip or
make two trips if needed rather than tempt disaster. Johnson became
known for a note that he kept taped to the dashboard of his plane: "If in
doubt, don't."

Besides income from hunting charters, Johnson bought a
commercial-fishing operation on the Kenai Peninsula in 1970. The
whole Johnson family participated in fishing the "set nets" used to

catch salmon in Cook Inlet. He continued to operate it until 2008. Also, in 1980, he bought Wildman Lake Lodge on the Alaska Peninsula.

He'd previously visited the area to hunt and occasionally tossed his bags at Wildman Lake Lodge. He fell in love with the surroundings, figuring it would be a perfect base of operations for a fly-in hunting destination. The site is located sixty miles from the small town of Port Heiden and rests on the spring-fed Ocean River. The nearest road to the lodge is three hundred miles away.

Just accessing Wildman Lake Lodge was an inspiring experience. The flight to the Alaska Peninsula presents the glistening Bristol Bay watershed and, beyond that, the snowy Alaska Range that connects to the Aleutian Islands. A visit from Anchorage or other airports typically required a stopover in the town of King Salmon, with another flight to Port Heiden and then a single-prop hop to the lodge. While the rustic lodge provided modern comforts as a home base, the actual hunting took place from spike camps proximate to the lodge.

Johnson's exclusive hunting in this area covered a swath of territory about 80 miles long and 35 to 50 miles wide. His hunters had the entire region to themselves, meaning some of the game animals had never set eyes on a human being. Besides being home to some of the best trophy brown bear hunting in the world, the area offered huge herds of caribou and moose as well as ducks and ptarmigan. Fishing for silver and sockeye salmon plus trout, char, and Dolly Varden served as a great side interest for clients. The hearty meals provided to lodge guests never lacked plenty of tasty protein and all the fixings.

The lodge's remoteness and the great experiences by clients led to huge success for Johnson. The lodge quickly became a favorite getaway of celebrities like singer Hank Williams Jr., astronaut Eugene Cernan, and pilot Chuck Yeager. At times it took three or four years for hunters to book an open trip at the lodge, a factor that made a trip donated by Johnson for the fundraising auction at the annual Safari Club International (SCI) convention in Reno, Nevada, one of the most prized and highly sought-after bidding items.

After Johnson sold Wildman Lake Lodge in 1996, he wasn't quite ready to retire. He bought into a deer-hunting ranch in Michigan, but it never equaled Alaska. He finally did leave guiding and set to work on writing *Unpredictable Giants*. As with all the family business ventures over the decades, Reta helped with the manuscript just as she'd done endless times in handling correspondence, accounting, booking schedules, supply ordering, and myriad other matters.

During his fifty-plus years in Alaska, Johnson donated a lot of volunteer hours to conservation groups and causes he believed in. He also served as a convincing advocate of ethical hunting practices among guides and hunters in both Alaska and the nation. Levelheaded and never losing his cool, Johnson spoke out in a responsible manner about antihunting elements seeking to restrict access to public lands or pushing for unreasonable regulations. Everyone—from hunters to game managers to political leaders—came to know Keith Johnson as an honest and forthright man.

Because of his integrity, Johnson received numerous professional honors, including recognitions by the Alaska Professional Hunters Association, the Alaska Bowhunters Association, and the Foundation for North American Wild Sheep. SCI named Johnson its "Professional Hunter of the Year for North America" in 1995. In Johnson's honor, Remington Arms produced a custom-made "dream" rifle engraved in gold leaf. The weapon was auctioned off for a large sum at an SCI convention.

Joni Kiser recalled an incident that revealed Johnson's character and how the old expression "what goes around, comes around" often comes true:

Before dad owned Wildman Lake Lodge, he was at the floatplane base in Anchorage and saw someone sitting with his gear and looking rather glum. He asked what was wrong and the young fellow—who was in the military—said he'd booked a hunt with a guide and paid for it, but the guide didn't show up. When dad found out where he was supposed to be dropped off for the hunt, he flew him there and days later picked him up. Dad simply didn't want anyone to have a bad impression of guides in Alaska.

On the flight back to Anchorage, he told dad that he didn't have the money to pay him. Dad said that he realized that and not to worry. But before they parted, he promised dad that one day he would somehow pay him. It was typical of dad to help people even if he knew it would cost him time and money.

Johnson with a Dall sheep, far and away his favorite quarry. Photo courtesy of the Johnson family.

Over twenty years went by after that incident. Dad had purchased Wildman Lake Lodge on the Alaska Peninsula and would attend conventions in the Lower 48 like Safari Club International to book hunters. During one such trip as he walked through the convention floor he heard a man calling his name. Dad turned around and didn't recognize him and said hello. The man said, 'You don't remember me, do you? Well. I remember you. You did something really kind for me many years ago and I've never forgotten it. Now I'm in a position where I can repay your kindness.'

It turned out that the man was very high up at Remington Arms. From that point forward, Remington Arms did all of their field-testing on guns at my dad's lodge. They would bring all of their new guns to the lodge with their staff, demo the guns in the field, hunt with them and then leave them for my dad and the guides. They ran full-page ads in the Safari Club's magazine for hunts with my dad that would say things like 'Book the hunt of a lifetime with Keith Johnson at Wildman Lake Lodge and Remington Arms.'

My dad's business really boomed. It was so amazing to see how his kindness and his honesty had come full circle and karma paid him back. Many years later, Remington Arms offered a 'Keith Johnson Special Edition' rifle for auction at the Safari Club International Convention. Dad designed the entire gun to his own specifications and his name was engraved on it with gold leaf engravings of bears. It was a one-of-a-kind Remington gun and auctioned off during the main auction event.

Reta believes that her husband's success in the guiding business had its roots in his career in education. "His real talent stemmed from his teaching experience," said Reta. "No matter what he did, he was still a teacher. In addition to field instruction, he showed new guides a video on how to judge bear and how to best hunt them. And when we ran the fishing business, he was always teaching the young men working there the most successful techniques to get the job done. He was a communicator."

As all good stewards of resources do, Johnson passed along his knowledge to guides, fellow hunters, and clients, but especially to his family. Daughter Joni, born and raised in Anchorage, inherited her dad's love for hunting and enjoyed innumerable trips into the wilderness with him aboard his bush plane. Joni, who became only the sixth woman to take a brown bear by bow, went on her first archery bear-hunting trip in 2012 when her dad was too sick to accompany her. She not only harvested a black bear with a one-arrow shot, she did the same on a huge brown bear that made the record book in the Pope and Young Club, a bow-hunting and conservation organization. As thrilling as that was, her main satisfaction was getting back home and telling her dad all about the shot.

Joni and her husband, Dave Kiser, own Full Curl Archery in Anchorage, a full-service pro shop. Both are Certified Archery Instructors with the National Archery in the Schools Program and also coach students for state and national tournaments. Joni is an archery instructor for the Alaska Department of Fish & Game's BOW Program and received the Diana Award for conservation from the Alaska chapter of Safari Club International.

"Over and over, when people come into our store they say he or she knew or hunted with dad," said Kiser. "While of course he receives many compliments about being a great guide, he's best known for always being fair and honest."

Johnson's youngest son, Jerry, obtained his Assistant Guide License and, for several seasons, guided hunts for moose, caribou, and brown bear at Wildman Lake Lodge. Daughter Linda worked a season as a cook's assistant at the lodge. Johnson and oldest son, Robert, both got their pilot's licenses, and Robert guided one season for sheep in the Wrangell Mountains for his dad.

Johnson had few equals as a spellbinding storyteller about the enviable occupation of making a living as an Alaska hunting guide. He also became a respected conservationist and a teacher to many about the majesty of Alaska's big game animals. While *Unpredictable Giants* justifiably portrays bears as the deserving masters of the Alaska wildlife hierarchy, it's a fitting parallel that Johnson himself ranks as one of the great Master Hunters in Alaska's history.

16

CECILIA "PUDGE" KLEINKAUF, 1936–PRESENT

Anchorage

Upon her arrival in Alaska, she realized that women lacked the respect and training opportunities normally afforded men in learning the rudiments of fly-fishing. As well as developing a professional niche based on resort packages offering classroom and in-the-field courses, she's also become an internationally sought speaker and seminar instructor at fishing clubs and conventions.

Cecilia "Pudge" Kleinkauf, a cancer survivor, has served as a lobbyist, university professor, and lawyer. Who could ever predict that a background like hers would produce one of the world's greatest advocates of fly-fishing for women.

As a small child, Kleinkauf was nicknamed Pudge by her dad when she contracted a rare form of anemia that made everything she ate go to fat. All that melted away after treatment and a cure. Even so, the moniker endured with family and friends, and then among the public. The owner of Women's Flyfishing, Kleinkauf has been an Alaska trailblazer on a mission to open doors previously reserved for men. For nearly thirty years, she's been Alaska's leading female fly-fishing instructor, guide, and fly-tier.

Bedecked in wading and fly-fishing gear, Kleinkauf readies to release a trout. Photo courtesy of Pudge Kleinkauf.

Kleinkauf's inevitable rendezvous with Alaska began when her parents headed to Denver after her dad received a promotion from Texaco, the petroleum corporation, and was assigned there. They stopped first in Sterling, Colorado, and spent several weeks. The family fell in love with the small town and decided to make it their home instead. Primary education came by way of boarding school for Kleinkauf and her three sisters in their mother's hope that it would make ladies out of them.

Kleinkauf recalled: "When I graduated, the head nun took me into her office and said, 'Please don't tell anyone you came to this school because we really don't like the way you turned out.' To her, I was a rebel because I'd sneak a cigarette or date boys, but to me it was simply enjoying life as a teenager."

After college, Kleinkauf married and had a son, Scott, but the marriage ended in divorce. She decided to become a veterinarian, but the head of the school where she applied informed her that it didn't admit women, a message all too familiar to women in those days. She switched to becoming a teacher while attending what was then Colorado A&M (later renamed Colorado State University). Kleinkauf taught junior and senior high school students in both Colorado and California, but then gravitated to social work and supervised a public welfare office while obtaining a master's degree in that field at the University of Denver.

By then remarried, Pudge moved to Anchorage in 1969 with her second husband. She headed the social-work department as a professor at the University of Alaska at Anchorage, working there for fourteen years. Early on, she became interested in fishing during her free summer months.

"I started with spin gear, but soon switched over to fly," said Kleinkauf. "That's because my son Scott always caught more fish than me using a fly rod. I'd often go off to practice by myself, casting all day and getting home in time to fix dinner. Soon women I knew or met on the water would ask about learning how to fly-fish and whether I taught classes. It gave me the idea that many women wanted to get into fly-fishing and would prefer another woman showing them how."

Kleinkauf did some checking around. In the 1980s, no one in Alaska could be found teaching seminars or offering fly-fishing classes specifically for women. Likewise, she noted the absence of magazine or newspaper articles written by women or female fly shop owners. So, she took fly-casting lessons from a man recommended by a friend. Once Kleinkauf started teaching fly-fishing, she also began leading small groups of women on excursions all around Alaska. Soon her classes and excursions became successful.

She initially ran into some resistance while rising in stature in Alaska. "I had to prove myself to a number of male guides," Kleinkauf recalled. "It was also quite a challenge to create awareness specifically to women about my business as well as getting connected with manufacturers in the fly-fishing industry."

Over time, other women guides and instructors arrived on the scene. "Women are now coming into fly-fishing much more and clubs have formed all over the country," she said. "I'm really glad to see that happen in my lifetime."

Kleinkauf's life was not always about teaching and fly-fishing, however. In 1983, a malignant melanoma was found under her chin, requiring removal of one side of her neck down to an armpit in order to cut out the cancerous lymph nodes.

"It made me pay attention to what I wanted to do with the rest of my life," she said. After five years with no recurrence of the cancer, Kleinkauf set out to accomplish what she'd added to her bucket list. In 1988, she enrolled in law school at the University of Puget Sound (now

Seattle University) since there weren't any law schools in Alaska. She obtained a law degree in 1991 and passed the bar exam in Alaska.

Kleinkauf put her legal education to good use in Alaska. She explained:

> I never litigated, but instead used that understanding of the legal system to practice public policy law. I became active in social worker groups nationally and in Alaska. At one point I worked with the Alaska legislature in Juneau as a representational lobbyist on social issues. For six years I worked on a blue ribbon committee established by the governor on laws having to do with senior citizens, food stamps, medical care and such. I really enjoyed doing that, but slowly but surely I got out of lawyering and lobbying—the fish goddess inside my head said it was time to do more fly-fishing.

Pudge now guides from Nome to Cordova and ten places in between and conducts a number of beginning fly-fishing classes in Anchorage. The instruction goes beyond the classroom by helping women apply their new skills on the water in pursuit of numerous species. She also offers an annual women-only fly-fishing school lasting four days at a lodge in Cordova. Women come from around the United States to master fly-fishing with both light- and heavy-weight rods used to catch fish ranging from pink and chum salmon to cutthroat trout and Dolly Varden.

Kleinkauf serves as an Alaska guide on trips composed of women and couples. She also leads at least one trip each spring to Mexico for saltwater fly-fishing and, every few years, takes a group to Sweden or Ireland. In addition to guiding, Kleinkauf instructs in all aspects of fly-fishing: casting, proper gear, and techniques. Her appearances at outdoor shows and conferences throughout the United States are hugely popular, thanks not only to her reputation as a champion of Alaska fly-fishing but also due to a high-profile media presence. Kleinkauf appears regularly on national TV shows and is a regular host on the *Alaska Magazine Television Series* on Public Broadcasting Service. She's frequently a featured speaker at fishing clubs around the country.

Kleinkauf (middle) greatly enjoys teaching women all the ins and outs of catching fish on fly. Photo courtesy of Pudge Kleinkauf.

Not surprisingly, Kleinkauf represents numerous fly manufacturers as a professional staffer, and she's been a member of the Guides Association of the Federation of Fly Fishers, Worldwide Outfitter and Guides Association, and the Alaska Fly Fishers. Kleinkauf is a one of the founders of the International Women Fly Fishers. Pudge is a fly-fishing ambassador for Patagonia, and her Women's Flyfishing business is a Trout Unlimited–endorsed company.

With her business humming in 2004 and all going well, another huge medical challenge arose that again threatened her very existence. Kleinkauf contracted a bacterial infection from which 80 percent of the victims die. In a coma for two weeks and stuck in a hospital for seven more weeks, she simply refused to give up.

"I kept telling myself that I've got to get back outside," she said. "I went into the hospital in January of that year and was back on the water and guiding in June." The following spring, Kleinkauf took top

A big smile from Pudge for a spunky char caught before release in Becharof Lake. Photo courtesy of Pudge Kleinkauf.

prize for the winning sailfish in a tournament based in Mexico, proving to any doubters that she hadn't lost a step.

When the busy spring and summer seasons turn into winter, Kleinkauf remains active at her home in Anchorage by updating her website and writing. She's a contributing editor for *Fish Alaska Magazine* and at work on a new book, her fifth. Titles authored by Kleinkauf include *Pacific Salmon Flies: New Ties and Old Standbys*, and *Fly-Fishing for Alaska's Arctic Grayling: Sailfish of the North*, and she's received the coveted Gold Medal Benjamin Franklin Award for *River Girls: Fly Fishing for Young Women* and a Silver Medal for *Fly Fishing Women Explore Alaska*.

Being in the Alaska wilderness as often as she is, bear confrontations inevitably occur. "I've been charged a couple of times and also bluff charged," she said, "but all clients and I have remained safe and sound. The key is to learn how to avoid bear encounters and then how to react when they happen." That wasn't always the case with Kleinkauf herself. "One of my sisters still gives me a hard time by reminding me that when I first moved to Alaska, I was afraid to even leave the house to go to Safeway because of bears," she laughed.

Clients are typically edgy about bear encounters too. "One of the first questions someone asks when booking a trip is about bear danger," said Kleinkauf. "I always reply that I'll show them what to do based on two established methods that start with the letter N: noise and numbers. Let your presence be known and stay together as a group."

Some clients don't always listen. "One year a woman insisted on fishing by herself," she recalls. "I said that I didn't want her going down the river away from our group in case a bear should appear. Well, she snuck off at one point and did it anyway. Sure enough, a bear appeared between her and the rest of us. Luckily it wasn't interested in causing trouble and walked away, but it really shook her up. She came back scared to the bone and exclaimed, 'Oh my god, you were so right.' She never strayed again after that."

Kleinkauf is always looking for something fresh and new for clients, and such an opportunity came knocking a couple of years ago. For decades she's guided most charter clients and students in Alaska to fish coastal rivers for species such as silver salmon because that's where fish tend to run larger and in greater quantities. However, when a former hunting guide who lives near Denali National Park in Interior Alaska got in touch about catching rainbow trout in lakes on his property, Kleinkauf didn't believe it.

"He invited me to come up and fish his lakes to see for myself, but I kept saying no because it just wasn't plausible that rainbows could survive year-round in Denali—the water is just too cold and most lakes freeze solid," she said.

However, on the next occasion when Kleinkauf needed to visit Fairbanks, out of curiosity she decided to drop by his place since it was on the way. "It turned out to be true," she said. "It was an amazing discovery. He'd been stocking his lake with rainbows and also had a resident number of Arctic grayling for many years, and he and his son fed them twice a week. Even though the ice freezes on the surface of his lakes during winter, the upwelling from deep springs provides enough water and oxygen to keep fish alive in the winter. Ever since then, I've been taking gals there to float tube the lakes, and it's become a very unique and popular trip."

Although Kleinkauf's path has been especially fraught with hills and valleys, she's endured the hardships thrown her way, emerging more determined than ever to find her calling in life and turn it into a success. Through it all she's not only survived, she's flourished.

"My main goal is to provide a safe and supportive environment for women to comfortably and confidently learn to fly-fish," she said. "It's a thinking person's sport and the progression of complexity is thoroughly challenging and fun. In particular, women must be brave and trust their instincts in forging forward even when things look dim."

Her son, Scott, has been the joy of her life, and she now shares that love with two grandchildren, Erin and Dylan. They're further validation for one Cecilia "Pudge" Kleinkauf, a true Alaska legend who advanced from a passion to a profession. In that regard, she's quite the symbol of strength, determination, and success to men and women alike.

17

DICK BISHOP, 1937–PRESENT
MARY BISHOP, 1937–PRESENT

Fairbanks

This husband-and-wife team became a powerful influence on Alaska's management of fish and game in the post-statehood period when effective leadership was desperately needed to focus on the proper stewardship to protect fish and game resources while balancing recreational and commercial interests. That leadership is still paying dividends for Alaska's great outdoors and resource users.

About twenty years ago as I sipped a brew in Juneau's Red Dog Saloon, Tag Eckles—better known by his stage name of Phineas Poon—was at his perch on stage behind a piano for another set of his wonderfully bawdy performances. But in a philosophical moment, he lamented about the exhaustibility of Alaska's resources.

"People have always *taken* from Alaska," he said. "First they came for the furs; then they came for the gold; then they came for the salmon; and then they came for the oil."

True enough. And people are still coming to Alaska, especially tourists and new residents wanting a piece of The Last Frontier. We reap what we sow when it comes to healthy fish and game resources as they must be enhanced in the present, or at least not reversed, for future generations to enjoy the pleasure of taking a fine moose or salmon.

Dick grew up in northern Minnesota where he learned to hunt and skin beaver such as this one in 1955 at Pequot Lakes. Photo courtesy of the Bishop family.

Well-managed fish and game populations can accommodate visiting fishers and hunters. At least that's been the goal of wildlife managers before and since statehood in 1959. And when it comes to combined efforts of the government and conservation organizations, Dick and Mary Bishop come to many minds as an important team in the formative years of the Alaska Department of Fish & Game (ADF&G).

As I dug into the research for this book, certain names kept cropping up time and again in the minutes of myriad meetings and in the bibliographies of countless research papers and studies. One was Dick Bishop. And while he can stand on his own merits, his wife, Mary, well deserves sharing the chapter with him. Many spouses to some degree become an integral part of the other's career, and Mary has been incredibly impactful as a driving force for sound rule-making outside ADF&G. As such, Dick and Mary have been a potent team.

Before we get into their good works and characters, Dick was quick to point out that when Alaska became a state in 1959 and immediately thereafter took over management of the state's fish and wildlife resources from the federal government, particularly from the U.S. Fish and Wildlife Service, monumental turf wars erupted, with some still going on to varying degrees. "The federal government controls nearly two-thirds of Alaska between the Bureau of Land Management, U.S. Fish & Wildlife Service, National Park Service, U.S. Forest Service and Department of Defense," said Dick.

That being the case, some of those in the trenches of ADF&G from its inception represent the state-employed pioneers battling federal game and fish agencies, lobbyists from every side of every issue, a public wary of more layers of regulations and laws, and the political jockeying in and out of the agency itself. Nonetheless, despite the attempts by federal regulators to usurp state authority, ADF&G moves on—sometimes bloodied, but generally unbowed—to establish laws affecting most animal species that walk the forests or swim the waters of Alaska, marine mammals being the most notable exception. The work boils down to ensuring sustainable fish and game uses ranging from recreational, commercial and subsistence.

Field studies conducted by state biologists at times conflicted with federal management directives. As if that weren't enough, battle lines were drawn over subsistence priority fishing and hunting by rural versus nonrural Alaskans. Another conflict involved the question of how predators affected the numbers of prey, with some biologists insisting that bears, wolves, and the like had little impact on game populations.

Given that background, let's delve into the parts played by Dick and Mary Bishop. Born in Devil's Lake, North Dakota, as the winds of World War II were stirring, Dick grew up in northern Minnesota and loved nothing more than hunting, trapping, and fishing the surrounding Jack pine forests. In the 1950s as Alaska inexorably headed for statehood, he'd already heard plenty about how The Last Frontier represented the altar at which all hunters and trappers worship. Bishop decided that that's where his destiny must lead, as he wanted to trap in the North.

The year 1961 proved to be a momentous one for Dick and Mary. He attended college at the University of Minnesota and graduated with a degree in wildlife management. During that time, he met Mary Walsdorf as she studied to obtain a master's degree in zoology. They tied the knot as Dick completed his U.S. Army Reserve duty. He'd also worked summer jobs between semesters, performing salmon counts in Bristol Bay and doing various chores at McKinley National Park. Those tastes of Alaska convinced Dick to move from Minnesota, and in October of that year, the couple arrived in Fairbanks in a house trailer just as temperatures began to plummet.

The going proved to be tougher than expected. Mary was eight months pregnant with their first son, Dan, and they initially lived in the old house trailer and later a converted garage. Dick took a job as a lab and teaching assistant at the University of Alaska Fairbanks (UAF) and also set out a few traps. He couldn't resist scratching that trapping itch. "We were long on enthusiasm and short on smarts," he joked while musing about their initial years in Fairbanks. "We weren't making much money, but we got by and loved living in Alaska."

Times got better. According to Mary's sister, Nancy Walsdorf of Charlotte Harbor, Florida, "Dick and Mary eventually moved to a log cabin home on Gus's Grind, which is several miles from Fairbanks. They have a big garden and depend largely on catching fish and shooting game for food. They share what they have with the families of their sons Dan, Sam and Doug."

Indeed, I found their home to be quite comfy, perched amid thirty wooded acres in the hills. A grizzly bear had been sighted days earlier in the neighborhood; we kept a watchful eye while I played tennis-ball fetch outside with their Lab.

I asked Dick about his ADF&G path after arrival in Fairbanks. He explained that he soon took on an assignment in Gambell, Alaska, to monitor the 1963 spring walrus harvest. He then worked toward obtaining his master of science in wildlife management from UAF, with his thesis focusing on the life history of harbor seals. His star rising, Dick went to work full time for ADF&G in 1965, assisting with moose, wolf, and lynx management and research in south-central and Interior Alaska.

One of his later ADF&G roles centered on serving as the area game biologist in McGrath, Alaska, on the Kuskokwim River in western Interior Alaska. That rural experience in McGrath deeply impacted Dick and Mary. They gained a huge respect for the dedication and knowledge that locals exhibited to live in the wilderness. The ability of those who decided to live off the grid with few modern conveniences, like electricity and running water, impressed them. That lifestyle had fascinated both of them from childhood.

In early 1975, Dick resigned from ADF&G to become a visiting professor for one semester in UAF's Wildlife Management Department. The influence of his McGrath assignment gnawing at him, Dick and Mary moved to a cabin in the center of the Interior at Lake Minchumina with their three sons aged nine, twelve, and thirteen.

"It was the best two-and-a-half years imaginable for us and the boys," said Mary. "It was a lot of work, but we came away better people on account of it because we learned to be independent and to

Mary, undaunted by a swamp wade, has been a leading voice in Alaska conservation issues. Photo courtesy of the Bishop family.

appreciate a more tranquil lifestyle." The boys ran their own traplines and dog teams, maintained a vegetable garden and helped put food on the table by hunting, fishing, and trapping. Mary always made certain her family was well nourished, and she served as doctor for minor injuries and illnesses.

While trapping, hunting, and fishing were personally satisfying, the trickle of income from it didn't make ends meet. Dick obtained a contract to conduct a study on local-resource uses for the proposed expansion of McKinley National Park, and then it was back to the real world in Fairbanks for the Bishops. Dick immediately secured a full-time job with ADF&G in 1977 as regional supervisor for the Game Division. While he surmised that the position would last maybe a few years before he could get back to living off the land, he instead stayed on until 1989 due to an intense interest in the challenges resulting from the adaptation of new and old federal laws.

Mary's story began on December 26, 1937, born to Opal and Lee Walsdorf in Ladysmith, Wisconsin, a small rural community about a hundred miles east of Minneapolis. Her father, who made a living in insurance and real estate, loved to fish and hunt.

"Dad often talked to the local biologist and forester, and I always tagged along with him on those visits and especially enjoyed fishing and squirrel hunting with him," she said. "He was a sharpshooter and early NRA member. Mom was a farm girl who didn't want to go back to the farm. As a family we did camping trips into northern Minnesota canoe country with my older brother and sister."

Mary became interested in zoology and biology even in grade school, her interest in animals spanning from insects to reptiles to dogs. As three sons soon were added to the Bishop family, it became practical for Mary to be a stay-at-home mom. She explained:

> We could have had more money if I was employed, but the added stress of day care and seeing other dual-career marriages fall apart was something we didn't want happening to us. When we moved into our present home in 1966, it was without electricity or water and the roof had only three inches of mouse-shredded insulation. We used rainwater and melted snow for most things, including water for the sled-dogs. Dick carried containers of drinking water on his back up to a mile at a time during the spring and summer when the road was too muddy to drive.

In 1969, the family moved to McGrath, the Bishops now residing in a more-modern home that ADF&G made available to whoever took on the role of resident biologist. "We liked McGrath, but it was too tough on the kids with all the heavy boozing taking place around the village," Mary recalled. "And so, in 1972 we came back to Fairbanks right around the same time Dick found out about Lake Minchumina. We finally moved there in June 1975 and it was marvelous. I cooked on an old wood stove, baked all our bread and made everything from scratch. I also learned how to prepare a big hunk of moose meat that would last several days and still taste delicious."

Mary homeschooled the three boys, and the family went through its share of challenges, which is part and parcel to anyone spending time in the Alaska wilderness. But Dick and Mary raised the boys to be able to cope with any problems they might face in the great outdoors.

Mary expressed her thoughts on the challenges of balancing state's rights versus federal jurisdiction. "I think the state's fish and game department was one of the best in the nation and still is, but the dual system of federal management on federal lands within Alaska causes a huge assortment of problems," she said.

> One of the biggest issues that still tears at the social fabric of this state is the preposterous idea that some of us, as individual Alaskans, wanted to repeal subsistence hunting. Not so! We wanted to repeal or amend a federal law that gives a priority for harvest to certain residents based simply on where they live. It's not a priority based on race, ethnicity or need. The priority was ruled unconstitutional under state law, but it's never been challenged in the U.S. Supreme Court—it should be.

Mary composed and edited the Alaska Outdoor Council newsletter for about twenty-five years. She's spent countless hours researching and commenting on fish and game management issues in both state and federal arenas. Of great debate to this day is the Alaska National Interest Lands Conservation Act (ANILCA) signed into law by President Jimmy Carter in December 1980 as he was about to leave office. ANILCA caused a vitriolic uproar when over 157 million acres instantly became national parks, recreation or wilderness areas, and refuges. Some Fairbanks citizens protested by hanging Carter in effigy and staging other protests.

Fortunately, Mary's life hasn't been one of just dealing with contentious environmental issues. Marilyn Kulibert of Ladysmith, Wisconsin, a high school pal of Mary's, spoke of her friend's lifelong interest in wildlife. "On a Girl Scout camping trip in our teen years, she came back to the camp with a large snake wrapped around her neck," said Kulibert. "Mary held out the head and tail for all the rest of us timid girls to look at, but we didn't appreciate her find."

Dick's accomplishments at ADF&G were exceptional during that formative era of great change and enormous controversy in Alaska's fish and game management. Mary pushed hard as well through the Alaska Outdoor Council. Initial hurdles included coping with federal mandates laid on the state's fish and game management, with the oil pipeline, with battles over subsistence priority fishing and hunting, and with predator control debates.

The latter issue encouraged the passage of the Federal Airborne Hunting Act, which prohibited public shooting of predators from the air. It caused another round of tumultuous clamor statewide. "In some areas we had a well-documented imbalance of predators to prey, making it difficult or impossible to manage some of the game populations and provide for people's wild food needs," said Dick. "It was really frustrating."

Dick often stood in the forefront of innovation. As early as 1968, he participated in collaring and tagging moose, including calves. He helped promote the use of radio collars that eventually replaced reliance on less-accurate recaptures of ear-tagged animals or sporadic reports of sightings. The collaring data turned out to be extremely successful in monitoring seasonal moose movements, identifying calving areas and determining causes of moose mortality.

"Cumulatively, those studies established that, in fact, predation can limit or depress populations of big game like moose and caribou," he said. "The myth that wolves only kill the sick and weak was refuted, but anti-hunting groups still believed the fabrications and opposed predator management."

In the face of so many controversial issues inside and outside ADF&G, Dick always kept his cool. He became known for his calm demeanor even when others lost their tempers during public hearings or when colleagues got out of line behind closed doors. After becoming the regional game supervisor for Interior Alaska, Dick was widely and favorably quoted in the newspapers when he said, "When there's something worthwhile saying, I'll say it."

While he didn't cross the line of being loud and overly outspoken, he was not a bit shy in making sure that the public be kept informed. "It's important that people know what's going on within the Department and in the field of wildlife management," he said.

Chris Batin, a veteran Alaska outdoors writer and videographer, confirmed Dick Bishop's quiet and responsible style: "He's a straight-shooter who always was, and still is, open to sitting down with journalists and interested citizens to discuss issues."

Bishop's son Sam once served as the editor of the editorial page for the *Fairbanks Daily News-Miner*. One Father's Day, he wrote a

The Bishops's home on Gus's Grind outside Fairbanks, offering privacy and mountain living. Photo courtesy of the Bishop family.

compelling piece, "A Father Who Listens," about his dad's special gift for understatement. The following excerpts are especially poignant:

> The ability to listen and find value in the thoughts and feelings of others has always seemed a respectable quality in my dad. I have many memories of him sitting for an evening of conversation with visitors to our homes, enjoying their perspectives and ideas even if they didn't always fit his own. Talking with elderly people, with their long experience in the world, appears to bring special enjoyment to him.
>
> Even when people lash out angrily and emotionally, he seems able to resist responding in kind and instead takes the kernel of the person's concern and deals with it.
>
> Not that he's a quivering wimp. I've heard enough sharp responses (plenty of them directed at myself) to know that he stands up forcefully to actions he believes are wrong. But his anger

is usually swathed in some sort of logic. (Except for lost tools. He's just not reasonable on that subject.)

After his retirement from ADF&G in 1989, Dick hasn't exactly loafed around in a rocking chair, and the same with Mary. Both are still active in wildlife research and public policy on resource management for fishing, hunting, and trapping. Besides the Alaska Outdoor Council, they're active in a number of organizations such as the Wildlife Society (composed of professional wildlife biologists), the Alaska Trappers Association, and the National Rifle Association.

From May to early June each year, they depart Fairbanks and hop aboard the mail plane to reach Lake Minchumina, where they maintain a small cabin. It's still an isolated, untouched portion of Alaska with only twelve residents. They return in the fall to hunt moose and ducks, pick berries, and bask in the beauty of nearby Denali. Some winters, Dick still does a bit of trapping.

"We like to watch the ice break up in spring and see all the birds flying in," said Mary. "The area always brings back fond memories of the days when our young family of five worked and played together—it was so challenging and exciting."

While many figures from the past fade into obscurity, Dick and Mary aren't forgotten relics. Former Alaska governor Sean Parnell presented them a trophy—a bust of a caribou—and a citation for their conservation work. The inscription reads: "Governor's Conservationist of the Year Award for longstanding dedication to the conservation of Alaska's fish and wildlife and for exemplary service to the people of Alaska and their outdoor traditions. Presented to Dick and Mary Bishop, February 23, 2013."

I think even ol' Phineas Poon at the Red Dog Saloon would have agreed that the Bishops have given much more than they've taken from Alaska.

18

DENNIS HAY, 1940–2015

Elfin Cove

He applied targeted publicity and executed smart marketing techniques to his creation of a viable sport-fishing-lodge operation at a remote location that no one else thought feasible. The lodge also paved the way for a greater appreciation and access to recreational fishing off Chichagof Island and the Gulf of Alaska.

When I first met Dennis Hay in Juneau in 1998, he personified the quintessential mountain man. Standing six feet, two inches tall, stocky, sporting a short but scruffy white beard, exuberant with a curious tilt of his head as he talked, Hay immediately conveyed the persona of an intriguing person.

We spent the night in Juneau before boarding his boat the next morning for a three-hour run to Elfin Cove. That ride itself was magnificent on this rare slick-calm day as we ran through Icy Strait, passed Glacier Bay to our right, rounded the northwest edge of Chichagof Island into the Gulf of Alaska and slipped into the protected waters of Elfin Cove. How beautiful that tranquil cove, and how fulfilling it was to stand on the balcony of Hay's lodge on a clear day and gaze across the salmon-swollen Gulf waters toward the mighty Fairweather Mountains and Brady Glacier. While countless vistas in Alaska earn the million-dollar-view rating, this one is a multimillionaire.

Hay looking every bit of a man with an adventurous spirit. Photo courtesy of Dennis Hay.

Hanging out with Hay was memorable. He bounced ideas off you constantly—some brilliant, some not—and one wondered when his brain might shut off. But there was no questioning him as an outstanding fisherman, guide, and lodge owner as well as an aggressive businessman. I quickly came to recognize Hay as a public relations genius of sorts, an entrepreneur driven by the rush of obtaining new clients, guiding them to impressive experiences with salmon and halibut, and organizing all the lodging components while providing unrushed time for guests to experience the astonishing environment and culture of Alaska.

Being affable, Hay connected well with his clientele. Despite his bulky countenance and notable presence once he entered any door, Hay never comported himself as a ruffian. He enjoyed camaraderie, a good joke, a glass of wine, and, as a lifelong bachelor, the sowing of plenty of wild oats with the ladies. Perhaps his high-octane energy level was simply too much for any woman to keep up with on a 24/7 basis, but he was sure fun to be around.

Another character of immense color was a cohort of Hay's named john bluefeather (all letters spelled at his insistence in lowercase). A former hippy who is still pretty hip, bluefeather became Hay's alter ego. While Hay might be impetuous and idealistic at times, bluefeather would be measured and practical. They were a Batman and Robin team, feeding on each other's strengths and idiosyncrasies. Though years older than Hay, bluefeather kept himself in peak condition and, like his borrowed name implies, felt an Indian-like spiritual connection to nature. But more on bluefeather later.

Hay's interest in fishing started at five years of age as he caught crappie from the lakes of Minnesota. Born January 22, 1940, in Mankato, Minnesota, his mother divorced Hay's father and wanted to start a new life in Washington near Tacoma. She, Dennis, and his brother left Mankato and traveled via train to Tacoma in the fall of 1946. His mother remarried in 1947 in Kent, Washington, which brought her not only a new husband but also three additional kids to raise.

"While a 12-year-old, a fishing pal named Forrey and I would sneak into a trout farm about two a.m. and catch a few sixteen- to twenty-inch rainbow trout," said Hay. "The next day, Forrey would flash our big catches to his two uncles, but never told them where we caught the lunkers—it drove them nuts trying to figure out the location of our honey hole."

Hay graduated from Kent Meridian high school in 1958 but not before letting his height and agility earn some athletic notice. In 1957. he was the leading scorer in the Puget Sound League, and the following year, his team placed third in the state basketball tournament. Hay was Second Team All-State and presented with a full scholarship to Seattle University. However, at the time his mother had cancer and was quite ill, and Hay dropped out after the first semester.

He labored at various jobs and played in town basketball leagues, and that's when he first met john bluefeather in 1960—a fellow he would not see again for over twenty years. Hay worked with his father in Phoenix prior to being drafted into the U.S. Army from August 1963 to 1965.

Once out of the army, Hay moved back to Kent and drove a dump truck until June 1966 when he had an opportunity to work on a basketball schoolmate's commercial-fishing purse-seine boat in Southeast Alaska. It was an awesome summer that included landing a sixty-two-pound king salmon while sportfishing off Hoonah, which is about

Hay bought an A-frame in 1979 and years later completed this 5,000-square-foot Elfin Cove Lodge in the ultraremote northwestern portion of Chichagof Island. Photo courtesy of john bluefeather.

forty miles west of Juneau in Icy Strait. The commercial boat caught over 50,000 salmon that summer, and Hay earned a $4,000 boat share. More importantly, he was now hooked on Alaska.

From 1967 through 1972, Hay visited Hoonah for summer getaways to fish with locals he'd befriended. Also from 1967 to 1974, he began to put his bubbling ideas to work by getting into the publishing and advertising business with a partner. They published business directories and tabloid shoppers, earning a respectable living. But the call of Alaska burned deeply within Hay's heart.

In 1973, he purchased a new twenty-three-foot Glasply boat, an inflatable boat, gear, equipment, and tackle, taking it all with a fishing buddy on the one-thousand-mile trip to Hoonah. They spent July, August, and September in a rented cabin in Spasski Bay, hand trolling for salmon in Icy Strait and Glacier Bay to cover expenses. The next two summer seasons, Hay commercial fished for salmon with his Glasply and decided he needed a larger boat. So in 1976, he bought a thirty-footer and a power-troll permit and, two years later, upgraded again to a thirty-six-footer.

Hay and a deckhand did well, earning about $50,000 during the spring to early fall season trolling off Deer Harbor for king and coho salmon. And then, Hay's big opportunity came knocking. In the fall of 1979, a nine-hundred-square-foot A-frame structure in Elfin Cove was up for sale, priced at $105,000. The owner wanted $25,000 down and would carry the balance.

Hay knew nothing about the hospitality business, but he could recognize a good deal when it fell onto his lap. He'd visited Elfin Cove several times, finding it a perfect setting for a fishing charter business. A natural outcropping protects the cove from the frequently harsh winds in the Gulf of Alaska. The site was pristine and beautiful, located seventy miles west of Juneau at the sparsely populated northwest section of Chichagof Island. It could be accessed from Juneau by floatplane in about thirty minutes and by boat in a few hours. Plus, Chichagof Island had potential too, being the fifth largest island in the United States with a population of less than fifteen hundred people and the highest population of bears per square mile in the world.

It was easy to envision making a success based on the unique setting of Elfin Cove Lodge (ECL). A picturesque wooden boardwalk surrounded the vintage fishing village, with no fast-food restaurants, gas stations, or even car access. You either floated in by boat or landed there by float-plane. The inner portion of the cove was idyllic, surrounded by thick forest and calm waters disturbed only by playful otters.

Hay's imagination went into overdrive. He designed all-inclusive packages: airfare from Juneau or boat pickup; comfortable accommodations and meals; fishing, and fish-packing for flights home; on-the-water and dock pictures of the catches; and more enticing services. It would be a highly sellable product, and Hay had the marketing expertise and hustle to make it happen.

Encouraging Hay further was Henry Vatne, a friend and father figure to Hay. Even before the deal was sealed, Hay had begun drawing up plans to establish the lodge, which the dozen or so residents welcomed. Commercial fishermen could continue to fish while at the same time, tourists would bring in additional dollars. It would spawn a small cottage industry of gift shops and a bar, with jobs for fishing guides and lodge maintenance. If ECL proved successful, other lodges would follow and spurt additional growth. But the small area could never support the commercialization that would spoil its remote charm.

Another benefit of Hay's lodge would be a modest increase in resident school children in the village. With a minimum requirement for the number of children needed for the state to provide a school and teacher in such far-flung places, additional families moving in might help the community reach that minimum. Otherwise, Elfin Cove kids would still have to be home-schooled or sent on the thirty-five-mile boat ride each day to the classroom in Hoonah—which isn't navigable in bad weather.

Hay sold his commercial boat and power-troll permit to focus all his energy on ECL. Vatne pitched in big time, contributing his skills as a boat builder, carpenter, and all-around handyman. From the summer of 1981 through 1987, the 900-square-foot A-frame grew to a 5,000-square-foot lodge poised on the base of a mountainside connected to the cove. It provided a crow's nest view across the Gulf of Alaska at the Fairweather Mountains and Brady Glacier. Looking below the lodge's balcony, one could watch the floatplanes landing and taking off, and witness the dock activity when the boats arrived with the day's catches. ECL became the first lodge not only in Elfin Cove but also in that remote portion of Chichagof Island.

Floating docks were put in and an on-and-off loading ramp for floatplanes. Hay installed a full kitchen; plenty of good food was imperative. It was no easy trick to build the new facility and to pull everything together given the logistics involved and absence of a work force, but soon the lodge was ready to accommodate twelve guests and six employees with an adjacent chalet for four more guests.

From 1985 through 1996, ECL was a cash machine. Hay booked 120 to 150 guests each season, some staying for weeks at a time. The operation grossed an average of $350,000 per season, topping out at half a million dollars in 1994. His prior years in the publishing field were a huge leg up for promoting and marketing. Besides depending on word of mouth, display ads, or booths at boat shows, Hay published a full-color eight-page tabloid with articles written by well-known outdoor writers like Doug Olander, editor in chief of *Sport Fishing* magazine.

Hay invited key members of the media, politicians, and others involved in tourism and the recreational-fishing industry. A few celebrities stayed at ECL such as NFL Hall-of-Famer Steve Largent, at the time a wide receiver for the Seattle Seahawks. Hay made deals with large fishing- and hunting-trip booking companies like Frontier Travel. Elfin Cove Lodge became established as a world-class fishing destination.

Not satisfied to lie back idly during the winter off-season, Hay acquired targeted mailing lists. He devised direct-mail marketing materials to include a response card, a questionnaire, and an airfare credit coupon. The effort kept the lodge in good stead year-round, and soon Hay needed more boats and guides because he couldn't cover it all by himself.

Besides running the lodge, Hay guided many of the fishing trips for halibut and chunky salmon like this one. Photo courtesy of Kelly S. Kelly.

"In early 1985, I was told that I was the first guy to get lists of all non-resident anglers from the Alaska Department of Fish & Game," he said. "They shipped four boxes of computer paper that included every lodge and vendor with lists of their clients, including addresses. It was a gold mine, and we immediately booked over one hundred new clients that spring."

In September 1981, john bluefeather arrived at Elfin Cove in his canoe, *The Prince*. He had also discovered the majesty of Alaska and the Yukon, and would spend a month or more each summer away from his native Montana, canoeing by himself. He'd float down a river, admire the blessings of nature, erect his tipi each evening, and tune in to the soul of the wilderness. He carried a single-shot .44 magnum Ruger Blackhawk handgun and a Bowie knife, never having to use either on a bear, moose, wolf, or wolverine—it was as if animals sense that bluefeather was no threat and he should be left alone.

Hay hadn't set eyes on bluefeather since they played basketball together all those years ago in Washington. "bluefeather was going to spend the winter at White Sulfur Hot Springs, but I convinced him to instead 'castle watch' the lodge," Hay said. "He spent 12 winters in Elfin Cove with his wife and daughter, living there and looking after the lodge. It was the most exciting time of my life to share those experiences with him."

bluefeather remembered a particular October day a couple weeks after the last guests headed south:

Dennis and I motored from the lodge in his twenty-six-foot dory the four miles across Port Althorp to the old abandoned cannery that served as a naval seaplane base during World War II. The muskeg meadows behind it were prime Sitka blacktail deer and brown bear habitat, so an extraordinary sense of awareness must accompany one when hunting there.

Dennis chose his area and I opted to explore a remote meadow that I had seen on the map a couple miles farther back. After a few hours, I heard a single shot and headed back down to find my adventuresome partner dragging a two-point buck to the dory about a quarter of a mile away. After re-boarding the dory with the young buck, Dennis wanted to try out some new lures sent to him by a manufacturer.

Within half an hour he'd landed two thirty-pound halibut. The next morning we ate a bountiful breakfast of fresh venison liver, poached eggs, homemade biscuits made from scratch, raspberry jam and hot chocolate—Dennis was an excellent cook. I smugly remarked that wherever and whatever King Farouk was doing that day, it could not compare to such a beautiful place as Elfin Cove and nowhere near the king's breakfast we were enjoying. Dennis just smiled, nodded and kept eating. It's simple memories like that together that make me smile too.

Hay never breached the bond between himself and bluefeather because of any "employer to employee" attitude. They were friends first, business associates second, and therefore equals in the most important sense. At the same time, each envied what the other had. bluefeather recalled:

After selling Elfin Cove Lodge, Hay often fished out of the picturesque fishing village of Pelican on Lisianski Inlet. Photo courtesy of Kelly S. Kelly.

I look back now and realize our time together was especially plea-surable when the last guests were gone in September and just prior to when Dennis would fly south to, as he put it, 'catch more guests for next year.' During one such time, we were alone in the spacious lodge with Dennis intently working on his taxes while across the room I was reading a book on metaphysics. After a cou-ple hours or so, he suddenly stopped and asked me, 'Would you be interested in an even trade of this lodge and my three boats for your canoe and tipi?' I shook my head and replied, 'No deal.' He then said, "I didn't think you would,' and went back again into another long period of silence.

In 1996, overwhelmed with ever-increasing state and federal fish-ery and business regulations, Hay tired of juggling the myriad balls of running a lodge operation. He sold it for $950,000—which he regretted.

"Looking back, I should have kept ECL for another 10 years," he said. Hay returned to Washington and kicked back for a few years, playing with a variety of ideas such as a lure company, a new downrigger design, and even a salmon cannery, but nothing panned out.

From 2001 through 2009, he headed back to Alaska each summer and operated a one-man charter business. He bought a small duplex in Pelican, a charming commercial fishing village ensconced on the quaint Lisianski Inlet in Chichagof Island. "I spent a lot of money but didn't earn much," Hay recalled. "But we can all look back and wish we would have done some things differently, as the road to success is always under construction."

Hay often celebrated good times with bluefeather. While in Pelican during July 2004, the two of them caught 159 king salmon commercial trolling off Deer Harbor and Yakobi Island aboard Hay's boat, the *FV Destination*. bluefeather ran the boat while the Ol' Cap tossed the big kings over his broad shoulders like they were herring.

One of Hay's enduring characteristics was being nonchalant no matter the gravity of the situation. I recall a time when a friend took the wheel of his boat and blithely ran too close to a shoreline and the rocky bottom blew out half the prop and bent the drive shaft. Luckily we were close to Elfin Cove and just barely putt-putted into the cove, but it put the boat out of commission for nearly a week. Hay's response throughout the ordeal: "It's alright, it'll be alright." It became his trademark comment no matter how calamitous the situation, a refreshing contrast to those who tended to get angry, blow up, and make matters worse.

I managed to play a practical joke on Hay after I'd visited him in Elfin Cove in the late 1990s. He'd rented a two-bedroom house along the inner rim of the cove. I occupied one room, bluefeather slept on the floor in his sleeping bag, and Hay took the other room with a pretty gal from Washington who appeared to be in her mid twenties. (Hay was about sixty at the time.) After I departed Elfin Cove and flew from Juneau to Seattle to await a connecting flight, a friend from Tacoma met me at the airport for lunch. I borrowed his cell phone, called Hay and disguised my voice.

"Excuse me, is this Dennis Hay?" I sternly queried. Hay acknowledged that it was.

"Sir, are you aware that my daughter—who I know you've been 'entertaining,' so to speak—is only seventeen years old?"

Crickets.

"Uh, well, no sir, I didn't think that was the case," he finally replied meekly. "At least I hope it's not."

When I told him who I was, he compared me to a certain bodily opening and didn't forgive me for months.

But turnaround is fair play. My wife, Kelly, and I were visiting Hay in Pelican one year when we decided to stroll across the boardwalk to Rose's Bar & Grill. Encouraged by Rose, the bar owner, to add a signed dollar bill to the ceiling, Hay told me to step atop the bar counter to affix it. As I did so and raised my hands up, Rose pulled my pants down to my ankles. The three of them practically turned blue laughing.

One of my most memorable experiences in Alaska took place aboard Hay's thirty-foot boat on an early September day. We shoved off from Elfin Cove and ran south down the coast of Chichagof Island. We'd just been passed by a large pod of orcas that had playfully, even curiously, surrounded our drifting boat. Hay then ran us into a deep bay while we quietly drifted near the confluence of two hillsides from where a stream flowed out. Hay warmed chunks of smoked king salmon on the stove, and we savored the taste while watching a brown bear less than one hundred feet away showing her two cubs how to fish. Along the bank we could see the footprints of moose and wolves. At the same moment, a loon's cry could be heard as a bald eagle cruised above us with wings fully spread.

"Is Alaska heaven?" I said in wonder.

"Yes, it is," replied Hay.

We can thank Dennis Hay for opening Elfin Cove—and our eyes—to still another little piece of Alaska that's very special indeed. But Father Time finally began to drain Hay's energy as he neared his mid seventies. In July of 2010—the last time Hay went fishing—he skippered a boat with john bluefeather and his daughter Violet out of Elfin Cove. While he had fun hanging out with his old friend, it became too much for Hay to be out on the ocean all day.

However, I called recently to check up on him, and he sounded like his old self. "There's no point just sitting around here in Washington and being bored," he said. "I'm going to move back to Alaska, buy a boat and spend my remaining years there." He spoke of settling in Gustavas, a beautiful little town on Icy Strait near the entrance to Glacier Bay.

It was definitely a wonderful idea, and I encouraged him to make that happen so he could close the final chapter of his life in his beloved Alaska.

"I've arranged to have my ashes spread in Elfin Cove when my time comes," he said.

How sadly prophetic. Shortly thereafter, Hay's health took a turn for the worse, and he passed on in 2015 after an intense battle with leukemia.

Dennis Hay will remain alive and vibrant in the minds of all those who knew and admired one of the most colorful pioneering spirits in Chichagof Island's—and Alaska's—outdoors history.

19

JIM BAILEY, 1940–PRESENT

Eagle River

His near-death escapes and adventures both in the air and on the ground as a Master Guide have been the fodder of numerous newspaper and magazine articles. His knack for living on the edge attracted the likes of John Denver and the president of Mercedes Benz, but his passion for flightseeing in addition to guiding anglers and hunters opened a revenue stream that exploded in popularity throughout Alaska.

Comparing most mortals to Jim Bowie would require quite a stretch but not in in the case of Jim Bailey. In fact it's doubtful the legendary southern woodsman possessed anywhere near the wilderness skills of Jim Bailey, who was a bush pilot, lodge operator, Master Guide, and so much more. Of course airplanes weren't around in the early to mid 1800s when Bowie made a name for himself, but it's also unlikely that he ever dueled one-thousand-pound-plus bears and even bigger bull moose, as Bailey has done.

With so much time in the air as a pilot, Bailey seems to be a cat with nine lives. One such close scrape occurred when flying a hunter with the plane only five hundred feet above the trees because of low clouds. The engine quit, and Bailey put the nose of the plane into the wind with full flaps and hit the top of the trees. "When that happens,

Paratrooper, bush pilot, Master Guide and lodge owner—Jim Bailey's done it all and still doing so. Photo courtesy of Jim Bailey.

you go straight down," he said. But that was just a minor incident; he's survived seven other crashes with five of them considered major catastrophes.

Bailey's prowess in a cockpit particularly serves a career tracking brown bears in the far reaches of Kodiak Island, and owning and operating a successful lodge near Denali National Park. His résumé includes licenses as a commercial pilot, Master Guide, and master marine in addition to earning a Master Parachutist rating and military service as a master sergeant.

Although he's always been an adventurous sort, the likelihood of beginning a life in arid Arizona and ending up near the Arctic in Alaska seemed far-fetched. Born in Middleton, Ohio, Bailey moved with his family to an area now known as The Why about twenty-five miles south of Ajo near the Growler Mountains in southern Arizona.

"My folks bought 25 acres there to homestead," recalled Bailey. "We lived in a circus tent for three years while building a small home. Even after that, we still slept outside most of the time on World War II wooden army cots due to the warm weather."

Getting ready for yet another jump with the U.S. Army 101st Airborne Division in December 1959. Photo courtesy of Jim Bailey.

To ward off scorpions, leg ends of their cots rested in coffee cans containing kerosene. But that didn't deter all desert critters from intruding. "One morning before I got up, a diamondback rattlesnake was neatly coiled in the shade beneath me," said Bailey. "Flash floods posed another danger. When that happens, everything normally living underground crawls aboveground, including snakes, scorpions and centipedes. One centipede climbed onto our screen door and it measured four inches wide and eighteen inches long—we'd never seen one so big."

Bailey's father worked for the border patrol out of Sonoyta, Sonora State, Mexico, and was gone most of the time. That left all the everyday chores to the four kids and mother. "We raised about six hundred Rhode Island Red chickens and sold eggs to neighboring Indians," Bailey said. "In turn, they'd help us round up wild horses and trap coyotes. They taught us a lot too, like hitching a just-caught colt or young mustang to a post for three days, after which you give it about a gallon of water to drink—right then and there the horse learns to trust you."

Bailey joined the U.S. Army in 1959 and was assigned to the 101st Airborne Division. He savored the excitement of parachuting from a tower or plane, looking forward to each jump. After a transfer to Guantanamo Bay, Cuba, he ended his service at Fort Campbell, Kentucky. By then he'd saved enough money to buy a new motorcycle, and he spent a month riding across America before returning home to Arizona.

He worked for a pest-control company in Mesa, Arizona, and, just for fun, converted a nineteen-foot school bus into a self-contained camper. He installed a 352-horsepower industrial engine and equipped the bus with a toilet from a Boeing 707 and a shower. The upgrading project consumed three years, and in 1967 he drove the camper to Las Cruces, New Mexico, where he obtained a commercial-pilot's license while employed by an aviation school.

As the tumultuous decade of the 1960s came to an end, Bailey made the big break: He drove the camper to Alaska and found employment on an oilrig at Trading Bay across from Cook Inlet, and later relocated to Middleton Island about 250 miles south of Anchorage. That job was short-lived; the rig ultimately was relocated to Singapore. But by then he'd become totally smitten with the magical splendor of Alaska. Rather than going to Singapore with others in the crew, Bailey stayed put.

Jobless in 1971, he filled out an unemployment compensation form. "I'd have rather just spent time flying rather than working, so I wrote down 'exterminator' on the form where it asked for your background," he said. "I figured no one would need an exterminator in Alaska, but to my surprise I was immediately contacted by Fort Richardson Army Base in Anchorage." (The base ultimately combined with Elmendorf Air Force Base and is now called Joint Base Elmendorf-Richardson.)

"Apparently cockroaches ride along in household goods shipped to Alaska, and the base had been on the lookout for an exterminator," Bailey continued. "I ended up employed there for 10 years."

During that time he also joined the Army National Guard's 38th Special Forces Unit, which later became the 207th Rangers. Bailey again became a parachutist and soon enough had jumped out of just about every aircraft the military flew, including a modified door on a Twin Otter. He ended his army stint earning a Jumpmaster qualification. But the big question for him became what to do with the rest of his life.

Bailey had spent all of his vacation time and holidays with a rifle or rod in Alaska in the forests, mountains, and streams. "Even as a kid I always loved hunting and fishing, and being a guide would be just the ticket," Bailey said. "But in May 1972 I married my wife Bonnie and we weren't so sure that guiding would provide a steady income. Luckily we'd saved some money and she worked full time, affording us the ability to acquire the needed Alaskan outdoor toys of airplanes, boats and snow machines."

While he felt comfortable in the wilderness in his own right pursuing deer, moose, caribou, wolves, sheep, goats, bears, and pretty much anything on four legs, he lacked experience in guiding the paying clients. He needed an apprenticeship, so he began toiling as a packer for guide Rick Halford on the Alaska Peninsula. He later did the same for guide Nick Botner at his Stephan Lake Lodge in the Talkeetna Mountains of south central Alaska, about 140 miles north of Anchorage.

Bailey loved everything about hunting and learned the ABCs of guiding from the ground up. In 1972, he became an Assistant Guide for Botner, continuing in that role until 1979 when Bailey passed the written and oral Registered Guide test. He then became a Master Guide in 1995 after providing the required documentation.

In 1980, Botner sold Stephan Lake Lodge to a group of Europeans who loved the area and the lodge's business profile. Ray Genet, a mountaineer, oversaw the lodge operations for the group, but he subsequently died during a climb of Mount Everest. That left the group of investors without the necessary representative in the United States. Although Bailey was battling medical complications due to inhalation of toxic chemicals during his many years in the pest control business, the group wanted him to step in full time. They trusted him; he knew the guiding business; he knew Alaska; and his effervescent personality perfectly suited dealing with well-heeled and sometimes eccentric clients.

The investment group gave Bailey the green light to give it a go for that summer season to see how things turned out. And give it a go he did, with that first management gig continuing for the next eighteen years. Bailey subsequently bought the lodge from the Europeans on a friendly basis.

"I met many wonderful people who came to the lodge for hunting, fishing, rafting, wilderness photography, hiking and flightseeing around Mt. McKinley in Denali National Park," said Bailey. "I was the manager, chief pilot, hunting guide, fishing guide, sometimes cook and entertainer. The flightseeing in particular boomed in popularity and soon became emulated all over Alaska."

Famed singer John Denver strums while Bailey, at right, smiles with approval. Denver and his family were guests on several occasions at Bailey's Stephan Lake Lodge in the mid 1980s. Photo courtesy of Jim Bailey.

Bailey guided many dignitaries, including the president of Mercedes Benz, Wolfgang Porsche's son, and Manfred Bruner, who at the time served as defense minister of Germany. But his prize client at Stephan Lake Lodge was John Denver, who stayed there several times.

"John visited the first time in 1983 for the filming of him obtaining a pilot float rating using my Piper Cub," said Bailey. "That segment later appeared in a TV show produced by Sir Edmund Hillary. The following year he brought his children, Anna Kate and Zack, to the lodge and a few years later he flew in to go fly-fishing. He was always very friendly and unpretentious—he even insisted on carrying his own bags."

An interesting side note to Denver's lodge visits is that he asked to keep his presence low-key. "He was worried about negative comments from extreme environmental groups about his fishing and flying trips," said Bailey. "They gave him a hard time by saying it was wasting natural resources for him to fly his plane to Alaska rather than using commercial airlines."

Bailey sold Stephan Lake Lodge in September 2012. But that hardly marked a time for him to fade away into the woodwork. Back in 1985, he'd purchased three acres on Kodiak Island and built four sixteen-foot-by-twenty-foot cabins. He continues to hunt spring and fall brown bears. He also operates a twenty-eight-foot diesel-powered boat so his hunters can access productive locations in and about the rivers.

John Morehouse, a friend of Bailey's since the age of twenty-one and a cycling buddy from Mesa, Arizona, has flown numerous times with Bailey. "He's always been a Harley rider, which alone requires a certain type of edge," said Morehouse. "An experienced bush pilot will routinely encounter occupational hazards like small airports surrounded by tall trees, unexpected storms or a plane weighted down with clients, gear and packed meat. But Jim thrives on that—he's still alive and so are all his clients, so that's living proof that he knows his stuff."

Chris Batin of Talkeetna, one of Alaska's most successful outdoors journalists, has chronicled in national magazines many of Bailey's adventures and close calls. Batin greatly respects his deep wilderness knowledge:

> Over the years I've learned a lot about hunting with Jim. He's taught me many things. For just one small example, on one occasion while snowmobiling together he put our lunch on the manifold so the food stayed warm when we stopped to eat—a great idea during the winter.
>
> And as a bush pilot he's incredibly talented. One time a fuel line broke and fuel was pouring down my leg. Jim banked the plane so it glided back to where we took off. His actions were those of a pro—deliberate and automatic, executed without thinking. Jim combines the art and adventure of skilled flying with the savvy and gut instinct of a saloon poker player. Each move is a calculated risk in a wild frontier filled with potential disaster that could result in loss of life, not to mention a $150,000 aircraft.

One such plane, a PA-11 Cub, still lies in the freezing waters of the Bering Sea. A huge fog bank had moved in quickly and Bailey turned the plane to head back to camp. But the fog and swirling snow caused a white-out, making it nigh impossible to determine positioning relative to water or land. Unable to get a bearing, Bailey opened the cockpit door and cringed to see crests of waves spinning the wheels of his plane. Ice formed on the wings as snow clung to the windshield. Unable to climb, inevitably the plane cartwheeled into the sea and ended upside down.

Jim and Bonnie Bailey enjoy the Alaska lifestyle at their home in
Eagle River. Photo courtesy of Jim Bailey.

Windshield glass imploded and cut Bailey's face and that of his assistant guide in the copilot seat.

Somehow they both surfaced, the storm raging and ten-foot waves making it a major hardship to keep hold of the plane's tail. But minutes later even that disappeared beneath the broiling brine, and Bailey figured they were doomed. He knew that the frigid water and pelting snow could foretell only one thing: hypothermia. But providence intervened, allowing a slight enough break in the weather, and as the men rode a wave swell they could just make out the shoreline in the distance. That adrenaline rush helped them summon all their remaining strength and stamina to swim in that direction.

"We swam for what seemed an eternity, and just as we were about to give up, our feet touched bottom," said Bailey. Their legs too weary to walk, the men slithered like snakes onto higher ground, first Bailey and then the copilot. Desperate to ward off the hypothermia close to killing them, Bailey retrieved from his pocket the most precious possession of his life at that moment: a water-resistant, military-issue container of matches. A series of fires provided reviving warmth, and hours later as the tide receded and a portion of the plane could be viewed, Bailey retrieved a .44-caliber magnum handgun he always kept under the pilot's seat.

The area was laden thick with brown bears, and Bailey kept the handgun at the ready as they walked thirty-four miles in two days to a Coast Guard light station at Cape Seniavin. Soon enough, Bailey saw a Super Cub, his frantic waving catching the eye of a Fish and Wildlife Protection trooper piloting the plane. Being too small an aircraft to carry several people at a time, the trooper left them a sleeping bag and a can of peaches until he could send a larger plane to retrieve the two survivors.

"I still don't know how I survived that one," Bailey said, as we sipped tea at the Fancy Moose Lounge in the Millennium Alaskan Hotel in Anchorage. Looking far younger than his age, Bailey exhibited vitality and quick wit while conversing and sorting through pictures he'd brought.

I asked how long he's been flying. "Fifty years with over 10,000 hours," he answered. "That's a lot of takeoffs and landings in Alaska, plus I do it year-round with floats, wheels and skis. My favorite floatplane is a Cessna 185 and for a plane with wheels it's a Super Cub."

Stories about Bailey surviving close scrapes in the woods and in the air are legendary. One such saga involved Bailey guiding a hunter in the Talkeetna Mountains one late September day. They tracked a huge grizzly until they spotted it feeding on a caribou. The client took aim and only wounded the bear in the belly with his .338 rifle. The bear ran off but then in a flash doubled back at them. His client froze, evidently gripped in fear, so Bailey wasted no time putting five shots into the bear with his rifle from thirty-five yards away. But even that didn't stop this charging mass of fury. Now out of bullets and his client quaking, Bailey grabbed the man's rifle and squeezed off a perfect shot right between its eyes. The bear fell dead a mere seven feet away and taped out at eight feet, four inches.

Bailey nodded when I asked him about that episode. He remarked, "The only sure kill shot when a bear is that close to you is hitting it in the head—if you don't, you're in big trouble."

Close calls or not as a pilot or a guide, Jim Bailey continues to approach each day with the robustness one would expect from a true Alaska adventurer. "I'd have rather done nothing else with my life," he mused. "Then again, I'm still living it."

20

WAYNE HEIMER, 1943–PRESENT

Fairbanks

~~~~~~

Many biologists become bureaucrats who mimic their agency's marching orders or become influenced by political pressures. Not this man, who stood up for the robustness of the research no matter what direction it led and became a leading authority and policymaker for one of the hunting world's most sought-after mountain species.

~~~~~~

Dall sheep were and still are Wayne Heimer's bailiwick, and few biologists involved in Alaska's fish-and-game-management history have delivered such an indelible legacy of significant work or caused more gnashing of teeth by bosses who found him arrogant and even a little scary.

On any level, Heimer is difficult to ignore and commands respect. A perusal of his published studies or public addresses or lectures reveals a heady command of vocabulary, coupled with a writing style exhibiting boundless depth in whatever subject he's involved. This he does with a simultaneous flippancy and wryness that reveal a man who's complicated on the surface and vulnerable at the core.

Heimer's self-deprecating humor deflects any hint of self-aggrandizement as witnessed in the beginning of a bio I asked him to provide: "Born April 25, 1943—the year of the lead penny

Known at Alaska Department of Fish & Game as the "sheep guy," a youthful Heimer embraces a lamb in the mountains. Photo courtesy of Wayne Heimer.

on Easter Sunday, the latest possible date for Easter on the Gregorian calendar. Might account for oversize ears."

Yet like most scientists, the plucky spirits of curiosity and discovery are always ready. Heimer grew up on a small grain farm in Holyoke, Colorado, and in 1961 left for college at Colorado State College. He moved on to Washington State University in 1965 and thereafter to Fairbanks in 1967, where for four years he attended the University of Alaska Fairbanks (UAF). His research area at that time? The biochemistry and physiology of heat production in mice.

This choice of fields was probably natural because Heimer's undergraduate degrees were in chemistry and biology. Next came a master of science in molecular biology/physiology with a minor in biochemistry, leading to the doctoral program in mouse physiology. At first glance, that seems to be a rather odd background for a wildlife biologist. However, it's precisely that unusual scientific breadth, ranging from biological chemistry to biological communities, that may account for the difference between him and more classically trained wildlifers. As he puts it, "Working with life from molecules to human politics will definitely mess with your mind."

Heimer (*right*) and fellow biologist Tony Smith scoping to locate and observe game animals in the wild. Photo courtesy of Wayne Heimer.

The book learning certainly provided credentials to work in the fields of Dall sheep research and general management at the Alaska Department of Fish & Game (ADF&G) for the next twenty-six years. But his real education took place in the field and not behind a desk. He now looks back and feels his efforts "changed the sheep management paradigm for the better, I'd say—others disagree." After his final years at ADF&G involved an exasperating effort to fend off the federal take-over of wildlife management in Alaska, he retired in 1997 on—quite fittingly, as Heimer puts it—April Fool's Day.

Along the way, Heimer fought hard to put Dall sheep-management decisions on a sound biological footing and to translate the behavioral ecology of Dall sheep into benefit-producing regulations. While he's authored a huge body of studies, technical publications, and works on Dall sheep, he's also covered topics such as predator control and the effects of weather on game populations.

His innumerable achievements raised the status of Dall sheep in the minds of Alaskans and sportsmen worldwide while building a cooperative relationship between sheep managers, hunters and guides. That was certainly his goal, which resulted in the first species

Heimer is known for his zaniness as well as his brilliance. Photo courtesy of Wayne Heimer.

management plan at ADF&G, even if stodgy decision makers above him failed, at times, to keep up. His discovery (for which he always credits his friends and partners, plus his critics) that ram-harvest rates can be raised by harvesting only mature rams remains controversial for some because it is counterintuitive (it turns out, the young rams need to get past their less-useful adolescence or they won't know how to court the ewes). Still, he says, "The data are still there."

One of Heimer's once-in-a-lifetime field experiences took place on one of his countless outings to trap and mark sheep as well as simply to watch their behavior. He described the incident:

I baited our sheep trap, which was a rocket net stolen from turkey trappers—if you can catch turkeys you can catch anything—with a salt block. About thirty sheep soon appeared and obviously headed for it. From years of stealing ideas from others, I'd learned that a low burping sound seems to put sheep at ease. So, I burped while not making eye contact, pawing the ground as they do while slowly easing into a sitting position near the salt block. On all fours, I began pretending to lick as if one of them, and soon a ewe did the same right next to me. And then another did so—pretty soon I was like one of the herd. It was an exhilarating feeling of acceptance, being surrounded by wild Dall sheep only inches away.

Heimer can be all business but also zany at times. An environmental group had filed a lawsuit challenging the ADF&G's wolf-control program, and a meeting on the topic was scheduled in the office of Bud Burris, Heimer's boss at the time. To mock the extremists' image of themselves as the indestructible defenders of nature, Heimer bounded into the somber and serious meeting wearing a Superman outfit (it was Halloween time). "Can I help?" he asked. "Yeah, fly away," retorted Burris. It was quite the hilarious moment.

Among his many organizational involvements, Heimer served two terms as director of the Foundation for North American Wild Sheep and yet another term after the group changed its name to the Wild Sheep Foundation. He rates his best work with the foundation as directing funds toward disease research that demonstrated domestic sheep could transmit pneumonia directly to bighorns. That contagion was a critical issue in the management problem of separating domestic sheep from bighorns in the West.

For twelve years, he was executive director of the Northern Wild Sheep and Goat Council. He's also a member of the Alaska Sportsmen for Fish and Wildlife, Sportsmen for Habitat, and the Alaska Wildlife Conservation Association. Heimer holds life memberships in the Alaska Outdoor Council, the Wild Sheep Foundation, and the National Rifle Association.

One of Heimer's mentors, generally acknowledged as the world's pioneering expert on wild sheep biology, is Val Geist, a professor emeritus of Environmental Science at the University of Calgary, Alberta. Now living in British Columbia, Geist was the world's trailblazer in sheep biology and management. He knows Heimer well, particularly his battles with those he considered short-sighted policymakers at ADF&G, who often cared more about political correctness, management traditions, getting along with federal agencies, and not offending cash-flush special interests than what was best for the resources, sportsmen, and Alaska citizens. Geist deeply admires Heimer, his science, and his ethics.

I am glad you count Wayne among Alaska's fishing and hunting legends. Ever since I met him, I saw in Wayne a courageous, ruthlessly honest and exceptionally bright man. He was a first-rate scientist and scholar, but later I saw another side of him—an advocate for sound, evidence-based public policy. My only regret back then involved not knowing Alaska politics well enough to appreciate all his efforts. And I do cherish his tenacity. No matter how he was put down, he rose again and again to make his point in beautiful prose. Hunters in North America, but especially in Alaska, owe him a loud vote of thanks.

In 1965, Heimer and wife Karen married, went to graduate school at Washington State in Pullman, and then moved to Alaska in 1967. That year, a great flood caused the Chena River to inundate most of Fairbanks. Heimer's wife was a high school home-economics teacher, and arrived during the height of the flood. Heimer came along about a month later "when it was safe," he jokes, but he actually was finishing his master of science degree in Pullman before driving the Alaska Highway north to his future.

After his doctoral program ran its course, Heimer was hired by the ADF&G. Needing a place to live and having fallen in love with the Chena River, he began to look for river land. At that point, memory of the great Chena River flood four years earlier still occupied everyone's mind. Nobody really wanted riverfront land for fear of another flood. Still, Heimer decided to take a chance and he acquired ten acres fronting both the river and Chena Pump Road just outside Fairbanks for the asking price of $12,000.

Borrowing what was then the considerable sum of $36,000, Heimer built a comfortable home on the river, where he pursues boating and hunting interests. The real estate from this humble beginning is now valued at roughly twenty times its original cost. When asked if he's a shrewd investor, Heimer modestly says, "Naw, I just wanted to live on the river and took a chance."

Heimer's first supervisor at ADF&G, John Burns, was willing to take a chance on a bright guy with an atypical background as the state's Dall sheep research biologist. After he'd worked for ADF&G for about four years, a daughter, Carrie, was born, and six years later, a son, Mark. Heimer is particularly pleased he was able to share some of his love for Alaska's Dall sheep, rivers, and mountains with his family as they grew. He stressed being adaptable and making do with what was at hand.

His family certainly recognizes the Heimer penchant for thrift. Daughter Carrie, an English composition teacher, eloquently writes about that trait and the values her dad instilled in her. I usually liberally edit most anecdotes from family, friends and associates, but Carrie's contribution is simply too eloquent and insightful to abbreviate:

I was the only student at West Valley High who drove around with a wall tent and fifty pounds of lead shot in the back of my car for ballast, both for the weight and because they might be 'useful if you're stranded.' I was also the only one whose headlight was held in place with the punctured inner tube of a bicycle tire, and who tucked in my '78 Ford Fairmont every morning under a 'perfectly good' comforter from the dump transfer site. All of these were Wayne Heimer's innovations.

My dad has always valued pragmatic and inventive solutions. He admires people who make creative use of what's at hand, and he strives to do the same. He respects trappers and homesteaders who operate on the 'lash-up' principle so central to the Alaskan ethos that you can make do with just about anything when the need is pressing. He knows, for instance, that when a bee stings you in the crotch while you're piloting a four-wheeler out of Granite Creek, you can improvise pretty well with baking soda toothpaste. He knows you can cobble a makeshift muffler for your Hodaka Ace 90 out of a juice can and steel wool.

Dad is a collector of rusted out snow-machine frames and trailer parts because 'you never know when they might come in handy.' He's also a collector of rusted out old-timers whose stories of the days when people really knew how to survive match his vision of Alaska's best years. His favorite tale of my husband's family is the one about Grandpa Buzby's plan to lash his wife Tiny to the blade of a dozer to get her back to camp after she fell and broke her hip on a berry-picking trip. He wishes he'd thought of that. His fascination with the intersection between need and invention is the mark of how his mind works; it's what drew him to Fairbanks and to sheep management.

My dad has always been "the sheep guy." It's more than a career: It informs his view of the world. As a leader in our church, he's famous for basing his illustrations of human behavior on Dall sheep. People count on him to explain that when you're holding a lamb to take a blood sample, you have to hold it tight to your chest or it will hurt itself flailing about. They count on him to draw the parallel to the kind of firm and gentle care our difficult relationships sometimes require, how sometimes we need to hug people in a gracious embrace while they buck and snort, giving them some boundaries and clear expectations so they don't wake up to a sprained or broken friendship when their panic has passed.

He has been this kind of mentor and friend, and while it means the occasional bruised ribs, he has never been the one to break ties or cut communication. He is willing to talk, always and often, even about differences, and all he asks is equal parts reflection and reason. He loves to change his mind—but only for something that makes more sense. The familiar Biblical metaphor for the faithful is sheep, but his years in Alaska have taught him that these weren't passive, domesticated blobs, but wild sheep, unused to training, unaccustomed to soft living. As the sheep guy, he's always had a tender spot for the wild sheep in the Kingdom, those who are a bit shaggy, a bit bold, a bit hard-headed. He feels a kinship there and hates to put too much restriction on them, loving what's wild, suspicious of what becomes too tame.

In my bedroom, two photos hang side by side. In one, I'm two years old and mom held the camera. I'm standing in my dad's Kelty pack, bottle by rifle, squinting with him in the sun. He's packing me up to the observation cabin he assembled at Dry Creek from a pile of odds and ends. When we arrive, I will toddle about and learn to love the fresh, cold water of the creek, the metal dipper hung on the nail in the tree beside it. In the other photo, I'm twenty-one while dad held the camera. I'm dressed in flannel and hip-waders, leaned back in the saddle of a mud-caked four-wheeler, dandelion between my teeth. I've been to the mountains with my dad and a tagalong named Leo. I've learned to deflate the front tires and lean over the handlebars to climb a steep incline. I've learned to lean back and center my weight in my heels to step-slide down the shale surface of a mountain so I don't stumble forward and skin my hands. In both pictures, he is doing what he loves more

Time to get in the
chopper! A tran-
quilized moose
starts to revive
as Heimer takes
a blood sample.
Photo courtesy of
Wayne Heimer.

than anything in the world. In both pictures, I am happy and I am
safe in a wild place.

Karen Rudolph from Boise, Idaho, referred to fondly by Heimer as
the "DNA woman," is a friend, coauthor, and collaborator of his. She
describes how she met Heimer and the impression he made then and
since:

I was first introduced to him in 1996 at a Northern Wild Goat and
Sheep Council meeting in Colorado. As my first wildlife conference, I was there to listen, learn and help present data on a bighorn sheep die-off in Idaho. When Wayne presented his talk on
wild sheep data, it was special. I took note of the way he kept it fun
while informative.

Soon after that, a new program for bighorn sheep was getting
off the ground and I participated in a field trip where Wayne and
others were on hand to get acquainted with the project and personnel. I came to appreciate even more Wayne's extremely broad
and deep knowledge of biology and all things sheep as he took
great interest in understanding our molecular biology-based
immunology project.

He also became instrumental in doing one of those things he
does so well—serving as a translator between the language of
technical hard scientists and the interested lay person or sheep

enthusiast or funding board. He's an amazingly prolific writer and presenter who always strikes a chord with readers—either very positively or very negatively. Without a doubt, there's never a dull moment in Wayne's World."

Echoing the sentiments about Heimer being a lightning rod for commentary is Ray Lee of Cody, Wyoming, a former president of what's now known as the Wild Sheep Foundation.

"Wayne's formal education in both macrobiology and microbiology gave him a somewhat different perspective on the world than is common to most people," writes Lee. "During our 11-member board meetings, more than one director would look quizzically at Wayne after he had offered his view on a particular issue—and there were a few votes that went 10 to 1 against him. More than one of his presentations could only be fully dissected in the confines of the nearest bar."

Chris Batin, a well-respected outdoor advocate and writer in Alaska for decades who often sought Heimer's input on articles, simply labels him "the most intelligent person I've ever met." That description is high praise coming from Batin, who has dealt with all levels of bright and earnest men and women during his long career as an outdoors journalist.

After my first long chat with Heimer, I could see what Batin meant. And like so many others, Heims (his nickname) has earned my respect for having the chutzpah to let the science dictate the direction to go rather than letting a conclusion-based direction decide where the science should go. That bravery at times made him a pariah around the offices of ADF&G and the water coolers of federal agencies.

His tongue and pen are indeed barbed and sharp. "Is conservation best practiced by inculcated, cooperative societal norms or mores, or by coercive governmental regulation?" he writes. "I fear the U.S. Fish & Wildlife Service (and most other agencies) which are staffed by 'trained' (i.e., brainwashed toward conventionally cultured 'scientific purity' by the academy) biologists are easy prey for the 'correct,' the 'pure,' and the 'scientific' without giving much thought to the actual conservation and management practices of a public which is ultimately responsible for the success or failure of conservation." As Heimer often good-

A recent picture of Heimer amid the Alaska wilderness. Photo courtesy of Wayne Heimer.

naturedly admits about himself, "It's difficult to flush the toilet just a little, and when pulling the handle with 'Wayne's World,' chances are you'll get the whole tankful."

Critical (or some say cynical) though he may be, Heimer still believes the good works of improving the fish and game resources in Alaska have outweighed the bad. To his friends who ask, "Did you actually *do* anything?" his answer is an emphatic *yes*. "Others may disagree, but I think things are better than they might have been in spite of the challenges faced over the years," he replies.

If more fish and game managers approached science and regulations as Heimer did and still does—in Alaska as well as everywhere else—the question about "doing anything" would never even have to be asked.

21

JAMES WILLIAMS "J.W." SMITH JR., 1943–PRESENT

Painter Creek

As opposed to laidback lodge owners who seldom harnessed the power of the press, he offered to high-profile writers and television show hosts in the Lower 48 complimentary trips to visit his camps hidden hundreds of miles off the beaten path. The subsequent flow of magazine features and TV segments generated many new visitors to the state and elevated him as one of Alaska's most successful fishing and hunting promoters.

A number of factors go into what makes a man or woman an Alaska fishing or hunting legend. It's more than being an expert angler or hunter, great journalist, top guide, brilliant biologist, or other stand-out. Countless people would qualify just on that basis. What makes the difference is the added element of how he or she contributed in a remarkable way to a practice, technique, or innovation that pushes forward the enjoyment of fishing and hunting in Alaska. One such man is James Williams Smith Jr., better known as J.W. ever since his boyhood in Clinton, Tennessee.

While many great lodges have existed in Alaska as far back as the late 1800s, most owners concentrated on making their guests' experiences memorable. Accommodations, food, guides, location, and access—all

Overview of J.W.'s Nakalilok Bay Camp in 1994. Photo courtesy of J.W. Smith.

had to be meticulously executed to bring in new guests and keep them coming back. But J.W. went a step farther; he also put great effort into achieving a high profile through skillful use of the media.

Most common marketing campaigns centered on running magazine ads and occasional mailings, but J.W. wasn't content to sit back and wait for the phone to ring. After he founded Painter Creek Lodge in 1981 and got it humming at a high level, he didn't wait for writers and TV producers to find him. J.W. researched the publications and shows that best fit his operation and got in touch to offer complimentary trips so they could relate firsthand to readers and viewers all that his operation had to offer.

Editorial coverage is far more convincing than a paid advertisement or a mailed brochure. As his lodge began appearing in regional and national magazines and TV hosts filmed shows based at his lodge, readers and viewers got a taste of what it would be like if they went there too. That was J.W.'s marketing strategy, which cost him some free trips here and there but the payoff became huge with increased bookings from the ensuing publicity.

Besides direct business, copies of the articles and samples of the shows were included in mailings to make them more effective. "The

A game warden in Tennessee in 1963 before heading to Alaska. Photo courtesy of J.W. Smith.

lodge itself didn't make me rich, but the whole experience served as a springboard for my current international booking business for fishing and hunting trips," said J.W.

But let's back up a bit and get a picture of J.W.'s upbringing and what led him to do business in one of Alaska's most remote wilderness regions.

He grew up fishing for trout and smallmouth bass with bait-casters and fly rods in the rivers and lakes of eastern Tennessee. He was named after his dad, a World War II veteran and chief accountant for Union Carbide in Oak Ridge, Tennessee. J.W.'s mom, Juanita, and his dad loved to fish and that rubbed off on him. His mother still goes swimming even as she approaches the age of ninety.

Juanita loves telling the story of how J.W.'s grandparents would put him in the car when he was a toddler and drive him around Norris Lake in Clinton. The outings were intended to soothe him to sleep. Instead, he'd brace his arms on the dashboard and study the water and woods as they passed by.

While attending college at the University of Tennessee, J.W. also worked for Bob Epperson, an electrical contractor who shared his Alaska hunting and fishing stories. J.W. left the university just before earning his business degree to accept a job in Atlanta as a service manager for Rich's Department Store. "Retail drove me crazy, and sent me back to the hills of east Tennessee," said J.W. "I became a game warden for four years with the state's Fish and Game Commission. At that time, the game warden doubled as a deputy sheriff when needed. By then it was in the early 1970s and I decided to move to Alaska, so I sold everything and off I went."

He spent the next fifteen years in law enforcement, including the Alaska Department of Fish & Game (ADF&G) as a game warden in Tok, Alaska, and then with the Alaska State Troopers (AST) Fish and Wildlife Protection Division when the state merged ADF&G with AST. He spent the remaining four years as a special agent with the U.S. Fish & Wildlife Service, covering the state while based in Anchorage, Alaska. On his off time, he escaped to the lakes, streams, and oceans of Alaska. As good as the fishing was around Clinton, it couldn't compare with The Last Frontier's resources and unsurpassable beauty.

Al Crane, a former state and federal game warden and special agent and pilot from Petersburg, Alaska, met J.W. back in the 1960s, when both were involved in law enforcement. "I knew J.W. was different when we first met," Crane said. "He was smart, intense and thorough, and lived life like there was no tomorrow. He was always well-honed, impeccably clad and liked the best restaurants and hotels. When it came to hunting or fishing, he made sure we also gave every ounce to that. It came as no surprise to me when he decided to strike out on his own to pursue a career in the private sector."

As 1981 rolled around, J.W. had grown tired of busting poaching rings. He placed into action something that had been on his mind for years: making a living in the great Alaska outdoors. So he launched Painter Creek Lodge, a hunting and fishing venture.

"I wanted a lodge far from the noisy crowds," said J.W. "Our guests never saw another angler on Painter Creek—they could have wilderness streams all to themselves. It took a lot of scouting and exploring to

Smith (*right*) celebrates this caribou taken out of Painter Creek Lodge.
Photo courtesy of J.W. Smith.

discover that pristine fishing area so distant from neighboring towns or villages."

To expand his clients' fishing success, J.W. sometimes hiked fifty miles or so from Painter Creek Lodge on the Bristol Bay side of the Alaska Peninsula to Amber Bay and Nakalilok Bay on the Pacific side, traversing the Chiginigak Volcano Mountains in the process. J.W. slept under a tarp and survived on fish and freeze-dried meals during the trip. "You couldn't carry enough butter to keep from losing weight," said J.W. "But the results of these reconnoiters were incredible. I couldn't believe the abundance of fish in the streams on the untouched Pacific side of the peninsula."

J.W. had the perfect personality to schmooze big-moneyed clients and the right good-old-boy temperament to manage fishing guides and cooks. Painter Creek Lodge, located about 400 miles southwest of Anchorage and 100 miles south of King Salmon in the heart of the Alaska Peninsula, was in the proverbial middle of nowhere. He reclaimed an abandoned 5,000-foot airstrip and built the lodge on 15 acres of private property, all of which is surrounded by the 4.3-million-acre Alaska Peninsula Wildlife Refuge and mountain peaks of the Aleutian Range.

Painter Creek Lodge became the only operation on a fifty-mile home-river and lake system that drains into Bristol Bay and is accessible by jet boats and wheel plane. It's one of the best fly-rod fisheries in Alaska, with unending action throughout the summer season for king, chum, and silver salmon fresh from the ocean. The stream fishing is also phenomenal, with a full range of river opportunities near the lodge and within a twenty-mile fly-out for trophy Arctic char, Dolly Varden trout, Arctic grayling and more.

After disputes arose among the lodge's partners, J.W. switched his efforts to a booking agency specializing in light-tackle fishing and wing-shooting. In 1988, J.W. joined forces with partner David Gregory to form Rod and Gun Resources (RGR) based in Kerrville, Texas.

J.W. and David have spent the last three decades growing the business from a small outdoor travel agency to its present status as a prominent international booking agency for fishing and hunting trips. The duo also started South American Fly Fishing (SAFF) in 2012, and they now represent outfitters and lodges throughout North and South America, concentrating solely where they've found the most abundant and consistent sporting opportunities. Bookings exceed a thousand clients per year.

"I knew J.W. wouldn't be entirely happy sitting behind a desk making calls," said Gregory. And so it was that J.W. established the Alaska Wilderness Safari Camp (AWSC) in 1988 on Nakalilok Bay on the southeast side of the Alaska Peninsula National Wildlife Refuge. He obtained a concession agreement with the federal government to operate wilderness caches, meaning any camps would have to be disassembled and stored after each season.

Talk about remote: King Salmon, 110 miles away, was the nearest settlement, and no road system existed within 350 miles. The only neighbors were brown bears, but having seldom encountered humans, they invariably scampered away rather than put up a fuss.

"No work was beneath J.W. at the office or in the field," said Gregory. "On one of my trips to Alaska, J.W. had me working alongside him to expand the outhouse holding capacity. For two days we enlarged the hole with shovels while wearing hip boots."

J.W. met his future wife, Dawn, during a Dallas Safari Club convention. "Dawn's dad was a senior test pilot for Bell Helicopter," said J.W.

Dawn Smith, who can fish and hunt with the best of them, displays her Kipchuck River rainbow trout. Photo courtesy of Dawn Smith.

"He'd actually flown geologists to some of the areas where we eventually established our Alaska Wilderness Safari Camps." J.W. and Dawn, married twenty-eight years, have a son, Steve, and a daughter, Crystal (who married another Smith, Jeff, one of J.W.'s guides). Both kids grew up working at the Alaska lodges and camps.

Theirs is a productive domestic and business partnership. "I often had strange cooks before my wife Dawn took over the kitchen when we formed AWSC," said J.W. "The guests loved her double entrée dinners of salmon, barbecued pork ribs and big thick steaks as well as homemade breads, pastries and desserts—eating well is hugely important to running a successful camp, especially in the wilderness."

Besides knowing her way around a skillet and oven, Dawn became an expert angler in her own right as she experienced the Alaska wilderness with J.W. Her education produced a degree in photojournalism with a minor in biology. "I told people that after graduation I planned to work for *National Geographic*," said Dawn. "Instead, I married *National Geographic*."

Accessing AWSC involves a one-hour plane flight across the mountains from King Salmon and landing on the beach at low tide. It's considered by those visiting the camp to be one of the most-scenic and -inspirational portions of Alaska, and that's saying a lot in Alaska.

"We tried to camp right on good fishing," said J.W. "On the early Kipchuck River float trips, I'd have some of the richest people in the world camping on river bars, sleeping on air mattresses, bathing in side pools and eating around an alder wood fire. But ordinarily, it required very little walking to get into big ocean fish with silver salmon running fifteen pounds and more right out our front door."

Best yet, when an offshore wind blows, you can wade in the ocean and sight-fish for salmon daisy-chaining along the beach in the surf, and then move upstream and battle ocean-fed Dolly Varden and char as large as eight pounds. Adding to AWSC's mystique is the natural silence so far removed from anything resembling civilization, save for the occasional bald eagle scream, a yipping fox, or a brown bear with cubs splashing in the river below camp.

Ever innovative, J.W. bought a Vietnam-era seismic sensor system and turned it into a perimeter defense system at AWSC. "The monitor sat beside our bed in our tent," he said. "At least once a week we'd hear the zuuut, Zuuut, ZUUUT alarm as a bear climbed the trail into camp. We'd fire off a shotgun shell to scare it off."

In addition to the fixed camps, J.W. operated spike camps on Gertrude Creek and Agripina Bay. Guests accessed them via wheel plane and helicopter. They camped in Eureka tents and hiked across tundra to fish for trophy rainbow trout in the twenty-five-inch class as well as grayling, Dolly Varden, and king and chum salmon.

Over the years, J.W. worked with several legendary bush pilots, the last being Sam Egli of Egli Air Haul based out of King Salmon. Egli began flying for AWSC in 1993 and still does so. In 2013, Egli received the Alaska Air Carriers Association's Pilot of the Year Award. He described J.W. and their relationship:

Smith admired the unpretentious nature of the legendary Johnny Cash, here with a salmon caught during one of his visits to Painter Creek Lodge. Photo courtesy of J.W. Smith.

I first met J.W. in July of 1993 when he approached me about flying clients and supplies to his AWSC, the location of which was yet to be determined. We really solidified our relationship when I flew him and Dawn to Nakalilok Bay on the Pacific side of the Alaska Peninsula. After landing on a sandbar, we walked into the brush and then hurried back due to the rising tide. When we reached the plane, a couple of the gear-packed dry-bags were starting to float away.

J.W. waded in up to his chest until all bags were retrieved, after which he took off the soaking wet pants to fend off hypothermia. He then said I'd better take off before the plane went underwater while assuring me that they had all the supplies needed until I returned. Passing by as I took off, the last thing I saw was J.W. standing barefoot on a big rock, naked from his shirttail down, Dawn standing at his side with her arm around his waist and the lush green of the untamed Alaska Peninsula as their back-drop.

In 2001 J.W. sold AWSC to his head guide, Rus Schwausch, who operates the camp and credits J.W. as a mentor. Nowadays, when J.W. isn't in the field checking out new destinations for RGR and SAFF, he finds time to do a bit of woodworking.

"I build furniture out of native hardwoods and use natural finishes that highlight the wood grain," he said. "I made all the furniture in our house. It's solid. I call it 'furniture that fat men can dance on.'"

He and Dawn like to grow unique vegetables and plants in their garden. But it's another hobby that fascinates him more: long-range shooting. He can hit a target with a rifle a thousand yards away if it's not too windy.

The lore and color of Alaska's fishing and hunting heritage includes many categories of talent. One such talent is the formidable ability to start a wilderness lodge operation from scratch and to build it through skillful use of the media and other outlets. Then to leverage that experience into a successful international booking agency propels J.W. Smith onto the stage as of one of Alaska's pioneering outdoors entrepreneurs.

22

WILLIAM C. GASAWAY, 1943–2011

Fairbanks

Everyone who treks the fields, valleys, and mountains of the world in pursuit of moose owes a debt of gratitude to this man. By devising a method for estimating moose populations that far exceeded the accuracy of all existing techniques, he righted many wrong directions being followed by game managers. His method is still employed with some modifications to this day.

Nicknamed "The Gasser" by coworkers and later "The Golden Gasser" when he became widely known, Gasaway pioneered groundbreaking research that revolutionized modern proactive wildlife management. When predator management was emerging as a management tool, Gasaway's work provoked new management perspectives and fresh understanding of animal behaviors.

His career stemmed from a love of the outdoors and hunting, especially for trophy-size animals. He also enjoyed statistical analysis and experimentations. Many wildlife researchers and managers end up lost in the anonymity of bureaucracy and become prisoners of conventional wisdom, unmotivated to push the pencil beyond what the bosses want. Gasaway was an exception to this rule.

Changing long-held perceptions is nigh impossible in any profession, but it's particularly difficult in a governmental agency. Ironically,

resistance to change is often due to being unduly influenced by professors who themselves inherited most of their beliefs from textbooks
and old-school professors. The syndrome is like a grandson who always
votes straight Republican or Democrat because that's the only political
philosophy he heard growing up.

And there's the push-and-pull of prevailing politics. Prior to statehood in 1959, Alaska's fish and game resources were decided by federal agencies from the Department of the Interior, particularly the U.S.
Fish and Wildlife Service (FWS) and National Park Service (NPS), as well
as the Department of Commerce's National Oceanic and Atmospheric
Administration (NOAA) that mainly oversaw marine fisheries. When
Alaska took over many of those decisions and became responsible for
management within state boundaries in and through what became
the Alaska Department of Fish & Game (ADF&G), the sparks flew in all
sorts of directions.

Some of those sparks were dutifully generated by a handful of
visionaries at ADF&G who dared to challenge the status quo. They
were intent on making policy based on sound research intrinsic to
Alaska rather than adapting and adopting what was doctrinaire and
at times outdated. Just as when fighting city hall, it's not easy to pre-
vail against the long-held beliefs of some bureaucrats, politicians, and
hard-line environmentalists. It's a challenge that to some degree will
always exist between federal and state authorities.

While he wasn't there at the beginning—his ADF&G tenure lasted
twenty years from 1972 to 1992—Gasaway turned out to be one hell
of a spark, but that wasn't apparent at the beginning of his career in
wildlife management. His master's degree work at Washington State
University dealt with an improbable study involving the feeding
of zinc to captive mallards until they got sick and died, after which
an autopsy was conducted. As morbid as that may seem, when later
drafted into the military, that peculiar background got him assigned to
the U.S. Army's Edgewood Arsenal in Maryland to help study biological
warfare agents.

Gasaway obtained a doctorate, with a thesis on the nutritional physiology of ptarmigan, at the University of Alaska's Institute of Arctic
Biology in Fairbanks. His research imparted an intricate appreciation of
the variables of nutrition in the wild, an important element of wildlife

Gasaway (*right*) with fellow biologist Wayne Heimer after a duck hunt in 1966 during their early years together at the Alaska Department of Fish & Game. Photo courtesy of Wayne Heimer.

management theory then and now. When Gasaway applied for a job at ADF&G in Fairbanks, he was hired to serve as a laboratory researcher.

With a predilection toward nutrition and a love for hunting moose, Gasaway focused his energy on what moose liked to eat, on how they digested food, and on related studies. Plenty of moose roamed the Fairbanks region in the 1960s and early 1970s, so experimentation on carcasses was easy. Gasaway knew about the existing theory that moose would essentially eat all the vegetation in one area and cause the population to crash. His research design applied to moose the same techniques that he used in studying the innards of ptarmigans. A moose would be killed and dissected in the field, and samples taken to the lab to be further analyzed.

Despite Gasaway's detailed nutritional work in the field and in the lab, his results didn't seem destined to affect wildlife management, which meant making healthy populations available for hunting, in his mind. All the work made for lots of complex studies too, but didn't change policy. And that led to an epiphany: Gasaway realized he'd become mired in his own minutiae and was making little impact on the big picture of wildlife, wilderness, and policy. He arrived at the conclusion that even as a soldier in a governmental agency, he must somehow become a leader, not a follower.

That realization fit with his prior dreams of becoming a major player in the betterment of wildlife and hunting. Gasaway decided to switch his research emphasis to the restoration of moose populations instead of concentrating on molecular details of their digestion processes. Fortunately, that was a "thinking big" game plan to which his bosses at ADF&G readily agreed.

Gasaway's first hurdle was to dispel the accepted notion among wildlife researchers that the "balance of nature" always works out just fine if the footprints of man can be eliminated. He already knew better because his many days as a hunter in Alaska's wilderness revealed stark fluctuations in game populations even in remote regions where hunters seldom ventured. Above all, Gasaway began to suspect that predators such as wolves impacted populations far more than serving as merely cleanup crews to the ecosystem. Wolves didn't just scavenge or kill only the weak or genetically unfit, and they certainly didn't regulate their reproduction to stay in balance with their prey. That behavior in turn translated to significant impacts to hoofed mammals such as moose.

When Gasaway mused about such "new think" with some of his peers in the late 1970s and early 1980s, he may as well have detonated a nuclear bomb. Climbing into the ring to beat the daylights out of him in the policy arena were any number of "Save the (fill in the blank)" environmental groups, a plethora of federal wildlife managers, and more than a few top-echelon honchos at ADF&G. The gun-shy reticence of Gasaway and others was largely a result of an earlier predator-control program pushed by ADF&G involving bounties on wolves that drew national rebuke. The outrage could not be rebutted. No evidence existed, however, to substantiate the program, and in fact it later became recognized by Gasaway and others that the estimated ratio of the wolf populations vis-à-vis prey populations prior to the 1980s was woefully inaccurate.

In the face of such entrenched resistance, Gasaway knew that only evidence gathered in the field through sound science would reveal if his concerns about controlling wolf populations held water. It would also be the only credible way to convince reasonable detractors of his theory. Gasaway first needed to assure colleagues that his open-mindedness about predator effects did not mean he favored unmanaged hunting or ignored other factors affecting prey resources, such as weather, snow depth, nutritional availability and in some cases migration habits.

In his landmark study, *Interrelationships of Wolves, Prey, and Man in Alaska*, published in1983, Gasaway and his coauthors offered a new theory to explain the decline of ungulate populations and the impact of wolf predation on them in Interior Alaska during the early to mid 1970s. In the following excerpt *ungulate* refers to a hoofed animal such as a moose or caribou:

> Predation by wolves can exert substantial control over ungulate prey populations, as demonstrated by wolf control experiments. In retrospect, errors were made in managing the moose, caribou and wolf populations in our study area during the early 1970s. Moose population size was not estimated accurately enough, and its rate of decline was initially underestimated. Consequently, appropriate hunting regulations were implemented belatedly. Also, biologists underestimated the combined impact of wolf predation and hunting on moose and caribou during the early 1970s and did not adequately manage wolves.

But how to solve the glaring problem of getting an accurate read on moose populations? That momentous breakthrough occurred when in 1986, Gasaway and others devised a moose-population census estimate that became known as the Gasaway Method. It involved a stratified count using aircraft, which proved to be far-more accurate simply because animals tend to run or hide from men on foot or in vehicles. With reliable statistical data that provided much better estimates of the prey and predator populations in a given area, ADF&G could better justify whether predator control was warranted.

There's a backstory to how this game-changing Gasaway Method came into being. The idea germinated during a break amid a statistical sampling workshop at the University of Alaska at Fairbanks. As Gasaway and ADF&G pal Wayne Heimer strolled around the campus and gazed out over the Tanana Flats, Heimer mused, "If you could define which areas of the flats where moose are more abundant or easier to see at survey time, a smart guy ought to be able to figure out, with some statistical boundaries, the overall moose population at the time of the survey."

The Golden Gasser with a healthy sheep in the Brooks Range in August 1971. Photo courtesy of Dave Harkness.

Gasaway lit up like a lantern. His mind raced on the concept of a high, medium, and low stratified aerial approach to perform a statistically valid census. Statisticians came up with a mathematical-probability formula that field biologists could follow. And thus, the Gasaway Census took shape. The ensuing wolf control in the Tanana Flats region resulted in the moose population rebounding.

His name grew in fame as the Gasaway Method blossomed world-wide into a model for game management researchers. His census method became widely quoted and referenced in innumerable studies—and still is—even as modifications continue to be made with refinements in population estimates through new technologies like the Geographical Positioning System (GPS) and radio-frequency tags.

In a more practical sense, Gasaway's innovation overcame the accepted notion that wolves, wolverines, foxes, bears, and other predators don't significantly alter game resources like moose, caribou, musk oxen, goats, and sheep. That mistaken mythology notion tended to load most of the blame for population decreases on hunters and trappers, often resulting in regulations unfairly slapped in place to limit human access or impose overly restrictive regulations.

The aerial survey also at times contradicted misperceptions of migratory habits. For decades prior to the Gasaway Census, many game researchers believed that some species such as moose seldom migrated. That meant that a traditional survey showing a significant decline between population in "survey A" and that in a later "survey B" might result in hunting closures because it wasn't known that the moose may have simply been elsewhere at the time of "survey B."

Gasaway's achievements made an indelible mark because whatever the project he had in mind or the scientific model he wanted to test, he began with a clean slate: nothing was taken for granted; nothing was assumed; there was no acceptance of presupposed "laws of nature;" no conclusion-based biases drove the science; no political influences tainted the data and analysis . . . these were just pure, unadulterated scientific methods that weighed all natural and human factors.

At some point, Gasaway became a pilot. Heimer recalled a humorous but telling incident when Gasaway had shot a large moose in the Brooks Range with Pam, his wife at the time:

His airplane didn't have a fantastic payload, so the idea was to ferry the moose from a small lake to a bigger one where there would be more takeoff distance for a larger load. The Golden Gasser loaded the airplane with camp gear, some meat, his wife, and he strapped the antlers to the wing struts. They taxied to the end of the small lake but the floatplane wouldn't fly.

He unloaded and tried again, but the same result. This went on a couple of more times until it was just him and the antlers as weight, and the plane still wouldn't fly. The Golden Gasser surmised that the curvature of the antlers was negating airflow over the lifting and control surfaces of the airplane. Adjustments were made and all the meat, gear and wife were safely transported back to Fairbanks.

On a trip with Gasaway to the Sheenjek River on the south side of the Brooks Range, Heimer recalls another moose story:

We flew in and camped overnight. The next day we spotted a forty-eight-inch moose making his way upriver about half a mile from camp. He was too small for us to shoot that early in the hunt, so we simply decided to see if we could call him in just for the fun of it.

By then, the moose was headed steadily upriver about six hundred yards from our camp. We were sitting on a high bank overlooking the Sheenjek and I gave a loud grunt and the bull immediately stopped in his tracks. He turned almost ninety degrees and began to walk straight at us. As he approached, I began to thrash

Fieldwork often entailed obtaining stomach samples to gauge feeding habits, such as with this moose on the Tanana Flats in June 1972. Photo courtesy of John N. Trent.

the brush a little with continued grunting and eventually shifted to that 'gluck' sound that moose make when "on final." The bull came right for us, entered the willows on the other side of the river and was out of sight for a while.

That's when the Gasser said, "I wonder if we can call him visually." He held up a couple of white caribou shed antlers that had been lying around camp as if each sprouted from his ears. I was riding "shotgun" on the bank, and I was to shoot only if the moose crossed completely out of the river to charge Gasaway—a predicament that we'd heard had happened to other researchers. Well, the moose came out of the willows, made the glucking sound with each display step and headed across the mud bar toward the river, which was between Gasaway and the moose.

I kept glucking as Gasaway stood and held up the caribou antlers while making display movements. The moose never hesitated. Apparently he saw the antlers and mistook Gasaway for a competing bull. The moose came steadily across the mud bar, waded into the river and crossed it to where he was within fifteen feet of Gasaway. But it kept one rear hoof in the water so I didn't shoot. With the moose that close, Gasaway lowered the antlers and the moose quickly turned and splashed back across the river toward the brush.

We thought that was a great experience, but wondered if we could do it again. Amazingly, we coaxed that moose to return two more times doing the same thing, but each time it stayed farther away before again dashing off until he tired of the game.

And so it was that Gasaway, "The Golden Gasser," contributed to better hunting as a famous wildlife researcher in Alaska. Motivated in good measure by his love of hunting and propelled by an analytical mind, he realized the goal of making important significant contributions to improving Alaska's moose populations. His career is a great testament not only to successful scientific accomplishment but thinking out of the box. That's the true legacy of a trailblazer.

23

BOB STEPHENSON, 1945–PRESENT

Fairbanks

> *With knowledge acquired from Eskimos and his extensive field studies, he came up with valuable insights about wolf behavior in Alaska that derailed the prevailing attitude by many researchers and hunters that wolves were always the culprits for reductions in populations of game animals such as moose and caribou. His work helped attain a true perception of the wolf's place in nature, which ever since has played heavily in determining ADF&G hunting regulations.*

I realize that appreciation for those who assisted in the publishing of a book traditionally appear only in the acknowledgments section, but in this case, the writing for this chapter belongs to Wayne Heimer. He and Stephenson became close colleagues and friends at the Alaska Department of Fish & Game (ADF&G), and Heimer strongly felt that it would be an injustice to leave Bob Stephenson out of *Legends of Alaska's Great Outdoors*. I concur, as Stephenson's body of work remains an important element in understanding the state's game animals, and no one knows his contributions better than Heimer. Here, then, is Heimer's portrait of Stephenson.

Born in Wisconsin, Bob Stephenson received his undergraduate education at the University of Wisconsin at Stevens Point. Thereafter he enrolled in the master's degree program at the University of Alaska in

Stephenson (*right*) with Johnny Rulland at the Punlatuuq Camp on the upper John River in spring 1980. Photo courtesy of Grant Spearman.

Fairbanks. Stephenson's time in graduate school and his early years at ADF&G were partly interrupted by service in the Army National Guard. His master's research had to do with the ecology of arctic foxes on Saint Lawrence Island.

Upon graduation, Stephenson's specialty in the basic biology of canine predation was attractive to ADF&G. Stephenson was initially hired in early 1970 as a temporary [employee], and then moved into a permanent position in the fall as the Interior Region wolf research biologist. Wolves were coming to be seen as more meaningful than just varmints, and a fresh mind on the subject was needed.

The view of wolves in the contemporary world was in the early stages of evolution prior to the 1980s. Man has always competed with wolves for food. Wolves are inherently better adapted to life in the Arctic than man. They are always adequately insulated, can travel great distances with relative ease, and are equipped to live off the land. About all man has going for him is his large brain and ability to adapt competitively.

I don't know that ADF&G leadership was figuring this out when they hired Stephenson, but the perception of wolves was changing from that of predatory varmint to wilderness symbol. Stephenson was well equipped to provide basic information on wolves because of his intuitive gifts and the understanding that even though he had a master's degree that involved *Canids*, he didn't know everything. He was characterized by a humble manner and an open mind.

Because of this perception, Stephenson didn't immediately undertake a large-scale research program to find out everything about wolves. Instead, he went where there was already substantial knowledge—to Anaktuvuk Pass in the Brooks Range. Anaktuvuk is a combination of Inupiat words for scats or droppings. Basically the word *anak* means feces. The Nunamiut word for caribou is *tutu*. Hence Anaktuvuk Pass means a place of caribou droppings.

The Nunamiut are an inland group of Eskimos who were traditionally caribou people. Their village at Anaktuvuk was an established place where caribou were dependably found in the fall/winter. Anaktuvuk residents lived on caribou and other wildlife and were known for their detailed knowledge of the wildlife and environment in the Brooks Range for a long time before Stephenson came on the scene. Their knowledge of wolves was well known among Alaskans.

It just seemed natural for Stephenson to go where the knowledge and understanding of wolf biology and behavior was. Consequently, when he was hired, he convinced his supervisor at ADF&G, John Burns, to let him periodically live in Anaktuvuk Pass with the caribou/wolf people during the first few years of his tenure. This was unlike anything remotely similar to what would happen today.

Stephenson was on the job before I showed up at ADF&G in November of 1971, but I'd heard about his Anaktuvuk Pass assignments. That time was well spent for Stephenson because it allowed him to learn about wolves and develop his intuitive gifts. He didn't ever become, or represent himself as, a wolf whisperer, but he acquired a knack for seeing the forest rather than the trees.

Stephenson's knowledge, acquired from the Eskimos, put him in a remarkably good position to deal with what was happening with wolves at the time. Knowledge about how wolves really live was becoming important because popular opinion was changing the perception of how wolves get along in nature, and what it means to all of us. The perception of wolves as varmints was largely because they competed with Europeans as the westward expansion of our nation involved raising livestock, which wolves readily killed and ate. However, when Stephenson came on the scene, the image of wolves was being reshaped by the emerging preservation lobby.

Wolves were promoted to what I call the biological toothbrush level. Rather than being known as killers, they had been cast as agents of evolution, brushing up the ecosystem and gene pool by removing unfit individuals.

Rudimentary knowledge of their behavior had also given rise to the myth that wolves always regulated their population size through social behavior to stay in balance with their prey base. Both of these notions have been proven to be myths, and Stephenson played a major part in demystifying the wolf. However, the natural preservation interests still get lots of mileage from that public relations coup.

Stephenson was later assigned to study wolves in the Nelchina Basin in south central Alaska, where moose and caribou were not thriving. ADF&G leadership, by then, had come to reflexively intuit that when prey populations weren't thriving, wolves were to blame. They sent Stephenson to live in a small trailer near Glennallen. Stephenson spent a year in the country, flying with local bush pilots and monitoring a dozen or so radio-collared wolf packs. He came back to his bosses to report that there's not only a wolf problem there but there's also a bear problem. Years of marginally successful wolf control and bear research subsequently showed Stephenson had been right. He made objective observations and reached the appropriate conclusions.

Eventually, ADF&G's priorities shifted to doing additional hard-core quantitative studies. Stephenson could have done that work, but emerging talents looked like a better investment to ADF&G leadership. These talented young biologists (who have now retired) did wonderful work building on the foundation Stephenson had provided in enumerating the actual impact of wolves and bears on prey populations, and thus made it possible to manage predators more as functional components of ecosystems rather than simply preserving them as wilderness symbols.

In the meantime, the Endangered Species lobby in Washington, D.C., had figured out that Alaska lynx are the same species as Canadian lynx. Lynx in Canada were considered threatened by some measures,

Stephenson getting ready to do some moose calling on the Tenana Flats in 1982.
Photo courtesy of Wayne Heimer.

and Alaska's fur trade (of which lynx are a vital part) was threatened by restrictions on lynx fur exports. Stephenson was assigned the task of evaluating the population status and management of lynx in Alaska.

Part of this involved live-trapping and radio-collaring lynx, and following them for a year. Using his skills at getting along with almost everyone, Stephenson forged cooperative relationships with skilled trappers and they allowed him to use parts of their best trap lines to capture lynx. Another part of the study involved analyzing decades of lynx harvest records.

Anticipating that he'd only have money to radio-track the lynx for one winter, Stephenson decided he would do it as long as the lynx and the collars lasted. His solution? Build an ultralight airplane to do the work on his own when he was off the clock at ADF&G. Bob selected plans for an appropriate enclosed-canopy ultralight powered by a snow-machine engine. He ordered the kit with his own money and began to put it together in his garage. I recall one particularly interesting day when he called me to help him set the camber on the wings. That involved a sheep biologist twisting the wings and measuring the angles with a schoolboy's protractor while a wolf/lynx biologist tightened the appropriate nuts and bolts. Would you fly in that thing?

Eventually, Stephenson trailered his airplane to a local strip where testing began. Learning to fly it seemed daunting, but he'd spent thousands of hours flying with some of Alaska's best bush pilots. Stephenson outfitted it with radio-tracking gear, spare fuel tanks, skis, and a ballistic-deployed parachute to allow a soft landing if anything went wrong. On one flight, an engine failure did result in something going wrong. As a result, Stephenson's little airplane was damaged in the field. He rebuilt it before flying it home.

Stephenson's work showed that Alaska lynx are not threatened, and lynx harvest and trade remains a functionally sustainable part of Alaska's fur industry. However, Stephenson wasn't done. Always appreciated for his abilities to relate to Alaska Natives in village situations, Stephenson was assigned as the ADF&G liaison to a challenging area in northeast Alaska. There, Stephenson was tasked with finding out why moose in the area weren't thriving and perhaps find ways to improve the situation.

His first effort was to drive a powerboat on the Porcupine River where there should have been more moose based on the habitat, and talk to moose hunters. The thought was that people and predators (wolves and bears) were overharvesting moose, and were keeping the population from expanding.

While traveling on the Porcupine River one autumn day, Stephenson and a friend stopped to visit a meadow and noted that the vegetation—silverberry and sedge—was similar to that used by a transplanted group of plains bison near Delta Junction. The next week, a federal biologist came to spend time with Stephenson, who suggested the plant community might be suitable for bison.

As it happened, the federal guy happened to be the endangered species coordinator for the Yukon Flats National Wildlife Refuge (where there are currently no endangered or listed species), and mentioned that wood bison stock is available in Canada. Wood bison were considered to be threatened in Canada but were recovering well after some rather heroic efforts by Canadian wildlife managers. Those Canadian biologists were looking for another safe place to transfer wood bison where they would not be contaminated genetically or be threatened by livestock diseases and could thrive in good habitat. Stephenson's area seemed ideal. Thus began a twenty-year saga of bureaucratic and administrative maneuvering required by law (and politics) to allow reintroduction of wood bison to Alaska.

Reintroduction? Yes. Through Stephenson's exercise of his gifts for getting along with Alaskans, he learned that it is quite likely wood bison were extirpated by man by around 1900. He and the Alaska Native residents of the area found wood-bison bones and horn cores that were dated to throughout the last ten thousand years, ending only recently, and the reintroduction effort was on. This confirmed and added detail to earlier findings by paleontologists showing that bison had survived the Pleistocene extinctions and persisted in Alaska and northern Canada until recent times. It has taken twenty years, but wood bison were released in spring 2015.

A facet of Stephenson's personality that might reveal his compassionate side was his interest in alternative medicine. He was exquisitely allergic to mercury in all its forms, and when his health began to fail, he learned that his silver fillings were an amalgam of silver dissolved in mercury. He replaced all his fillings, and his health improved, which propelled him to explore alternative medicine.

Having an open mind, particularly to things beyond conventional medicine, Stephenson was the office health consultant. Actually, he was an evangelical zealot where alternative medicine was concerned, and helped many people. For example, Stephenson has maintained that improvements in microscopy actually make it possible to see things smaller than the wavelength of visible light. Recently the Nobel Prize for Chemistry was awarded to some guys who had done exactly that. Stephenson was on the leading edge of much alternative medicine and convinced a number of dentists in Fairbanks that the health of their patients would improve if they stopped using silver amalgamated with mercury as a dental filling material.

I fondly recall the time Stephenson was helping me helicopter a prefabbed building for use as a field camp into the Alaska Range. I went in with the first sling load that was to be the floor. Stephenson was to come in with the second load of walls and roof stuff. He didn't come for quite a while, and when he did, there was no building.

He said they had lost the sling load when the rigging rope broke and it was a thing of beauty to watch the walls and roof spiraling down like autumn leaves before disappearing into the spruce forest. "However," said Stephenson with a smile, "I did bring you a hamburger."

Thanks again for your insights about Bob Stephenson, Wayne. Other colleagues had some interesting tidbits about him too.

Grant Spearman, who for thirty years lived in Anaktuvuk Pass, knew Stephenson from his early work for ADF&G.

Stephenson was indeed fortunate to step amid the long-standing tradition of researchers working with the Anaktuvuk and Nunamiut people. He certainly came prepared, with an appropriate level of scientific background, but he brought much more with him than academic credentials—nimble wits and an ability to learn quickly.

Stephenson is also an openhearted and very likable man. His respect for elders and ability to easily and seamlessly adapt to new and novel circumstances won him friends, but an incident that impacted the village one winter cemented his deep and abiding connection to the community that remains strong to this day.

The village was hit with a severe flu epidemic in late winter of 1971, which fell heavily upon every household. Stephenson's mentor and friend there, a fellow named Bob Ahgook, was the designated Community Health Aide. As the only two people still on their feet, they worked ceaselessly for three days tending to everyone's needs. They went repeatedly from house to house, administering shots, helping to feed people and give them water, keeping fevers down especially among infants, pumping fuel oil to keep homes warm and just providing lots of encouragement.

Before this incident, people already liked Bob Stephenson; afterwards, they loved him dearly. In appreciation for his help, Ahgook gave Stephenson his own Eskimo name of Talliq, meaning forearm—a great gesture of affection for a non-Native.

Spearman also reflected on Stephenson's kindly affection for dogs: "His generosity of spirit—in many ways a classic quality of his Midwestern upbringing—is something he possesses in spades and it

At his desk with a 1983 version of a state-of-the-art computer.
Photo courtesy of Wayne Heimer.

especially extends to animals. He has never been without a fleet of good-natured and well-loved dogs. He's always ready to take in a stray animal that needs a home or medical treatment."

Dave Mech, a world-renowned expert on wolves, hails from St. Paul, Minnesota. Mech first met Bob Stephenson in Alaska in the late 1970s. He describes Stephenson as a jack-of-all-trades and master of many. "From Arctic foxes to wolves, with lynxes and bison in between, Stephenson helped inform science and the public about all those iconic species and many others," he said.

Through his field work and writings on wolves alone, Stephenson contributed information about ecology, predation, management, physiology, reproduction, homing behavior and population dynamics. He's examined countless carcasses, flown endless miles and tracked umpteen wolves. As such, he was long the major source of information about wolves in Alaska and met with other wolf specialists from around the world to help various countries deal with research and management issues.

Mech offered additional insights into Stephenson's character. "Stephenson has always welcomed me to Alaska and introduced me to his colleagues," Mech continued. "My most memorable time with Stephenson was when he and pilot Al Lee stuffed me atop my travel bag in the baggage compartment of Lee's Super. We took off near Fairbanks and radio-tracked wolves all the way to Denali Park. I'll never forget peering down at a wolf-killed moose with a huge grizzly bear lying on top of it."

Stephenson worked in the professional service of Alaska's wildlife and people for forty-three years. Thanks to his intuitive and good-hearted contributions, Bob Stephenson paved the way for a clearer understanding of the true impacts and roles that wolves play in Alaska's management of wildlife resources. In turn, that science has greatly affected hunting regulations on a wide range of big game species.

24

JIM LAVRAKAS, 1952–PRESENT

Homer

~~~~~~

While he could produce quality writing as needed for news stories and features, his greatest contribution to the escalating numbers of outdoors enthusiasts was and still is his professional photography. During the heyday of daily newspapers and international access to press images, his frequently viewed pictures of wildlife provided readers near and far with proof positive of Alaska's unparalleled fishing and hunting opportunities.

~~~~~~

Few Alaskans have captured the heart and soul of The Last Frontier better than Jim Lavrakas. As a photographer for thirty years for the *Anchorage Daily News*, his images ranged from news events, wilderness lifestyles, and portrayals of Alaska's people to fish, fishermen, game animals, and hunters.

He published a book of stunning photographic images, owned and operated a charter-boat business, worked for a chamber of commerce, and undertook all sorts of other interesting pursuits.

Born in Lowell, Massachusetts, he moved with his family to the dairy-farm community of Dunstable, Massachusetts, at the age of six. Their property included 120 acres of pine-wooded forest bordered on one side by Salmon Brook—ironically, a waterway devoid of salmon in modern times.

A steelhead caught in the Anchor River by Lavrakas in 2008. Since then, he releases fish without removing them from the water. Photo courtesy of Kevin Klott.

Lavrakas credits his father, Vasilis "Babe" Lavrakas, with introducing him to photography. At the age of twelve, Babe familiarized him with different types of cameras, explained intricacies such as f-stops, film speed, and shutter speed, proper lighting techniques, exposure tricks, and dark room skills. Those lessons inspired a passion that grew from a hobby into a profession, eventually propelling Jim to the most-prestigious photographer's job in Alaska.

Lavrakas took the first step toward a career in photojournalism at age fourteen by working part time as a stringer for the *Lowell Sun* newspaper. Before graduating from the University of Massachusetts with a bachelor of arts in English, he spent the summer of 1973 with college friends in Alaska. They ended up in Girdwood because one of the men had a place to stay there.

It was a beautiful bluebird day when they arrived in Girdwood with the peaks still snowcapped. Lavrakas turned to his friend and asked, "How do you ever get used to this?" His friend replied, "You don't." Over forty years later, Lavrakas still agrees with that sentiment.

An example of Lavrakas's award-winning photography—look closely to see the rainbow trout fingerling in the pike. Photo courtesy of Jim Lavrakas.

With no jobs to suit him in Girdwood, he ended up in Kodiak to investigate an opening in a "slime line" in a fish-processing plant. Finding that unappealing, Lavrakas learned of a job available for a bush-camp caretaker with photography skills. He got hired and spent six weeks at a remote bush camp on Kodiak Island. His main duty consisted of dog-sitting two Saint Bernards and a hound, but his employer got evicted from the site, and Lavrakas never received any pay.

That ended his stint in Alaska, which was a failure in terms of making money. However, the experience was the greatest of his life, and Lavrakas decided he must return to Alaska after college and somehow become a photojournalist. In 1975, Lavrakas did move to Alaska, his first position being at the Alyeska Resort in Girdwood. That didn't work out, and in short order neither did any other jobs in Girdwood. He finally secured steady employment as a gandy dancer (track leveler) on the Alaska Railroad.

"I worked on a mobile work crew that roamed along the line in a self-contained unit that included sleeping cars, a dining car, a generator and a water tanker," said Lavrakas. "That job lasted three years and I saw some gorgeous country, which was a great introduction to remote Alaska. But I knew a laborer's life was not for me. It was time to seek employment in the field that I'd listed as my ambition in my high school yearbook: photojournalist."

Lavrakas lacked two essentials of a photojournalist: camera gear and training in journalism. He had a degree in English, but that wouldn't be enough. He therefore hired on at Sandy's Photo Center in the Sears Mall in Anchorage. His employer, Sandy Ross, was tough but encouraging. The three years Lavrakas spent there under Ross's tutelage helped him attain pride in professionalism and a work ethic he was to carry for the rest of his career.

"To get the two newspapers in Anchorage to notice me, I started a photo freelance business specializing in the performing arts," Lavrakas said. The newspapers began carrying his photos of the productions and indeed took notice. In 1979, Lavrakas filled in for a vacationing photographer at the *Anchorage Times*, which led to a full-time job.

However, the larger *Anchorage Daily News* was expanding and needed photographers. Lavrakas worked part time for the *Daily News* for nearly two years until in January 1981 it went full time. Lavrakas had finally achieved his dream job in his beloved adopted state. At the time, there were less than a dozen photojournalists in Alaska, making the position all the more elite. A dozen years later, the *Anchorage Times* was bought out and closed down, leaving the *Daily News* the only game in town.

"I believe the twelve years between my hiring and the *Times* closing was the best time to be in the newspaper business in Alaska," Lavrakas recalled. "As a result of that fierce competition, more often than not story ideas pitched to the ADN [*Anchorage Daily News*] editor by the photo staff got the green light. That meant trips to Quinhagak, Barrow, Unalaska, Kodiak, Noorvik, Bettles and more places than I remember.

"I went to the Calgary Olympics in 1988 just to photograph the single alpine skier from Alaska and the two Nordic skiers. But hands down, the best photo assignment ADN offered to its photographers was, and still is, the Iditarod Trail Sled Dog Race."

Lavrakas and a reporter would hire a pilot and spend two weeks traveling the trail to obtain behind-the-scenes stories about more than just the race leaders. He ended up covering nine races over his career.

Jeff Schultz still hails from Anchorage and has been the official photographer of the Iditarod since 1982. "I first met Jim in the late 1980s on
a gym floor in Unalakleet, Alaska," he said. "We were playing a pick-up
game of basketball after dark during the Iditarod sled dog race.

> Earlier that day and throughout the last six days of the race, we
> crossed paths several times while photographing. Jim was a
> relentless photojournalist, seeking out the best pictures of the
> race to send back to the newspaper. He would always be in places
> where the real race was happening between the checkpoints.
> When he became a fishing guide in Homer, I hired him to take
> me and a colleague out for salmon fishing. He was just as relent-
> less in his guide work, putting us onto fish and going beyond the
> call of duty—including untangling our lines from the propeller.

But it wasn't all fun and games during those days either; Lavrakas
battled alcoholism. "I was producing excellent work before I become
sober in 1991, but I was sleepwalking through life with relationships,
my maturity, and my artistic expression stunted," he said.

> Ironically, ADN won the Pulitzer Prize for Public Service in 1989.
> At the time, I wasn't traveling for work because my home life was
> falling apart. My efforts for "A People in Peril," the series that won
> the Pulitzer, were Anchorage-bound. In my state of mind, the irony
> was that the series was about alcoholism and self-destructive
> behavior by Alaska Natives. I surely could identify with them.

The *Daily News* helped Lavrakas get sober and keep his job. He could
see things clearly again and gained a positive outlook on life. His work
improved through the 1990s, and he won many state and national
awards, but going digital in the year 2000 opened a whole new frontier.
Lavrakas became the digital guru of the photo department, but when
the newspaper industry went into a tailspin in 2005, the writing was
on the wall.

Budgets for trips and staff sank, layoffs began, and finally in October
2008 Lavrakas left the *Daily News* after thirty years. At age fifty-six, he
was in good physical condition, mentally alert, and still had the pride
and professionalism to succeed. He had all the photography skills one

At the wheel of the *Skookum*, a 27-footer custom built in Homer. Photo courtesy of Jim Lavrakas.

could achieve, possessed a deep knowledge of computer software, and had penned some stories for the travel section of the *Daily News*.

Many of his colleagues in those days at the *Daily News* still remain friends. Richard Murphy, a former supervisor and photo editor from Anchorage, admired Lavrakas's determination and tenacity. "When he went out to get a picture, he usually came back with it," said Murphy.

> I'll never forget one occasion when Jimmy needed a pair of snow-shoes for an assignment. The newspaper had little in the way of equipment in those days, so I loaned him a pair of top-of-the-line wooden beavertail webs. The snowshoes were not new, but they were stout, tough and very well cared for.
>
> Jimmy was known for being rough on gear, but there was little he could do to damage these beasts . . . or so I thought. The webs came back destroyed. The snowshoes were not merely broken, cracked or bruised, they were demolished. It looked like they had been run over by a truck. I don't remember the exact details of the explanation, but the real answer was rather simple—there was a

big patch of Alaska-tough alder between Jimmy and a picture he wanted to take. Since he could not go around or over it, Jimmy just bashed his way through the center. He made it through and back, and came home with the pictures; the snowshoes were just not as tough as he was.

Lavrakas served as an adjunct instructor teaching photojournalism at the University of Alaska at Anchorage and did likewise for Alaska Pacific University. But that's not all Lavrakas had going for him. He had a love of the outdoors. His first memories of camping were with his father as a preteen in the semiwilds of Maine's Baxter State Park. He hiked the Appalachian Mountain Trail with his father and as a Boy Scout, scaling mountains, and sleeping in bunkhouses or utilizing the system of spare shelters along the trail.

Lavrakas became adept as an angler and hunter. He won the annual Ship Creek King Salmon Derby in 2004 with a 45.2-pound king salmon. He'd been fishing the creek, which runs through downtown Anchorage, since 2000 for a web video series called "The Fishing Dude" for the *Daily News*. He nailed the big king on the second day of the ten-day event and had to sweat out the rest of the tournament in hopes no one would beat it. As it turned out, the second-largest fish ended up weighing about ten pounds less.

Fishing next to Lavrakas on that day was his pal Andy Sorenson, who would die at the age of only forty-eight from a heart defect. As a memorial, Lavrakas started (and he still oversees) the Andy Sorenson Sportsmanship Award for the tournament, which is now called the Downtown Soup Kitchen Slam'n Salm'n King Salmon Derby.

A former college roommate can attest to Lavrakas's fishing skills. Carl Lopes, who hails from Massachusetts, fished with his son as Lavrakas guided them to a halibut hotspot in Kachemak Bay near Homer. "Within seconds, my rod was jerked down below the water surface and the line began stripping from my reel," said Lopes.

Jim kept telling me to keep the line tight as my arms began burning. Jim grabbed the largest net I had ever seen. In twenty minutes the giant halibut finally appeared at the surface and Jim readied his net for the big scoop.

He quickly maneuvered his net under the fish and scooped upwards. The giant halibut gave one last effort, using its powerful tail and muscled out of the net. It headed straight down to the depths with the zinging sound of the line being ripped off the reel. My arms were in for another serious workout. I could see on Jim's face that he felt terrible for missing the netting because we all saw the open tear in the lip of the fish where the hook entered.

After ten more strenuous minutes the halibut again appeared on the surface. Jim covered the fish perfectly this time and the giant was ours. Once the fish was under control, it took all three of us to hoist it onboard.

Lavrakas enjoys hunting, particularly for blacktail deer on Kodiak Island at the beginning of each November. However, one day on a trip in 2004 a potentially disastrous bear confrontation developed. After his party of four had shot seven deer by the end of the week, they were ready to fly out. But before the charter flight arrived, Lavrakas walked half a mile from camp and started using a call that emulated a fawn bleating. Here's how Lavrakas described the scene:

Over my right shoulder, the slightest of sounds made me turn. Watching me intently about fifty feet away was the largest Kodiak brownie I had ever seen. I faced it fully and I bellowed, "Hey bear!" as I flipped off the safety on my rifle. We looked at each other for a few seconds and then I took a step backward—and tripped over a log.

The instant I was on my back I felt the desperation of knowing that the bear might take advantage. I got back up on my feet as if on springs. The bear hadn't moved while I was down, but then suddenly took three deliberate strides toward me, each faster than the other until it was only twenty feet away.

"Back off bear, back off now!" I said sternly, trying to sound mean and dangerous. It stopped and we stood there frozen again, eye-to-eye, neither of us sure of what to do. Then, slowly, it turned and walked away, pausing for a moment to look back at me before disappearing into the bush. I scrambled sideways to put as much

His first buck, taken on Kodiak Island in November 2006. Photo courtesy of
Jim Lavrakas.

distance between us as possible without running. The lesson I
learned: Don't go off by yourself when with a hunting party.

Lavrakas and his second wife, Ruth, have been married for seventeen
years, and he has thirty-one-year-old twin sons, Nick and Gabe. He and
Ruth moved to Homer in 2010 where Lavrakas ran Skookum Charters,
a saltwater fishing charter business. After the first year it became a
dining tour whereby he took clients out for rockfish and brought the
catch back to the cabin, cooking them as a bouillabaisse. In 2013 and
throughout the following year, Lavrakas served as executive director of the Homer Chamber of Commerce. However, Lavrakas is thinking about restarting Skookum Charters to handle trips exclusively for
Tutka Bay Lodge in Kachemak Bay.

Speaking of Tutka Bay, when Lavrakas's father retired, both he and
his mother became avid fishermen. In the 1980s they began spending
summers in Alaska to fish and in the early 1990s built a family cabin in
Little Tutka Bay. Once his father hit eighty-five about ten years ago, his

parents stopped coming to Alaska and Jim and Ruth bought the cabin from him.

In 2012, Lavrakas published his first book, *Snap Decisions: My 30 Years as an Alaska News Photographer*. I have a copy, and it's a fascinating sampling of the pictures he took while a staffer at the *Anchorage Daily News*. It sits alone on my coffee table and every houseguest becomes engrossed paging through it.

A fishing guide and hunter though he may be, Jim Lavrakas made his mark as one of Alaska's most preeminent photographers. He's still clicking away.

25

CHRIS BATIN, 1955–PRESENT

Talkeetna

With the grit and soul of a wilderness veteran who's equally adept with a rod or rifle, his creative nature and journalistic talents have driven him to become one of Alaska's most prominent outdoors communicators. His constant presence for the past forty years in print, TV, video, websites, blogs, and newsletters, and on seminar stages have most certainly ignited enormous interest in fishing and hunting in Alaska and resulted in far greater appreciation of the state's natural abundance and conservation challenges.

In the late 1990s, I served as editor of *Sport Fishing* magazine at what was then World Publications in Winter Park, Florida. Doug Olander, the magazine's editor in chief, came into my office one morning and said a fellow named Chris Batin would be dropping by. "He's a true wilderness expert and a very knowledgeable angler and hunter," said Olander. "Chris is going to do some writing for us, and if we need anything in Alaska, he's our man."

When Batin later arrived, he appeared to be fit and healthy, but I'd envisioned more of a grizzled ruffian befitting a hard-living mountain man. Just as a misjudgment of Bruce Lee's slight frame by an opponent would be a fatal mistake, my initial uncertainty as to whether Batin had the mettle to conquer the wilds of Alaska would prove to be way off the mark.

Batin with a sixty-inch bull moose he harvested three miles from base camp on a remote drop-off hunt in western Alaska. Photo courtesy of Chris Batin.

Chris was aptly nicknamed "Moose Shoulder" by several knowing friends, but my prior assessments of Batin's constitution vanished when I visited his beautiful Talkeetna home in the summer of 2014. We'd discovered that beavers had plugged up a culvert on his property. The disrupted water flow caused the road leading to his home to flood as well as other drainage imbalances. To my amazement, Batin stood in chest waders wielding a pickax and worked tirelessly for over an hour clearing the culvert. There were no rest breaks, no slowing down, no complaining. I couldn't believe his strength and stamina even though he was nearing sixty years old.

We also hiked from his home through thick brush and alders on a narrow bear trail leading to a nearby creek. Batin fearlessly led the way, trailblazing like Daniel Boone himself as I dawdled behind. Geez, I thought, this guy is tough as they come. Add to that all the campfire tales about Batin and his literary legacy, and it left no doubt in my mind that he's indeed the essence of a true Alaska mountain man and wilderness expert.

You can find plenty of Type A personalities wielding a rod or a rifle in Alaska, of course. But what makes Batin special is a rare talent for communicating his experiences in an insightful and entertaining manner. The man lives the Alaska outdoor lifestyle while artfully imparting his techniques to others.

John Beath, an accomplished writer and angler from Washington with deep Alaska experience as a guide and instructor, described Batin this way: "I've seen him time and again fly-fishing the same stream as twenty or more people using spinners, and he always catches more fish than all the others combined. He focuses so hard on the task at hand—catching fish—that his energy transforms into an efficient, focused fishing machine that few can match in fresh or salt water. His talent is limitless."

I can attest to that. Batin and I once fished with mutual pal Bill AuCoin in Tampa Bay. AuCoin guided us in his skiff on the flats of several islands edged with mangrove trees, ideal habitat for redfish, trout, and snook. Even though AuCoin and I were used to this style of Florida fishing and figured we'd show the cagy Alaskan a thing or two, Batin ended up releasing more fish than we did.

Another honoree of Batin's advanced fishing prowess is Joe Nye, the former dean of the John F. Kennedy School of Government at Harvard University. "Chris takes underwater pictures and videos of how a fly acts in front of a fish in different situations, and in the evening plays those films to reinforce his coaching on how to improve your presentations the next morning," said Nye. "I always come away from each visit to Alaska a better angler because of Chris."

Jim Rainey, for many years the executive director of the Outdoor Writers Association of America, recalled a fishing story about Batin that still makes him laugh:

I was wading a tributary of the Talkeetna River with Chris about fifty yards downstream of me. Up ahead I noticed a large dark tree stump. I continued casting, but Chris suddenly started waving and shouting. As I got closer to the stump, Chris shouted even louder. Now only about fifteen yards away, what I'd thought was a tree stump stood up, waddled out into the stream, grabbed a salmon and dashed into the woods.

Afterwards I figured Chris would be excited like I was about the imminent danger of that bear, but instead he calmly and good-

One of his favorite pastimes is wading remote rivers and fly-casting to in-migrating salmon. Photo courtesy of Chris Batin.

naturedly admonished me. "Jim, when fly fishing in Alaska, we make a cast, drift the fly and if no strike it's picked up and cast again," he said. "Only then do we pause, lift our heads and look around before repeating the process." It just goes to show what a perfectionist Chris is.

Batin is every bit as adept in the woods as in a stream. Mike Citrone, an Idahoan and longtime moose- and deer-hunting partner of Batin's, spoke about a fly-in trip years ago in northeastern Alaska. "On the ninth day of our hunt, Chris called in a nice bull and the other hunter with us made a clean shot. We went back to the same location the next day and darned if Chris didn't call in two bulls this time within thirty yards of us. It's amazing how talented he is at that. And after packing out all that heavy moose meat the day before, Chris rallied us by literally sprinting the mile and a half back to camp with an entire 150-pound moose hindquarter on his back—the guy is Superman."

For decades, Batin's byline has appeared on the mastheads of numerous magazines including *Outdoor Life* and *Western Outdoors*. He's presently the editor and publisher at Alaska Angler/Alaska Hunter Publications and the Alaska editor for *TravelAge West*. Batin's published article and photo credits run into the thousands with more than eighteen magazine covers and a listing of all his journalistic awards that would take up several pages. He's produced seven award-winning books including classics such as *Hunting in Alaska: A Comprehensive Guide* and *How to Catch Alaska's Trophy Sportfish*.

Ken Shapiro, editor in chief of *TravelAge West*, knows a thing or two about Batin's frequent wilderness jaunts. "He's given our editors here in Los Angeles a new appreciation for the term 'reporting from the field,'" Shapiro said.

As a travel magazine, we're used to working with writers all over the world—sometimes in very remote areas. But an art director once came to me complaining that Chris wasn't responding to her emails even though she figured he should be able to get a Wi-Fi signal wherever he might be.

Finally, Chris wrote back and explained that he was hunting a remote area in Alaska and politely said he'd do his best to send photos as soon as he field-dressed an animal before the bears could get to it. After that, the art director never complained again when Chris took an extra day or two to reply.

While it's true that an inability to reach the outside world can be problematic for a journalist, other challenges can be far more serious. In that regard, Batin has survived dangerous encounters with bears and moose, walked away from bush plane crashes, battled violent storms, toughed out precipitous mountain tumbles, and faced a plethora of other threats during forty-plus years of potentially dangerous exploits, any of which could have been fatal.

But nature hasn't been the only curveball tossed his way. In recent years Batin underwent major surgery to remove from one of his kidneys a cyst that was showing signs of cancer. Postsurgical complications arose: pneumonia, respiratory failure, internal bleeding, and shock. Those not in Batin's great physical condition probably wouldn't

A successful day in eastern Alaska during a wilderness backpack hunt. Photo courtesy of Chris Batin.

still be among the breathing. But true to form, he rebounded and is again living the life of the true Alaska sportsman. Any way you measure him, this fellow is one tough man.

I have one regret in getting to know Chris Batin. Sometimes we form later-in-life friendships with people and wish we'd begun that friendship earlier. Apart from learning about the great Alaska outdoors from him, I admire his intellect and sophistication when discussing wide-ranging interests—some deep, some playful. An example of the latter is that both of us are transfixed by the movie *Jeremiah Johnson*, and our frequent emails and conversations are laced with quotes from it. During our hike together on the bear trail, I even sang songs from the movie, as much to amuse him as to repel any grizzlies.

During one of our philosophical email exchanges, I proffered the opinion that while he's a mountain man for real, I'm a mountain man at heart. Is there really any difference? Here's his reply that includes a reference to Bear Claw Chris Lapp, a central figure and experienced mountain man in *Jeremiah Johnson*:

Ah, the mountain in the mountain man. Does the mountain exist for the man, or the man exist for the mountain? Or are the two as one? Some men have more sensitivity to the harmonics of the mountain, its energy and atoms; we drink the water that contains the elements of the dissolved mountain, and the mountain takes our cells from urine, or feces, and turns it into the food for life. The symbiosis of mountain man and mountain is transcendental. Bear Claw said it best: "You can't cheat the mountain, Pilgrim, the mountain has its own ways." Indeed, it is what it is. You don't hear it or feel it, and no amount of human reasoning will change it. You just exist with it … inseparable, as one.

People can try to separate the two, but it's like separating a raindrop once it's fallen into the ocean. Those who truly know the mountain, or the eastern woodlot, or the Florida salt flats, also become the human manifestation of these special places, of everything in creation, and more. My belief is that this not only embraces elements of Christian theology, but also the tenets of Taoism, with a touch of Zen philosophy and transcendentalism tossed in. Simply put, I know Alaska in a metaphysical way, and Alaska knows me. From an alpine meadow where I whistle to complement a flock of warblers performing their sopranic solos, to internalizing the purification of scouring snowflakes falling on me in sanctuaries of towering spruce, this communion with Alaska takes me to a super-heightened level of human and spiritual completeness. It give me a joy and energy unlike anything else on earth.

Chris's younger brother Bill relates a story that further brings into focus Batin's special sensitivities and mindset. "In the summer of 1986 when I was eighteen years old, Chris led a group of us fishing in interior Alaska," he said.

After a week of great fishing, we waited for a riverboat to pick us up. I sat alone at the water's edge of a nearby creek and watched the crystal clear, cold water lapping over the rocks. While the sunlight reflected off the ripples like miniature strobe lights, nothing else existed in my life except the contemplation of the natural patterns and randomness of the water's flow.

Batin specializes in one-on-one, weeklong seminar courses for students of all ages, such as budding angler Andrew Patterson pictured here crossing a remote Alaska stream. Photo courtesy of Chris Batin.

Chris found me and asked what I was doing. Still numb from being lost in thought, I replied, "Nothing." He paused and softly replied, "Really? Nothing?" Now out of my trance, I told him, "I know it's silly, but I'm just watching the water lap over a rock." Chris smiled and said to keep doing so because it's good for me. His understanding of my experience became a seed that forever blossomed deep within me, and it's something I always remember when observing nature. It illustrates a great gift about my brother—showing you the way without saying, "Look, there it is."

Batin often refers to his Talkeetna property, Batinwoods, in sacred terms because it represents his inspirational and therapeutic domain. A recent email to me exemplifies that:

It's a drizzle-and-rain day, a gray sky that is the opposite of yesterday: full sunlight, Denali in clear view, my lupine field heavy

Butchering a bull moose that he called in. Photo courtesy of Chris Batin.

with purple blossoms and bees going about their tasks pollinating nearby wildflowers. A moose cow and her two calves are feeding near the woodpile, and salmon are spawning in the creek. It's no wonder I took the day off and went on a three-hour hike with camera. Today, however, is for staying inside and working the physical mind, fueled by the spiritual nourishment of yesterday. Isn't that the way it is, though? We live for select times in our lives, tolerating what we need to do to survive. But here at the cabin, there's nothing to tolerate. I eagerly embrace what may be mundane tasks for some, despite the gray, ghostly curtains of heavy rains rolling in from the Susitna Valley. The energy of this place—the trees, the ponds, the meadows, and the wildlife outside the window, flows through me and into the tasks of the day. I'll back up photos, sort tackle and repair gear, charge solar batteries, start the broth for a pot of moose stew, outline several story assignments, and if time permits, write a few more pages in my next book. All things I need to do, and greatly enjoy. But nothing makes my heart sing as much as walking my beloved Batinwoods.

Batin is an Alaska individualist who's found his own path to happiness and self-fulfillment. He consumes fish and game that he harvests himself, enjoys splitting firewood for exercise and continues to adhere to a robust outdoor lifestyle. I suspect it's his inner energy and his love and connection to Alaska's outdoors that fuels who he is, what he does, and why he does it. That's why he's still able to hop around with half a kidney while packing out moose and climbing mountains.

He defines his forty-year Alaska residency and his love for the state in a simple statement: "I am proud to be born an American, but I choose to be an Alaskan."

It might be tempting to write a biography that makes a person appear larger in life than he or she actually is or was. But when it comes to Batin, no such exaggerations are necessary. To be great, and to do great things, isn't given to many men. But if in the hereafter there's ever a balloting on who was the essence of Jeremiah Johnson in our era, my vote will go to Chris Batin.

26

JOHN BEATH, 1960–PRESENT

Angoon

He is a highly respected journalist on the national scene and an out-standing charter-boat captain, and his mastery of all things halibut are legendary. However, it's his knack in all phases of media for clearly conveying the intricacies of his deep "how-to" and "where-to" knowledge and experience that places him in a class all by himself when it comes to fishing for this enormously popular species.

When a title like "The Halibut Professor" is hung on you, there's pressure to live up to it. John Beath does that in grand style. In fact, it's doubtful that anyone has walked this earth who knows more about how halibut tick than he does.

Chris Batin, a Talkeetna outdoors journalist (see chap. 25) and friend of Beath's for twenty-five years, puts it most aptly: "Most halibut guides feel like they are back in school when he's onboard their boats. John's life revolves around halibut; he's studied them and designed and manufactured tackle specifically for them.

"I recall fishing with John a few years back on the outer edge of Noyes Island, which offers some decent halibut fishing," said Batin. "But we weren't getting any hookups. Even the king salmon weren't cooperating. John tied on one of his UV Fat Squids, dropped it down, and within minutes was fighting a thirty-pounder. After landing and

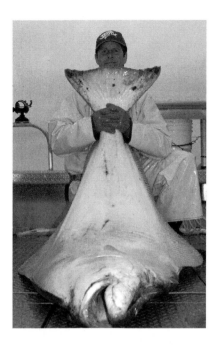

Well known as "The Halibut Professor," Beath knows where to find the monster flatties. Photo courtesy of John Beath.

releasing another five fish, he handed a lure to the guide. Soon every-one was into fish."

Beath's seminars on halibut at fishing expos consistently draw standing-room-only crowds, especially at the annual Great Alaska Sport Show in Anchorage and the Fairbanks Alaska Sport Show. "John's seminars are the best you'll find anywhere," Batin remarked. "They're not among the best—they're *the* best. His presentations are dynamic, scientific and easy to understand. He truly is Alaska's Halibut Professor and an Alaska fishing legend."

Like most legends, Beath openly shares his techniques and knowl-edge, even with other guides, instructors, and retailers. He operates fifteen websites and ten online stores of his own, learning from experi-ence how to make a site sticky and profitable.

The winner of numerous national and regional awards for articles in newspapers and magazines, he's also served as a syndicated radio show host (including the first-ever on the Internet) and produced DVDs on fishing. He's one of the featured charter captains on *Alaska's Fishing Paradise* TV series on the Sportsman Channel. Besides a U.S. Coast Guard Master's License, Beath holds a pilot's license and has served as

Although his specialty is halibut, Beath regularly puts his clients on chunky salmon such as this one. Photo courtesy of John Beath.

president of the Outdoor Writers Association of America. That degree of diversification is fed by the well of ambition and a constant desire to keep learning.

Beath studied subjects such as psychology and creative writing in college, and also received training in schools and institutes offering courses in tax and investment fields as well as real estate. He soaks up seminars, webinars and workshops about contract negotiating, conflict resolution, and team building.

The list of training certifications and accomplishments go on and on. Some of the more remarkable include being the manager of a major resort, an instructor at community schools, and a host for group fishing trips throughout Alaska and Central America. Although his halibut catches are legendary, he also set a world record with a 51.25-pound Chinook salmon caught on only six-pound-test line. He also holds four fly-tippet world records.

All that said, Beath is more widely known for being the king of flat-fish. While it's true that halibut will strike just about anything put in front of them, it's knowing the when and where that makes a big differ-ence in who usually catches the big ones and who doesn't. He's learned these nuances by employing underwater video, studying movements of the big flounders until his data stream produced a massive dossier on habits and preferences. Employing factors such as depth, scent, sound, and clever use of UV lighting above the bait, Beath and his cli-ents consistently nail the larger halibut as well as other species like lingcod.

Those criteria also led him to besting a massive 325-pound halibut that measured seven feet, one inch in length. An even greater feat involved winding home a hundred-pounder on only ten-pound test line—a 10 to 1 feat. Records aside, Beath is a big supporter of releasing halibut, especially the larger breeding females.

Bob Baran of Loudon, Tennessee, climbed aboard a charter with Beath and became an instant fan.

I first met John in August 2013 when he guided out of Angoon, Alaska. My wife Linda and I were assigned to John's boat *Jil* for our week of fishing. After a very successful morning the first day catching silver salmon, John suggested we try bottom fishing. He changed locations a few times and just when I'd about given up by day's end, my rod violently bends up and down, giving it what's known as the 'halibut dance' as it tried to shake the hook.

In about fifteen minutes of hard fighting, John yelled, "Color," and a big halibut neared the surface. He measured the fish as 63 inches, which translated to about 127 pounds. The icing on the cake was that it was also my birthday—what a great present. By week's end we headed home to Tennessee with 300 pounds of fillets consisting of salmon, halibut and rockfish. The following year, we again fished with John and I raised my personal best to a 67-incher estimated at 155 pounds.

Testimonials about Beath's skills as a guide are common, and same for comments about his personality. It's his congenial manner that makes him special, even when showing his intensity and direction

Beath's seminars on halibut fishing are extremely popular, and he's invented lures and techniques specifically for them. Photo courtesy of John Beath.

on the bridge. He's also constantly imparting tips and suggestions to make everyone aboard a better angler.

Veteran writer Tom Stienstra, a nationally acclaimed journalist from San Francisco, once wrote about a remarkable experience with Beath at the helm:

> The plastic contraption on the inventor's fishing line looked like nothing I've ever seen, maybe something you'd put on your Christmas tree. He dropped it from his fishing rod into the briny green and the plastic hunk seemed to come alive: It was a squid, glowing in effervescence, the tentacles undulating in the current. A separate wire arm called a spreader bar also glowed and extended to the side to keep the sinker clear of the lure.
>
> John Beath, who created this new lure and rigging for halibut, lingcod and just about anything that swims in the sea, set up another and inserted a tube-like light inside the squid body. He squirted a fish scent into a small container in the lure and added a half of herring on a big hook, hidden in the tentacles. When our sinkers hit the bottom, within seconds we both hooked up with twenty-pound halibut. It was only the start.

Beath makes no secret of his path to success. "I'm just curious and keep experimenting with different ideas," he said. "People always say to me, 'I've always done it this way or that and it works.' I don't disagree, but that type of limited thinking doesn't let you grow and learn new and possibly better ways of doing things."

An exploratory mind is one thing, but turning thoughts into action distinguishes a backbone from a wishbone. John Beath has successfully combined an inventor's inquisitiveness with outstanding skills as a writer, broadcaster and instructor. He's leveraged all those talents to make the pleasure of fishing a lucrative business venture with a variety of income streams. And in the process he's made clients, colleagues, viewers, and listeners better for it as well.

27

ANDY MEZIROW, 1964–PRESENT

Seward

When it comes time for serious competition versus other boats, few can match the tournament record of this skipper. His ability to think like a fish and gently instruct even neophytes to world-record catches aside, it's been his broad understanding of fisheries in general that has enabled him to sit on state and federal management councils and advisory boards as an extremely capable representative of recreational saltwater fishing in Alaska.

He's sassy, polite, ribald, gentlemanly, and always a ton of fun to be around. In fact, Captain Andy Mezirow is one of those interesting characters you meet once and never forget. That explains why his client loyalty keeps growing even after twenty-five years in the chartering business. Once one fishes with Mezirow, a return trip is a slam-dunk.

But personality alone gets one only so far. Mezirow combines his colorful persona with an intricate knowledge of the North Gulf Coast of Alaska. That translates to stellar catches on a consistent basis of halibut, salmon, yellow-eyed rockfish, lingcod, and most anything else plying Alaska's briny waters.

His specialty is halibut—giant halibut in the eighty-inch-plus class. During the month-long Seward Halibut Jackpot Tournament from 2010 to 2014, Mezirow's anglers reeled in flatties easily raising the

A happy client poses with Mezirow (*right*) and a 189-pound halibut caught on a live herring with thirty-pound test. Photo courtesy of Andy Mezirow.

scales to 250, 251, 323, 313, and 337 pounds. The last one was eighty-six inches and the largest halibut landed in Seward in the previous five years. In 2014, the 313-pound fish caught on the last day of the month-long event garnered a jackpot of $10,000 for his lucky Russian client. It also gave Mezirow his third title in four years in the month-long event along with numerous daily prizes.

No one knows the man better than Captain Jeff Seward—a descendant of Secretary of State William H. Seward who was responsible for buying Alaska from Russia in 1867. Seward mates for Mezirow and also at times skippers all of the three boats in the *Crackerjack* fleet. Seward, who earned the nickname "Poucher" due to his penchant for gaffing big fish in the belly or pouch, has worked a decade for Mezirow as a deckhand and as second-in-command captain.

Andy can be a bit of a practical joker and prankster sometimes, but all in good fun. I like to think of him as that crazy uncle I never met but heard plenty about. As a deckhand, that kind of behavior keeps me on my toes and heightens my "situational awareness" as I never know when I might get a fillet of herring in my sandwich, water sprayed down my butt crack or a hookless plastic jig-tail flying at my head.

Most seasoned deckhands tire of these antics and quickly choose to run a boat of his or her own when becoming a captain. I, however, prefer working for Andy because it's so darn much fun and the practical experiences are invaluable to me as a relief captain and fishing guide. Andy's grasp of marine biology and economic impacts on the fishery help him educate clients on just how important a twenty-pound halibut is for the future—it's all about conveying that sport fishing in Alaska has come a long way from the old "fill-the-freezer" mentality.

Mezirow holds a U.S. Coast Guard Master's License for vessels up to two hundred tons, which is honored on any of the world's oceans. Besides working *on* the water, he's also a student of what's *below* the surface: baitfish congregations, migration patterns, bottom contours, and the effects of tides, currents, and temperatures. All can change from one moment to the next. Mezirow stays way ahead of the game, a testament to over thirty light-tackle world records for his anglers along with innumerable tournament victories. His competitive spirit boils to the surface in tournaments with the motto: "If you're not first, you're last."

One never knows what's going to come to the surface, such as this leather grouper caught off Clarion Island. Photo courtesy of Andy Mezirow.

Since he hails from Alaska, friends refer to him as "Frosty" because his complexion is as white as a snowman. Married to wife Nici (short for Nicola and pronounced like Nikki) for nearly twenty years, he enjoys spending time with her and stepsons Brian and Tom. The family also owns a house in Kona, Hawaii, where they spend a few months during the winter and do spring fishing for marlin and tuna.

Mezirow also appreciates a widely held admiration for his uncanny ability to catch a fish every time he wets a line. "That's true, but the rest of my life is pretty much a train wreck," he said with a laugh.

Mezirow regularly maneuvers the forty-six-foot *Crackerjack Voyager* from atop the bridge while below 810-horsepower turbo diesels churn the boat at up to twenty-four knots. That's fast enough to zip out for half-day trips in adjoining Resurrection Bay or sleep up to eight anglers for days at a time at distant salmon and halibut fishing grounds.

Since some clients fish hard, others less intensely, and most somewhere in between, Mezirow is ready for all comers. His boat provides a full fish-around deck as well as an entertainment system, satellite

Mezirow doubles-up on two
beautiful lingcod. Photo courtesy of Andy Mezirow.

communications, and, of course, the latest electronics. But what's really
cool is that he also offers special vessel-based spring black bear and fall
Sitka blacktail deer hunts.

Peter Hardy, an experienced lecturer and book author on halibut
fishing from Anchorage, can attest to Mezirow's tenacity. Invited on a
May preseason scouting trip to Prince William Sound, Hardy watched
another angler on the boat hook what they thought was a huge halibut. When it finally could be worked to the surface, all aboard realized
that instead a 250-pound salmon shark was on the line.

"Galvanized into action, Andy grabbed a short-handled gaff while
someone else prepared a harpoon," said Hardy. "He sunk the gaff into
the fish and it exploded in a thrashing frenzy, threatening to escape.
The harpoon was fired but it bounced off the armorlike hide, so I
plunged it instead into one of the vertical gill slits. A second gaff helped
heave it aboard. Andy leaped on the shark's back like a rodeo rider and

concussed it with multiple swings from an aluminum bat. I was told later that that shark was tasty."

In the offseason, Mezirow stays plenty busy when not traveling to Hawaii or other exotic fishing destinations. He's a representative for the International Game Fish Association and serves on a variety of advisory boards for the Alaska Department of Fish & Game and the National Oceanic and Atmospheric Administration's North Pacific Fishery Management Council. He also freely shares his knowledge of seamanship as an instructor at the State of Alaska Maritime Training Center. He also owns a twenty-one-foot boat in Hawaii named *Pai Aki*, which is Hawaiian for sea salt. He also gets a kick out of restoring Volkswagen vans.

The infamous Mezirow sense of humor apparently is a family trait. Doug Olander, editor in chief of *Sport Fishing* magazine, himself a practical joker when the notion hits him, once turned the tables aboard the *Crackerjack Voyager*.

The first time I fished with Andy was for a feature on fishing the Seward area because it hadn't as yet become well known nationally as a sport-fishing destination. Joining me on the overnight trip were my brother and son. At the fishing grounds, I discovered a pair of ladies panties—very pink—that I certainly hadn't packed with my stuff.

I found out later that Andy's mischievous missus, Nici, had done the dirty deed. But no matter: Not one to waste the opportunity, late that evening I persuaded the deckhand to quietly lower the tallest VHF antenna on the boat and affix to it said panties before restoring it to its locked and upright position. We steamed back into port in Seward on a sunny August afternoon, proudly flying those pink colors—unbeknownst to Capt. Mezirow. They were, however, most definitely noticed on the docks. Andy loved it and ever since then, flying some item of ladies' lingerie has become de rigueur aboard the *Crackerjack Voyager*.

Not surprisingly, articles about Mezirow appear with regularity in Alaska and national media. A few of these outlets are *Fish Alaska*, *Alaska Fishing and Hunting News*, *ESPN Outdoors*, *Great Lakes Angler*,

Christmas 2009, the Mezirow family—hound dog included. Photo courtesy of Andy Mezirow.

New Zealand Fishing News, *Sport Fishing*, and *Western Outdoors*. In 2014, *Saltwater Sportsman* named Mezirow one of the top fifty charter-boat captains in the world.

Apart from all the accolades, Mezirow keeps his head on straight. He knows that the tournament victories and the world records will always come as long as he enjoys what he's doing and works hard at it.

"My greatest achievement is that I still get stoked each and every day to be out on the water," he said. "The closer I get to the dock in the morning, the faster I walk."

28

MORE LEGENDS OF ALASKA'S GREAT OUTDOORS

In addition to those depicted in the preceding chapters, many hundreds of other men and women could justifiably be included as legends of the rod or rifle in Alaska. All the journalists, biologists, bush pilots, photographers, guides, lodge owners, and others who have also contributed in a remarkable way to the huge success of fishing and hunting in Alaska would require a volume of books to document all the worthy names.

Insufficient records, uninterested parties, or lack of a reliable vetting source also frequently disallowed sufficient material to merit a full chapter on some worthy individuals. Even so, the following names, volunteered by many prominent Alaskans, kept popping up on the candidate lists for the book.

ANNABEL, RUSSELL
He is a prolific writer and book author of Alaska's outdoor history and lore, much of which is based on his own experiences.

BONDURANT, DALE
He drafted federal court briefs and testified at many state and congressional hearings about proper resource use and equal rights for all Alaska anglers and hunters.

Bud Branham holding a caribou mount on the porch of Rainy Pass Lodge, one of the lodges owned by the Branham brothers. Photo courtesy of Keith Perrins.

BRANHAM, BUD AND DENNIS
Both Master Guides, they were pioneers in establishing hunting lodges in the 1930s.

CURTIS, BOB
A pioneering lodge owner, he hosted many journalists throughout his career to sample and write about Alaska's great fishing and hunting opportunities.

ELLIOT, BOB
He was a bush pilot based out of Fairbanks who provided a prolific fly-out service to fishing camps throughout the wilderness.

ELWELL, LUKE
A surveyor, dog-team musher, and gold miner who with his wife,

Mamie, opened a fishing and hunting lodge on Upper Russian Lake in Cooper Landing in 1939.

ENGLE, CLARK

A well-respected Master Guide, lodge owner, and driving force in the Alaska Professional Hunters Association. He died while piloting a bush plane in 1987.

FORTIER, EDWARD

An Army counterintelligence officer in World War II, he was a member of the first Alaska Big Game Guide Board, a book author, and, for ten years, executive editor of *Alaska Magazine*.

GAUDET, JOHN JAKE

A Master Guide, hunter, and fishing guide, he owned and operated Jake's Alaska Wilderness Outfitters.

GRAY, CHUCK

A bush pilot and Master Guide from Fairbanks, he was also a deputized game warden prior to statehood and active in fish and game management.

GUFFEY, KEN

His taxidermy service, based in Anchorage beginning in the latter part of the twentieth century, gained a worldwide reputation for outstanding fish mounts.

HARBO, SAM

He was originally a trapper and then became an influential biologist for the U.S. Fish and Wildlife Service and, after statehood, for the Alaska Department of Fish & Game.

HELMERICKS, BUD

He obtained Master Guide License number four in the 1960s and was a skilled bush pilot and successful book author and writer.

Left to right: Mel Horner, Oscar Dahl, Harry Johnson, and Fred Henton in Seward in 1945. Henton and friends inspect a new rifle in an era when most men commonly wore a hat. Photo from the Fred Henton Collection, Anchorage Museum, B1965.018.225.

HENTON, FRED

A Cooper Landing hunting pioneer, he owned several lodges with his wife, Bernice, beginning in the 1940s and photographed many historic images of Alaska during that era.

LANE, KARL

A Juneau bear guide, he helped protect forests and block timber sales on Admiralty Island.

LIMERES, RENE

Journalist, book author, and guide, he has led fishing trips across remote regions of southwest Alaska and of Russia.

Considered the original Kodiak Island hunting guide, Madsen shows his strength by holding up a brown bear near Karluk Lake in the early 1930s. Photo from the Harshman Collection, Kodiak Historical Society, P-612-2-3.

MADSEN, CHARLEY
Kodiak Island's original professional bear guide, he marketed to the Lower 48 brown bear hunts from his camp beginning in the 1930s.

MASSEY, JAY
He was one of the first Alaska outdoor writers and an expert in bow hunting and moose hunting.

MAXEY, JOE
An expert pilot and the owner of Painter Creek Lodge on the Alaska Peninsula.

MCNUTT, RAY
He held Master Guide License number 38 from Tok and Chisana. He specialized in sheep and moose hunting in the Wrangell Mountains.

Howard Pollock campaigning in 1967. He would become Alaska's U.S. congressman and assist in sponsoring legislation favoring hunting and fishing rights. Steve McCutcheon, McCutcheon Collection, Anchorage Museum, B1990.014.5.Pol.02.12.

MORRIS, NANCI

She is a highly accomplished Naknek River fishing guide based in King Salmon on the Kenai Peninsula.

POLLOCK, HOWARD

A big game guide and hunter, he won Alaska's seat as a U.S. congressman, later served in the Nixon administration as deputy director of the National Oceanic and Atmospheric Administration, and became president of the National Rifle Association.

POWERS, DICK

A former National Forest Service employee, he opened the Angoon Trading Company on Admiralty Island and operated a B&B lodge.

RUNYAN, ANDY

For over forty years, he was one of the great Master Guides (license number 34) on Kodiak Island.

SEIFERT, VERN

He was an Alaska bush pilot, polar bear guide, and falconer beginning in the 1930s.

Guy Waddell (*second from right*) with guides, hunters, and pack horses at Eielson Pass in what is now Denali National Park in the 1920s. Fritz Nyberg, CIHS Collection Anchorage Museum, B1975.134.47.

SMITH, ROGER
A biologist, he contributed greatly to the understanding of Kodiak Island brown bears.

STEPHENS, STAN
He became a major player in developing charter fishing in Prince William Sound and was a leader in the Alaska tourism industry.

STOCKHOLM, KEN
His career included serving as a bush pilot, professor of criminal justice at the University of Alaska, and owner of Wood River Lodge.

SUITER, LARRY
He was an acclaimed Kenai River and Naknek River fishing guide.

SWENSEN, EVAN
He is the author of Alaska outdoor books, a bush pilot, magazine and newspaper publisher and producer/host of radio and TV shows.

WADDELL, GUY
A pioneering Alaska hunting guide whose career stretched back to the early 1900s.

WALATKA, JOHN

He started an air service out of Dillingham in the 1930s, founded sport-fishing lodges in Bristol Bay, and the Walatka Mountains in Katmai National Park are named after him.

WAUGAMAN, BILL

A noted hunting guide and outfitter beginning in the early 1950s known for his conservation ethics, he acquired a variety of camps on the north side of the Alaska Range.

WILSON, DEAN

He was a fisherman, hunter, and prominent trapper and fur buyer in Interior Alaska for over thirty years.

BIBLIOGRAPHY

Batin, Christopher. *Hunting in Alaska: A Comprehensive Guide*. Rev. 7th ed. Fairbanks: Alaska Angler/Hunter Publications, 2006.

——. *Chris Batin's 20 Great Alaska Fishing Adventures*. Talkeetna: Alaska Angler Publications, 1991.

Batin, Christopher and Adela. *How to Catch Alaska's Trophy Sportfish*. Fairbanks: Alaska Angler Publications, 1984.

Beath, John. *How to Catch Trophy Halibut*. Monroe, Wash.: Pacific Lure Communications, 2000.

Bennett, Bo. *Rods and Wings*. Anchorage, Alaska: Publication Consultants, 2000.

Brooks, James W. *North to Wolf Country: My Life among the Creatures of Alaska*. Kenmore, Wash.: Epicenter Press, 2003.

Clark, Marvin H. Jr. *Pinnell and Talifson: Last of the Great Brown Bear Men*. Wasilla, Alaska: Great Northwest Publishing & Distributing Company, 1985.

Gates, Nancy. *The Alaska Almanac*. 33d ed. Portland, Ore.: Alaska Northwest Books, 2011.

Gasaway, William C., et al. *Interrelationships of Wolves, Prey, and Man in Alaska*. Wildlife Monographs, no. 84. [N.p.]: The Wildlife Society, 1983.

Hammond, Jay S. *Chips from the Chopping Block: More Tales from Alaska's Bush Rat Governor*. Kenmore, Wash.: Epicenter Press, 2001.

——. *"Diapering the Devil": How Alaska Helped Staunch Befouling by Mismanaged Oil Wealth; A Lesson for Other Rich Nations*. Homer, Alaska: Kachemak Resource Institute, 2011.

——. *Tales of Alaska's Bush Rat Governor: The Extraordinary Autobiography of Jay Hammond, Wilderness Guide and Reluctant Politician*. Fairbanks, Alaska: Epicenter Press, 1994.

Huntington, Sidney, and Jim Rearden. *Shadows on the Koyukuk: An Alaskan Native's Life along the River*. Portland, Ore.: Graphic Arts Center Publishing, 1993.

Johnson, Keith N. *Unpredictable Giants: 40 Years of Alaskan Brown Bear Tales*. Glenwood Springs, Colo.: Gran Farnum Printing and Publishing, 2001.

Keim, Charles J., and Julia Waugh. *Alaska Game Trails with a Master Guide*. Anchorage: Alaska Northwest Publishing Company, 1977.

Kleinkauf, Cecilia. *River Girls: Fly Fishing for Young Women*. Boulder, Colo.: Johnson Books, 2006.

Kleinkauf, Cecilia, and Michael DeYoung. *Fly-Fishing for Alaska's Arctic Grayling: Sailfish of the North*. Portland, Ore.: Frank Amato, 2009.

———. *Fly Fishing Women Explore Alaska*. Kenmore, Wash.: Epicenter Press, 2003.

———. *Pacific Salmon Flies: New Ties and Old Standbys*. Portland, Ore.: Frank Amato Publications, 2012.

Lavrakas, Jim. *Snap Decisions: My 30 Years as an Alaska News Photographer*. Homer, Alaska: Far North Press, 2012.

Lawing, Nellie Neal. *Alaska Nellie*. Seattle, Wash.: Seattle Printing and Publishing Company, 1940.

Limeres, Rene, and Gunnar Pedersen, eds. *Alaska Fishing*. Roseville, Calif.: Publishers Design Group, 2005.

Rearden, Jim. *Alaska's Wolf Man: The 1915–55 Wilderness Adventures of Frank Glaser*. Missoula, Mont.: Pictorial Histories Publishing Company, 1998.

———. *Sam O. White, Alaskan: Tales of a Legendary Wildlife Agent and Bush Pilot*. Missoula, Mont.: Pictorial Histories Publishing Company, 2007.

Waugh, Hal, and Charles J. Keim. *Fair Chase with Alaskan Guides*. Anchorage: Alaska Northwest Publishing Company, 1972.

ACKNOWLEDGMENTS

While I cannot possibly thank all those who have been generous with their suggestions, the following alphabetized list takes a stab at it. But first, I must single out a number of those who proved to be of indispensable help. I start with my wife, Kelly Kelly—yes, that's really her name. Some call her K2 or K Squared for short. An accomplished writer and photographer in her own right, she proofed every word in this book and provided suggestions for corrections and clarity.

My daughter, Lynn Kelly, who generously put her advanced search and Excel skills to work to ferret out and organize a giant volume of online background data for each chapter. Without her I'd still be lost in a jumble of multiple files and lost notes.

Chris Batin, a guy who wasn't born my brother but whom I now consider to be one, offered unlimited counsel and list vetting. His wide knowledge of Alaska and innumerable contacts has been so immensely valuable that *Alaska's Greatest Outdoor Legends* simply wouldn't be what it is without him.

James Engelhardt, former acquisitions editor for the University of Alaska Press, combined his broad understanding of quirky writers like me with a friendly disposition. Krista West, who took over for James in the production process, was an absolute pleasure to work with.

Wayne Heimer, one of the chapter subjects, who not knowing me from Adam, wasn't too sure about my project when I first approached him. Besides serving as a chapter subject himself, he became an important collaborator on other Alaska game biologists worthy of inclusion. Thanks, Heims.

Doug Capra, an Alaska historian and author from Seward who kindly vetted my chapter on "Alaska Nellie," provided images of her from his private collection. You could have knocked me over with a feather when he offered that level of support to this starving writer.

Jim Rearden, the veritable dean of Alaska outdoor writers who, with the wonderful assistance of his incredibly talented wife, Audrey, generously contributed anecdotes, images, and vetting for several of the chapters.

Dick Bishop did a lot of extra spadework searching in my behalf for various images of hard-to-get characters.

And with that I now introduce only a small portion of other helpful folks and agencies who submitted candidates for the book, tipped me off about fruitful sources, and provided valuable support: Alaska Department of Fish & Game, Jean Ayers, Bonnie Bailey, Jim Bailey, Bob Banghart, John Baran, Peter Barela, Bill Batin, Carl Battreall, John Beath, Georgia Bennett, Dick and Mary Bishop, Jodi Bishop, John Bishop, Sam Bishop, john bluefeather, Boone & Crockett Club, Beatrice Brooks, Martin Buroker, Wayde Carroll, Mike Citrone, Bo Cline, Doug Corl, Al Crane, John DeLapp, Don Dodds, Harry Dodge, Sam Egli, Jennie Engebretsen, Darrell Farmen, Jim Fox, Hal Gage, Val Geist, Roberta Graham, Jackie Gengler, David Gregory, Matt Hage, Sheri Hamming, Peter Hardy, Shari Hart, Barbara Hecker, Carrie Heimer, Steve Henrikson, Larry Hibpshman, Chris Hieb, Agnes Huntington, Kurt Iverson, Reta Johnson, Sandra Johnston, Bruce Keith, Ketch Ketchum, Joni Kiser, Kevin Klott, Marilynn Kulibert, Gus Lamoureux, Koreen Lamoureux, Linda Lamoureux, Lorraine Lamoureux, Carl Lopes, Jim McCann, Laura McCarthy, Dan McDowell, John McIntyre, Dave Meck, Andy Mezirow, John Morehouse, Richard Murphy, Joe Nye, Doug Olander, Diane Olthuis, Sonny Petersen, Keith Perrins, Keith Perkins, Jim Rainey, Karen Rudolph, Alice Ryser, Safari Club International, Jeff Schultz, Jeff Seward, Ken Shapiro, Bill Sherwonit. Dawn and J.W. Smith, Nancy Ketchum Smith, Sandra Snell-Dobert, Grant Spearman, Justin Spring, Rhonda Stark, Tom Stienstra, Michael Strahan, Henry Tiffany IV, Zane Treesh, Holly Van Pelt, Nancy Walsdorf, Debra Way, Donna Westphal, and Dennis Zadra.

If you'd like to comment on any aspect of *Alaska's Greatest Outdoor Legends*, email AlaskaFishHuntLegends@gmail.com.

INDEX

A

AAC (U.S. Army Air Corps), 88–89, 94, 133

ADF&G. *See* Alaska Department of Fish and Game (ADF&G)

Admiralty Island, 286, 288

aerial hunting: of bears, 123; and predator control, 118, 123, 125, 182; and spotting game, 60, 99; of wolves, 25, 118, 125, 182

agriculture, 90, 107

Agripina Bay, 226

Ahgook, Bob, 246

Airborne Hunting Act, 182

airplanes: crashes, 203–205; and guiding, 160; and hunting, 60, 99, *115*; turbo-prop service, 65; ultralight, 243–244. *See also* aerial hunting; bush pilots

Alaska Air Carriers Association, 226

Alaska Air Command's Clear Air Force Auxiliary Field, 90

Alaska Airmen's Association, 109

Alaska Angler/Alaska Hunter Publications, 263

Alaska Aviation Heritage Museum, 65

Alaska Big Game Guide Board, 285

Alaska Board of Fish & Game, 145

Alaska Board of Game, 83, 146

Alaska Bowhunters Association, 162

Alaska Canada Highway, 95, 150

Alaska Central Railroad, 11

Alaska Department of Fish and Game (ADF&G): and Alaska Statehood, 176–177, 230; BOW Program, 164; and Brooks, 122; early years, 123; guide board, 99; and guide marketing, 191; and Hammond, 105–108; and Harbo, 285; and McIntyre, 92; and Mezirow, 280; and Smith, 222; and White, 53; wildlife management, 102, 176–177, 180–182, 209–212, 216–217, 231–237. *See also* predator control

Alaska Fish and Wildlife Conservation Fund, 152

Alaska Fishing and Hunting News, 280

Alaska Fly Fishers, 171

Alaska Game Commission (AGC), 49

Alaska Historical Society, 147

Alaska Humanities Forum, 108

Alaska Land Use Council, 108–109

Alaska Magazine, 145, 285

Alaska Magazine Television Series, 170

Alaska National Interest Lands Conservation Act (ANILCA), 153, 181

Alaska Nellie (Lawing), 9, 13, 22–23

Alaska Nellie's Wildlife Museum, *12*, 19, 21

Alaskan of the Year, 109
Alaska Northern Railway, 11
Alaska Outdoor Council, 85, 181, 211
Alaska Pacific University, 255
Alaska Peninsula Wildlife Refuge, 223
Alaska Permanent Fund, 101, 109
Alaska Professional Hunters Association, 64, 162, 285
Alaska Railroad, 115, 251
Alaska Range, 290
Alaska Road Commission, 117
Alaska's Fishing Paradise TV series, 270
Alaska Sportsmen for Fish and Wildlife, 211
Alaska Sportsmen's Association, 151
Alaska State Council on the Arts, 147
Alaska Statehood Act, 122
Alaska State Troopers Fish and Wildlife Protection Division, 222
Alaska's Wolf Man (Rearden), 28–29, 147
Alaska Territorial Department of Fisheries, 53
Alaska Territory, 45
Alaska Trappers Association, 184
Alaska Wilderness Safari Camp (AWSC), 224–228
Alaska Wildlife Conservation Association, 211
alcoholism, 83, 253
Amber Bay, 223
Anaktuvuk Pass, 241, 246
Anchorage Daily News, 249, 252–255, 258
Anchorage Times, 252
Andrews, Marguerite, 129
Andy Sorenson Sportsmanship Award, 255
Angler's Paradise Lodges, 69
Angoon Trading Company, 288
Annabel, Russell, 283
Anvik Mission, 76
archery, 160, 162, 164–165
Arctic grayling, 224, 226
Ark, 78
Athabascan culture, 74–75
AuCoin, Bill, 261
AWSC (Alaska Wilderness Safari Camp), 224–228

B

Bading, Christa, 125
Bailey, Bonnie, 200, *204*
Bailey, Jim, 197–205, *199, 202, 204*
Baran, Bob, 272
Bates, Nellie, 10. *See also* Lawing, Nellie Neal
Batin, Chris, 203, 216, 259–270, *260, 262, 264, 266, 267*
Batinwoods, 266–268
Battle Camp lodge, 69
Bear Creek claim, 79
bears, 14–15, 22–23, 71–72, 173
bears, black, 52–53, 81, 279
bears, brown: aerial hunting, 123; and Bailey, 198; Chicagof Island, 189; and Johnson, 156–157, 161; and Kodiak Island, 33–35, 38–44, 289; and Lamoureux, Gus, 97; and Lamoureux, Rene, *94*; and Lavrakas, 256–257; and Madsen, *287*; and Smith, 226; and Waugh, 60, 63–64
bears, grizzly, 42–43, 47–48, 52, 53, 80–83, 205
bears, polar, 92, *99, 115*, 120, 123, 124, 288
Beath, John, 261, 269–274, *270, 271, 273*
beavers, 123, 260
beluga whales, *112*, 120–121
Bendix Corporation, 145
Bergeron, Steve, *34*
Bering Strait, 118–120
Berlin Airlift, 133
Bifelt, Victor, 75
Big Delta, Alaska, *27*
Big Delta Army Air Base, 90
binoculars, 64
Bishop, Dick, 92, 175–184
Bishop, Mary, 175–184, *179*
Bishop, Sam, 182–183
bison, *27*
bison, wood, 244–245
Black Rapids, Alaska, 27
bluefeather, john, 186–187, 191–196
Bondurant, Dale, 283
Boone & Crockett Club, 98
Botner, Nick, 201
Bouffard, Rose Emma, 93

bounty systems, 123, 146, 232
bow hunting, 92, 160, 162, 164–165, 287
BOW Program, 164
Branham, Bud, 284, *284*
Branham, Dennis, 284
Bristol Bay, 65, 69
Bristol Bay Air Service, 69
Brooks, Beatrice, 125
Brooks Camp lodge, 69
Brooks, Jim, 111–127, *112, 119*, 144
Brooks, Lewis Knox Polk, 113
Brooks, Lewis Patrick, 119
Brooks River Falls, 71–72
Bruce (the dog), 131
Bruner, Manfred, 202
Bulchitna Lake, *139*
Burns, John, 212, 241
Burris, Bud, 211
bush pilots: Bailey, 197, 203; Egli, 226;
    Elliot, 284; Gray, 285; Hammond, 101,
    104, 105; Helmericks, 285; Johnson, 155,
    157, 160; Ketchum, 129; McIntyre, *89*;
    Petersen, 65; Seifert, 288; Stockholm,
    289; Swensen, 289; Waugh, 60; White,
    51. *See also* airplanes

C
cache, *61*
Cache Lake camp, 96
Calhoun, Alice, 21, 22
California Creek gold mine, 16
campgrounds, 151
Capra, Doug, 10, 22
caribou, 52, 161, *284*
Carter, Pres. Jimmy, 153, 181
Cash, Johnny, *227*
Castner's Cutthroats (Rearden), 147
Cavanaugh, U.S. Marshal, 14
censusing, 145, 182, 233–234
Cernan, Eugene, 161
Chapman, Rev. John, 76
char, 161, *172*, 224
Chicagof Island, 185, 189
China, 106
Chips from the Chopping Block
    (Hammond), 107
Chugach Mountains, 96

Citrone, Mike, 262
Civilian Conservation Corps (CCC), 114
Clark, Kenny, 136
Clark, Vie, 136
Collman, Henry, 13–14
conservation: access to public land,
    151–153, 283; Airborne Hunting Act,
    182; and the Bishops, 184; and Brooks,
    113; ethics, 80; and Hammond, 108;
    and Heimer, 216–217; and Huntington,
    80; and Johnson, 162; and Lane, 286;
    and Mezirow, 277; and Rearden, 146;
    and Waugaman, 290; and Waugh, 62;
    and White, *50*
Conservationist of the Year, 85
Cooper Landing, Alaska, 285, 286
Copper River Delta, 121–122
Cordova, Alaska, 121–122
coyotes, 25, 31, 95, 123
crabs, king, 126
Crackerjack fleet, 277
Crackerjack Voyager, *278*, 280
Crane, Al, 222
Cripple Creek, Colo., 9–10
culture, 73, 76, 78, 81–83, *81–84*, 118, 241
Curry, Alaska, 18
Curtis, Bob, 284

D
Dahl, Oscar, *286*
Darga, Norbert, 98
Dead Horse Hill, Alaska, 17
Deadman Bay, 59
deer, blacktail, 256, *257*, 279
Denali National Park, *289*
Denver, John, 202, *202*
Diana Award, 164
Diapering the Devil (Hammond), 108
Dillingham Air Service, 118
Dodge, Harry, *34, 43*
Dodson, Jim, 69
dogs, 17–18, 116, 124, 246–247, 252–253
Dolly Varden, 161, 224, 226
Downtown Soup Kitchen Slam'n Salm'n
    King Salmon Derby, 255
ducks, 161

E

eagles, 123
economy, 137
Egan, William, 105, 123, 124
Egli Air Haul, 226
Egli, Sam, 226–227
Eielson Air Force Base, 90
Eielson Pass, *289*
Eklutna Vocational School, 76
Elfin Cove, Alaska, 185
Elfin Cove Lodge, 188–196, *188*
Elliot, Bob, 284
Elmendorf Army Air Corps Base, 95
Elwell, Luke, 284–285
Elwell, Mamie, 285
Engle, Clark, 285
Epperson, Bob, 222
Ervin, Harold, *27*
Eskimo culture, 118, 241
ESPN Outdoors, 280
ethics, 80. *See also* conservation; fair-chase hunting

F

Fairbanks, Alaska, 90, 117
Fairbanks Alaska Sport Show, 270
Fairbanks Trappers' Association, 85
fair-chase hunting, 60, 64, 92
falconers, 288
Fanning, Ken, 146–147
Father of Alaska's Sport Fishing Lodges, 65
federal vs. state authorities, 152–153, 181, 230
Field & Stream, 35
Fish Alaska, 280
Fish Alaska Magazine, 172
Fisher, Dale, *34*
fishing: and Batin, 261–262; and Beath, 269–274; Bristol Bay, 65, 68; commercial, 160–161, 187–188, 194; fly-fishing, 167–174, 224, 261–262; Frontier Sporting Goods, 91–92; gill nets, 114, 122; and Lamoureux, 96; and Lavrakas, 255–258; lures, *273*, 274; management, 114, 120–122, 144–145; and Mezirow, 275–281; and Morris, 288; processing industry, 80; saltwater,

170, 257; and Suiter, 289; and tourism, 69; tournaments, 275–277, 281; trophy, 224, 226. *See also* lodges; subsistence fishing and hunting
"The Fishing Dude" web video series, 255
flightseeing, 201
fly-fishing, 167–174, 224, 261–262
Fly-Fishing for Alaska's Arctic Grayling: Sailfish of the North (Kleinkauf), 172
Fly Fishing Women Explore Alaska (Kleinkauf), 172
Ford, Pres. Gerald, 147
Fort Greely, Alaska, 90
Fortier, Edward, 285
Fort Richardson Army Base, 200
Fort Wainwright, Alaska, 90
Fort Yukon, Alaska, 50–51
fossils, 97
Foss, Joe, 98
Foundation for North American Wild Sheep, 162, 211
foxes, *156*, 240
Frontier Flying Service, 90
Frontier Sporting Goods, *88*, 91–92
Frontier Travel, 190
Full Curl Archery, 164
FV Destination, 194
FWS. *See* U.S. Fish and Wildlife Service (FWS)

G

Galena, Alaska, 85
game laws, 43, 49–53
gandy dancer, 115, 251
Gardiner, Bella, 106
Gasaway Method, 233–234
Gasaway, William C., 229–237, *231*, *234*
Gaudet, John Jake, 285
gee, 116
Geist, Val, 211
Genet, Ray, 201
Gertrude Creek, 226
Gibson, Jennie Jane, 8
gill nets, 114, 122
Girdwood, Alaska, 250–251
Glaser, Frank, 25–32, *26*, *27*, *29*, *30*
gold, 10, 14, 16, 74, 79

"The Golden Gasser". *See* Gasaway, William C.
Grandview roadhouse, 11–13, 16
Gray, Chuck, 285
Great Alaska Sport Show, 270
Great Falls Army Air Base (Mont.), 95
Great Lakes Angler, 280
Gregory, David, 224
Grosvenor Camp lodge, 69
grouper, *278*
Guffey, Ken, 285
Guides Association of the Federation of Fly Fishers, 171
guiding: advertising, 40–41, 55, *96*, 190–191; and air travel, 35, 160; gear, 41–42; licenses, 38, 100, 158; and the media, 219–228; policies, 60, 99. *See also* Kodiak Island; Master Guide
Gus's Grind, *183*

H

Halford, Rick, 201
halibut, 269–277, *276*
The Halibut Professor, 269, *270*
Hammond, Bella Gardiner, *102*, 106
Hammond, Jay Sterner, 65, 101–109, *102*, *104*, *105*, *108*
Hancock, Lee, 95
harbor seals, 121–122, 178
Harbo, Sam, 285
Harding, Pres. Warren G., 19–20
Hardy, Peter, 279
Harris, Charlotte, 130
Harris, Joseph R., 131
haw, 116
Hayden, Jim, 11
Hay, Dennis, 185–196, *186*, *191*
Hazard Express, 89
Heimer, Carrie, 212
Heimer, Karen, 212
Heimer, Mark, 212
Heimer, Wayne, 51–52, 121, 207–217, *208*, *209*, *210*, *217*, *231*, 233–237, 239–246
helicopters, *115*, 126
Helmericks, Bud, 285
Henton, Bernice, 286
Henton, Fred, 59, 286, *286*

Hickel, Walter, 123
hiking, 91–92
Historian of the Year, 147
Holden, Kenneth, 18, 19
Homer Chamber of Commerce, 257
Hoover, Pres. Herbert, 19
Horner, Mel, *286*
Hot Foot (coonhound), 9
Howard, Steve, *34*
How to Catch Alaska's Trophy Sportfish (Batin), 263
hunting: ethics, 60, 64, 80, 92; Frontier Sporting Goods, *88*, 91–92; game laws, 43, 49–53; license, 55; vessel-based, 279. *See also* guiding; subsistence fishing and hunting; trophy hunting
Hunting in Alaska: A Comprehensive Guide (Batin), 263
Huntington, Anna, 74–75
Huntington, James (Jimmy), 74, 76, 81, 83
Huntington, Sidney, 73–85, *77*, *79*, *84*

I

Iditarod mining district, 14
Iditarod Trail Sled Dog Race, 252–253
International Game and Fish Association, 280
International Women Fly Fishers, 171
Interrelationships of Wolves, Prey, and Man in Alaska (Gasaway), 233
Irwin, U.S. Marshal, 14

J

Jake's Alaska Wilderness Outfitters, 285
Jay Hammond Day, 109
"Jay Hammond's Alaska" TV series, 108
Jeremiah Johnson, 264–265, 268
Jil, 272
Jim Dodson Air Service, 69
Johnson, Harry, *286*
Johnson, Jerry, 158, 165
Johnson, Keith, 155–165, *156*, *159*, *163*
Johnson Kiser, Joni, 158, 162, 164–165
Johnson, Linda, 158, 165
Johnson, Reta, 157, 162
Johnson, Robert, 158, 165

K

Kaiugnak Bay camp, 96
Katmai Air, 69
Katmai National Park and Preserve, 65, 68, 290
Kenai Lake, *23*
Kenai River, 289
Kern Creek roadhouse, 16
Ketchum Air Service (KAS), 134–138
Ketchum, Clyde, 129–130
Ketchum, Craig, 133, 138
Ketchum, Edwin, 132
Ketchum, Lindley "Ketch," 129–139, *132*
Ketchum, Marguerite, *130*, 131–133, *132*
Ketchum, Nancy, 133, 138
Ketchum, Northrop, 132
Ketchum, Oakley, 132
Ketchum, Steven, 133
King Salmon, Alaska, 288
Kipchuck River, 226
Kiser, Dave, 164
Kiser, Joni Johnson, 158, 162, 164–165
Klein, Herb, 98
Kleinkauf, Cecilia "Pudge," 167–174, *168, 172*
Knowles, Tony, 152
Kodiak Bear, 56
Kodiak Island: and Bailey, 198; blacktail deer, 256, *257*; and Lamoureux, 96; location, 36–37; and Madsen, *287*; National Wildlife Refuge, 38; and Pinnell and Talifson, 33–35, 38–44; and Runyan, 288; and Smith, 289; and Waugh, 56–59. *See also* bears, brown
Kotzebue, Alaska, *26*
Koyukon culture, 78, 81–83, *84*
Kulibert, Marilyn, 181
Kulik Camp lodge, 69
Kulis Air National Guard Base, 151

L

Ladd Army Airfield, 90
Lake Minchumina, 178–179, 180
Lamoureux, George Norbert, 93
Lamoureux, Gus, 96, 97, 100
Lamoureux, Lana, 97
Lamoureux, Linda, 97–98

Lamoureux, Lorraine, 95
Lamoureux, Paul, 97
Lamoureux, Rene "Frenchy," 93–100, *94, 99*
In the Land of Alaska Nellie (film), 22
land surveying, 47–49
Lane, Karl, 286
Langlois, Ken, *34*
Largent, Steve, 190
The Last Frontier, 148, 175
Lavrakas, Gabe, 257
Lavrakas, Jim, 249–258, *250, 254*
Lavrakas, Nick, 257
Lavrakas, Ruth, 257
Lavrakas, Vasilis "Babe," 250, 257–258
Lawing, Alaska, 20–21, *23*
Lawing, Billie, 18, 20–21, 23
Lawing, Nellie Neal, 7–27, *8, 17, 47*
Lee, Al, 248
Lee, Ray, 216
Lemay, Gen. Curtis, 92
Libby, Burt, 121
Limeres, Rene, 286
lingcod, 272, *279*
Lisianski Inlet, *193*, 194
Little Diomede Island, 119–120
Little Tutka Bay, 257
lodges: Bristol Bay, 65, 69, 290; Elfin Cove Lodge, 188–196, *188*; National Park Service, 65, 69; Painter Creek Lodge, 222–224, 287; Rainy Pass Lodge, *284*(2); Stephan Lake Lodge, 201–202; Tutka Bay Lodge, 257; Wildman Lake Lodge, *156*, 161; Wood River Lodge, 289. *See also* roadhouses
Lorraine camp, 96
Lucky Shot Mine, 115
Luke, Jenny, 79
lures, *273, 274*
lynx, 242–244

M

Madsen, Charley, 33, 39, 56–57, 287
Malmstrom Air Force Base (Mont.), 95
Marine Mammal Protection Act, 124
Massey, Jay, 287
Master Guide: Bailey, 197–198, 201;

Branham Brothers, 287; Engle, 285; Gray, 285; Helmericks, 62, 285; Johnson, 155; Lamoureux, 100; Oldham, 158; Pinnell, 39; Talifson, 39; Thompson, 158; Waugh, 56
Maxey, Joe, 287
McDowell, Dan, 149, *151, 152*
McDowell, Sam, 149–153, *150, 151*
McDowell v. Alaska, 152
McGrath, Alaska, 178, 180
McIntyre, Alex, 87
McIntyre, Cordelia, 87
McIntyre, Dick, 87–92, *88, 89, 91*
McIntyre, Irene, 88, 92
McIntyre, John, 92
McKinley, Chuck, *43*
McKinley National Park, 179
McNutt, Ray, 287
Mech, Dave, 247–248
medicine, 245
Menin, Al, 145
Mezirow, Andy, 275–281, *276, 278, 279*
Mezirow, Nici, *278*
migratory habits, 234
Mile 26 Satellite Field (Alaska), 90
Mileur, Scott, *34, 43*
military, 90, 118, 133, 199, 200. *See also* World War I; World War II
Miller, Dale, 59
mining, 10, 16
Molchan, Mike, 97
moonshine, 83
moose: and Batin, *260*, 262, *267*; and Bishop, 182; and Gasaway, 231–237, 244; and Huntington, 80; and Johnson, 161; and Massey, 287; and McNutt, 287; and Petersen, *68*; regulations, 123; and White, 52
"Moose Shoulder," 260
Morehouse, John, 203
Morris, Nanci, 288
mountain man philosophy, 264–268
Murkowski, Frank, 109
Murphy, Richard, 254
museums, *12*, 19, 21, 65

N
Nabesna Guides, 96
Nakalilok Bay, *220*, 223, 224
Naknek River, 288, 289
National Marine Fisheries Service, 126
National Oceanic and Atmospheric Administration (NOAA), 230, 280, 288
National Park Service (NPS), 65, 69, 179, 230, *289*, 290
National Register of Historic Places, 23
National Rifle Association, 184, 211, 288
Neal, Nellie. *See* Lawing, Nellie Neal
Neal, Wesley, 10
Nelchina Basin, 242
New Zealand Fishing News, 281
Nonvianuk Camp lodge, 69
Northern Airways, 69
Northern Consolidated Airlines, 69
Northern Wild Sheep and Goat Council, 211
North Pacific Fishery Management Council, 280
North to Wolf Country (Brooks), 112–113, 117, 120
nuclear bomb, 122
nuisance animals, 123. *See also* predator control
Nunamiut Eskimos, 241
nutrition research, 230–231
Nye, Joe, 261

O
Oasis home, 11
O'Hare International Airport, 66
oil industry, 62, 101, 124, 134–135, 137
Olander, Doug, 190, 259, 280
Oldham, Kenny, 158
Old Nan (rifle), 63
Olga Bay, 37
Orrell, Reta. *See* Johnson, Reta
Outdoor Life, 35, 39, *41*, 145, 263
Outdoor Writers Association, 261, 271

P
P&T (Pinnell & Talifson), 35–44
Pacific Salmon Flies: New Ties and Old Standbys (Kleinkauf), 172

Pai Aki, 280
Painter Creek Lodge, 222–224, *227*, 287
Pal (the dog), 114
Panama-Pacific International Exposition, 10
Parnell, Gov. Sean, 184
Patterson, Andrew, *266*
Pelican, Alaska, *193*, 194
Petersen, John, 66
Petersen, Ray, 65–72, *66*, *68*, *69*, *71*
Petersen, Sonny, 66, 69, *71*
photography, 31, 60–61, 249–258, 286
pike, *251*
Pilot of the Year Award, 226
Pine Mountain Boarding School, 87
Pinnell, Bill (also P&T), 33–45, *34*, *44*
Pitka, Angela, 80
Poe, Pat, 65
Pollack, Frank, 117
Pollock, Howard, 99, 288, *288*
Pope and Young Club, 164
porcupines, 100
Post Lake Camp, 59–60
Powers, Dick, 288
predator control: aerial hunting, 118, 123, 125, 182; bounty systems, 123, 146, 232; and Brooks, 121–122, 123, 126; and Gasaway, 234; and Glaser, 25, 32; of wolves, 28, 126, 232
The Prince, 191
Prince William Sound, 122, 289
Professional Hunter of the Year for North America, 162
Prohibition years, 16
Prudhoe Bay, 124
ptarmigan, 161, 230
Punlatuuq Camp, *240*

R
race, 73, 76. *See also* culture
radio collars, 182
railroads, 11, 16, 115, 251
Rainey, Jim, 261
Rainy Pass Lodge, *284*
Real Alaska Coalition, 146
Rearden, Audrey, 106, 148
Rearden, Jim, 28–29, 85, 106, 119, 123, 141–148, *142*, *145*

Registered Guide Licenses, 100, 158
reindeer, *29*, 120
Remington Arms, 162–164
Rhode, Clarence, 27–28
Rice, Bob, 135
rifles, 31, 38, 42, 63–64, 162–164
River Girls: Fly Fishing for Young Women (Kleinkauf), 172
roadhouses, 11–13, 16–18, 20–21, 27. *See also* lodges
Rochelle, Dick, 56
Rod and Gun Resources (RGR), 224
roe, salmon, 125
Rogers, Will, 21
Roosevelt, Alaska, 18–21
Roosevelt, Pres. Franklin Delano, 22
Ross, Sandy, 252
Rowe, Peter Trimble, 76
Rudolph, Karen, 215–216
Rulland, Johnny, *240*
Runyan, Andy, 96, 100, 288

S
SAC (Strategic Air Command), 89–90, 133
Safari Club International (SCI), *159*, 161, 162, 164
salmon: and Alaska Wilderness Safari Camp (AWSC), 226; and Batin, *262*; and Beath, 271, *271*; and beluga whales, 120–121; and Hammond, 107; and Hay, 187–188, *191*, 194; and Johnson, 160–161; and Painter Creek Lodge, 224; regulations, 125
Saltwater Sportsman, 281
Samis, Earl, 97
Schaeffer, Bertha Mae Jane, 118, 124
Schodde, Toni, 69
Schultz, Jeff, 253
Schwausch, Rus, 228
sea lions, 122
Seifert, Vern, 288
Seward, Capt. Jeff, 277
Seward Halibut Jackpot Tournament, 275–277
Seward, William H., 277
Shadows on the Koyubuk (Huntington and Rearden), 78, 147
Shapiro, Ken, 263

shark, salmon, 279–280
sheefish, *26*
sheep, Dall, 121, 159–160, *163*, 207–217, *234*, 287
Sheep Guy, *208*, 213
Ship Creek King Salmon Derby, 255
Simons-Waugh Guide Award, 64
Skoog, Ron, 144
Skookum, 254
Slowe, Bob, 35
Smith, Crystal, 225
Smith, Dawn, 224–228, *225*
Smith Jr., James Williams "J.W.," 219–228, *221, 223*
Smith, Juanita, 221–222
Smith, Roger, 289
Smith, Steve, 225
Snap Decisions: My 30 Years as an Alaska News Photographer (Lavrakas), 258
Snead, Sam, 39
snoose (snuff), 29
sonar, 145
Sorenson, Andy, 255
South American Fly Fishing (SAFF), 224
Spearman, Grant, 246
spike camps, 13, 16, 33, *61*, 62, 98, 226
Sport Fishing, 259, 280, 281
Sports Afield, 35
Sportsmen for Habitat, 211
Sprucewood, 144
statehood, 122, 176–177, 230
State of Alaska Maritime Training Center, 280
state vs. federal authorities, 152–153, 181, 230
Stephan Lake Lodge, 201–202
Stephenson, Bob, 239–248, *240, 243, 247*
Stephens, Stan, 289
Stienstra, Tom, 274
St. John's-in-the-Wilderness Episcopal Mission, 76
Stockholm, Ken, 289
Strategic Air Command (SAC), 89–90, 133
subsistence fishing and hunting: and the Bishops, 177, 181; and Brooks, 125; and Glaser, 25; and Huntington, 81, 84; and McDowell, 149, 151–152; and Pinnell and Talifson, 35

Suiter, Larry, 289
surveying (land), 47–49
Swallow, 46, 49
Swanson, Charlie, 78
swans, trumpeter, 31
Swenor, Jim, *34*
Swensen, Evan, 289

T

Tales of Alaska's Bush Rat Governor (Hammond), 107
Talifson, Morris (also P&T), 33–45, *34, 43*
Talkeetna, Alaska, 266–268
taxidermy, 95, 113, 285
technology, 145, 272
Teller, Edward, 122
Temple, Lonnie and Brad, 95
Territorial Department of Fisheries, 120–122, 144–145
Thompson, Denny, 158
"three hides" ad (Pinnell & Talifson), 39, *41*
tourism, 69, 91–92, 102, 105, 201, 224
tracking, 57–58
Trans-Alaska Pipeline, 101, *105*, 137
transportation, 31, 35, 48, 117. *See also* airplanes
Trapper and Conservationist of the Year, 85
Trapper of the Year, 85
trapping: Alaska Trappers Association, 184; and Bishop, 177–178; and Brooks, 116–117; and Glaser, 26, 31; and Hammond, 103; and Huntington, 77–79; and Lawing, 9; and Wilson, 290
TravelAge West, 263
trophy hunting: and Batin, 263; and Brooks, 124; and Gasaway, 229; and Johnson, 156, 159, 161; and Lamoureux, *94*; and McIntyre, 91–92; and Pinnell and Talifson, 33–44; and Waugh, 58, 60–61. *See also* guiding
Trosper, Homer, 16
Trosper, Nellie, 8. *See also* Lawing, Nellie Neal
Trosper, Robert N., 8
trout, 161, 226, *250, 251*

Trout Unlimited, 171
Tutka Bay Lodge, 257

U
Ugashik Lake camp, 96
University of Alaska: and Brooks, 118,
    126; and Gasaway, 230–231; and
    Hammond, 109; and Huntington, 83,
    85; and Kleinkauf, 169; and Lavrakas,
    255; and Rearden, 143, 147; and
    Stockholm, 289
*Unpredictable Giants: 40 Years of Alaskan
    Brown Bear Tales* (Johnson), 156, 158,
    161–162
U.S. Army Air Corps (AAC), 88–89, 94, 133
U.S. Coast and Geodetic Survey (CGS), 47
U.S. Coast Guard Master's License, 270, 277
U.S. Fish and Wildlife Service (FWS): and
    Alaska Statehood, 176–177, 230; and
    Brooks, 119; and Hammond, 103–104;
    and Harbo, 285; and Heimer, 216–217;
    and Pinnell and Talifson, 37–38; polar
    bear research, 124; predator control, 25,
    28, 32; and Smith, 222

V
Valdez Oil Spill, 137
Valley of Ten Thousand Smokes, 71
Vatne, Henry, 189, 190
Veterans of Foreign Wars, 109

W
Waddell, Guy, 289, *289*
Walatka, John, 69, 290
Walatka Mountains, 290
Wallet, Lt. Col., 136–137
walruses, 119–120, *119*, 123, 178
Walsdorf, Mary. *See* Bishop, Mary
Walsdorf, Nancy, 178
Walsdorf, Opal and Lee, 179
Walters, Roger, *34*
Waugaman, Bill, 290
Waugh, Hal, 33, 39, 55–64

Waugh, Herman, 57–58
Waugh, Julia, 56
Weasel-heart, 83
weather, 48–49, 78, 98, 119–120
Weeks Field, 117
Western Outdoors, 263, 281
whales, beluga, *112*, 120–121
whiskey, 16, 51, 83
white mule, 16
White, Sam Otho, 45–53, *46*, *50*, *52*, 80
Wien Air Alaska, 49, 51, 69
Wien, Noel, 49
Wien, Ralph, 49
Wien, Sig, 49
wildlife management, 102, 176–177,
    180–182, 209–212, 216–217, 231–237
wildlife refuges, 38, 223, 244
Wildlife Society, 184
Wildman Lake Lodge, *156*, 161
Wild Sheep Foundation, 211, 216
Williams Jr., Hank, 161
Wilson, Dean, 290
wolverines, 123
wolves: aerial hunting, 25, 118, 125;
    and Brooks, 127; and Johnson, *156*;
    population control of, 28, 126, 232;
    and Rearden, 146; and Stephenson,
    239–248; and White, 52
Women's Flyfishing, 167, 171
Wonderon, 127
Wood River Lodge, 289
World War I, 45
World War II, 35, 88–89, 94–95, 103,
    117–118, 133
Worldwide Outfitter and Guides
    Association, 171
Wrangell Mountains, 287

Y
Yeager, Chuck, 161
Yukon Bush Air Charter, 51
Yukon Flats National Wildlife Refuge, 244

AUTHOR BIO

Doug Kelly, whose early career entailed locating clandestine listening devices worldwide, is a veteran newspaper and magazine writer and editor, and a former radio and TV show host. Author of *Florida's Fishing Legends and Pioneers* (University Press of Florida, 2011), a Representative for the International Game Fish Association, and a member of the Society of American Travel Writers, Safari Club International, Boone & Crockett Club, and the Southeast Outdoor Press Association, he's been writing about Alaska and other exotic destinations for over thirty years.